Asia's Rise in the 21st Century

ASIA'S RISE IN THE 21ST CENTURY

Scott B. MacDonald and Jonathan Lemco

 PRAEGER

AN IMPRINT OF ABC-CLIO, LLC
Santa Barbara, California • Denver, Colorado • Oxford, England

Copyright 2011 by Scott B. MacDonald and Jonathan Lemco

All rights reserved. No part of this publication may be reproduced, stored in a retrieval system, or transmitted, in any form or by any means, electronic, mechanical, photocopying, recording, or otherwise, except for the inclusion of brief quotations in a review, without prior permission in writing from the publisher.

Library of Congress Cataloging-in-Publication Data

MacDonald, Scott B.
  Asia's rise in the 21st century / Scott B. MacDonald and Jonathan Lemco.
    p. cm.
  Includes bibliographical references and index.
  ISBN 978–0–313–39370–9 (pbk. : alk. paper) — ISBN 978–0–313–39371–6 (ebook)
1. Economic development—China—21st century. 2. Economic development—Asia—21st century. 3. China—Economic conditions—21st century. 4. Asia—Economic conditions—21st century. 5. Asia—Economic integration—21st century. I. Lemco, Jonathan. II. Title.
HC427.95.M337   2011
330.95—dc23   2011025912

ISBN: 978–0–313–39370–9
EISBN: 978–0–313–39371–6

15 14 13 12 11   1 2 3 4 5

This book is also available on the World Wide Web as an eBook.
Visit www.abc-clio.com for details.

Praeger
An Imprint of ABC-CLIO, LLC

ABC-CLIO, LLC
130 Cremona Drive, P.O. Box 1911
Santa Barbara, California 93116-1911

This book is printed on acid-free paper ∞

Manufactured in the United States of America

CONTENTS

PREFACE

Several centuries ago, Asia was ahead of Europe in many areas. Around 1500 the two regions started to diverge, and Asia fell behind. The West (which came to include North America) went ahead—economically and militarily—and has long been the dominant force, pushed along by the globalizing tendencies of Iberian-, Dutch-, French-, British-, and currently U.S.-dominated international systems. That is changing, however, with the sustained resurgence of Asia's economies since the second half of the twentieth century. The rise of China is a particular catalyst in this process, a development that is complemented by advances in other emerging Asian economies, in particular India, Korea, Singapore, Thailand, and Indonesia. In a very broad sense, Asia is closing in on the West in terms of economic and political power. With this highly significant development, it is critical to understand that the terms of the debate about global power and globalization are changing. Globalization, the process by which local markets and cultures are becoming more uniform and standardized as to international norms and practices, is no longer a Western phenomenon. It is increasingly a composite with growing Asian content. This is a major change from the 1990s and early 2000s when globalization was synonymous with the United States. If nothing else, the global economic crisis of 2008–9 underscored that for the global economy to stay afloat and move to a recovery mode, policies needed to be synchronized and that Asia, China in particular, had a very important role to play.

It is important for the rest of the world to understand these trends and their implications. For the business community, be it finance, retail, or manufacturing, the need to have a better comprehension of the changing Asian economy and the region's rising power is more important than ever. Ignorance of the outside world does not stand as an excuse in a globalized economy. Americans should heed the words of Singapore's former ambassador to the United Nations and dean of the Lee Kuan Yew School of Public Policy at the National University of Singapore: "No country did more than the United States to spark the rise of East Asia. But paradoxically, America is among the countries least prepared to handle the rise of East Asia."[1] Indeed, ignorance of the rest of the planet is an invitation for misunderstandings and the spread of xenophobia, isolationism, and protectionism, all detriments to the advances of the exchange of goods, services, and ideas.

This book is meant to inform and make people think, even if they have profound disagreements with our views. Along these lines, we believe that the twenty-first century will be defined by the rise of Asia, the impact of a China-dominated region, and the response of the West to these trends. Certainly part of the equation is the nature of the Sino-American relationship, but it is also defined by China's interactions with Brazil, Russia, India, and China (the BRICs) and other emerging market countries, such as South Africa, Turkey, Indonesia, and Colombia. Considering the importance of emerging markets to global economic growth, the rise of Asia must be observed through its linkages to non-Western countries.

The audience for this book includes people conducting business in Asia, business students that are soon to enter the job pool, and students of Asian studies and international economics. Considering Asia's already wide-ranging impact on the West, the trend appears to be accelerating in the 2010s, making the need to understand the region all the more important in terms of strategic planning, business development, and even personal lifestyles. If nothing else, Asia and the West remain very closely linked, their economic strategies mutually reinforcing, with their objectives largely in the same zip code. A world of synchronized economic policies provides a far better business environment than a world of out-of-control economic and political rivalries. And we have observed that shift before in the early twentieth century when the rise of Germany helped end a globalizing economic order.

Although many hands helped stir the creative pot, the authors take full responsibility for their work. The views expressed here are our own and do not in any fashion represent those of Aladdin Capital Management, LLC, or Vanguard, though the support of these institutions is appreciated. We would like to thank Andy Murkerjee of *Bloomberg* (Singapore); Leslie Norton of *Barron's* Professor Emeritus Richard L. Sims of the School of

Oriental and African Studies (London); Professor William W. Grimes of the Department of International Relations, Boston University; Ricardo Hernandez of National Bank Financial; Dr. Dale Smith; Takahiro Onishi of Mitsubishi UFJ Securities International; Anusha Shrivastova (PhD) of Dow Jones; Li Zhu (PhD); and Steve Xia (PhD) of Vanguard's Risk Management and Strategic Analysis group for their comments and time. Professor Elizabeth Hansen of the Department of Political Science, University of Connecticut was also a useful source with whom to discuss ideas, especially on globalization and India. Thanks are equally extended to Professor Yu Zheng, Department of Political Science, University of Connecticut. We also benefited from discussions on globalization and Japan with Kenji Kobiyashi of Mitsubishi Corporation. David Levey, formerly of Moody's, was most helpful in supplying a number of thought-provoking articles.

Last, but hardly least, the authors, Scott B. MacDonald in particular, would like to acknowledge their gratitude through the years to Professor Albert L. Gastmann, Department of Political Science, Trinity College, who passed away in 2007. He was always ready for rigorous intellectual debate, entertaining tales, good food, and fine wine. His presence as friend and mentor is sorely missed, especially his ability to point out important nuances as he did in the early stages of this book. Gratitude is also extended by MacDonald to another Professor of Political Science at Trinity College, Ranbir Vohra, who was a significant influence in his looking East—all of those seminars on Chinese politics did pay off.

The authors would also like to thank their families for their support and indulgence. Without them, none of this work would be worth it.

Chapter 1

INTRODUCTION

Imagine it is 2030. Shanghai is the world's primary financial hub. The number one selling automobile on the planet is China's 2030 Mao Class Red Guard sedan, partially made in the East Asian country but assembled in Indonesia, South Africa, Turkey, and Colombia. China's clothing industry is chic, with an Italian-like design, while its shoe industry is high end and in demand in Paris, London, and New York. The industrial side of the economy continues to be robust, but the air is clean, the result of a revolution in green technology that weaned the East Asian economy from its coal and imported oil. Beyond China's immediate borders, the rest of Asia is a region of dynamic economic growth, with content upwardly mobile middle classes (who consume their fair share of regionally produced goods and vacation in Europe and North America). This Asian region has extensive linkages to China as well as to other large emerging market economies. Asia's combination of economic growth, its correspondent wealth, and its centrality to global industry and finance as well as its political stability means that all the major foreign companies—American, European, Middle Eastern, and Latin American—are represented. If you are not in Asia, then you are not competitive.

The above is a very glossy, overly optimistic vision of Asia in 2030. Asia in the early twenty-first century has numerous challenges, and there are major hurdles to achieving this glorious future, even if the clock is pushed further ahead to 2050. There can be the usual derailing factors to human endeavor—war, famine, disease, and natural disaster. Yet, the scenario is not as wild as it seems at first blush. Asia—in particular countries such as China and India, with the largest populations—is on the move to something different from the ill-fated historical paths that marked the region from India and Pakistan to Korea since the sixteenth century. The latest wave of change commenced with the Great Recession of 2008–9 and is likely to continue for the next several decades.

The rise of China, India, and other Asian economies in the late twentieth century, and even more so in the twenty-first century, represents a seminal turning point in history. As Asian economies long ago fell behind Europe and then North America (now collectively referred as the West), they are now closing the gap and quite possibly gearing up to surpass the West. According to International Monetary Fund and World Bank data, China is the world's second largest economy, pushing ahead of Japan in 2010 and lagging only behind the United States. Korea is also a significantly sized economy and a member of the Organization for Economic Cooperation and Development (OECD), while India and Indonesia are also climbing into the ranks of the largest global economies. China has the world's highest level of foreign exchange reserves, in excess of $2 trillion. It is also coincidently the world's largest holder of U.S. Treasury bonds. Equally important, the combination of Japan, Korea, Taiwan, Singapore, and Indonesia has amassed over $2 trillion in foreign exchange reserves, making Asia's financial clout very significant indeed. This wealth has provided Asia with a global reach that extends its business and influence into some of the world's farthest corners, ranging from Zambia and Sudan to Bolivia and Peru.

Asia's economic convergence with the West is noticeable by other measures. East Asia's share of global gross domestic product (GDP) has risen sharply from around 12 percent in 1970 to close to 25 percent in 2008. In terms of global trade, East Asia's share has expanded more dramatically from 10 percent in 1975 to over 30 percent in 2008. In 2004 China's manufactured exports surpassed those of Japan for the first time, and in 2006 Chinese exports went past those of the United States.[1] Indeed, China's total merchandise exports grew from $183 billion in 1997 (3.3 percent of the world total) to just under $1 trillion in 2006 (8 percent of the world total). In 2009 China went past Germany as the world's leading exporter.

Asia's growing significance is not limited to manufactured goods. Asia's buildup in foreign exchange reserves has made it one of the largest foreign creditors of the United States. This means that Asian savings had a large role in financing the rapid expansion of U.S. consumer debt during the 1990s and early 2000s and helped the subsequent bailout of the U.S. economy in 2008–9 via the large-scale purchases of U.S. government debt needed to finance the U.S. government's massive fiscal deficits.[2] Asia's buildup in foreign exchange reserves, in part a by-product of current account surpluses, also has given the region additional financial clout through the development of sovereign wealth funds (SWFs), which provide the various governments an instrument with which to invest national wealth around the world. Along these lines, globalization has given Asia newfound financial muscle and, with that, greater influence in world affairs. Although this financial interconnectiveness can be a double-edged sword as demonstrated by the market indigestion during the 2007–8 subprime market upheaval, Asia remains a net saver of capital, an out-and-out advantage over the spendthrift Americans.

China, along with Japan, India, Singapore, Korea, and others, is leading the way to a new structure in the global economy, which de-emphasizes the West and potentially raises Asia as the core of international growth. The United States had a fleeting moment as the sole superpower in the aftermath of the Cold War, but it could well have squandered its capacity to lead in the morass of Iraq and its inability to live within its means (i.e., placing too much emphasis on consumption). The last was pushed along by an excessive use of leverage, both on a personal and corporate basis, that led to a near-collapse of the financial system and a steep and brutal recession reminiscent of the 1930s. The consequences of deleveraging and structural adjustment are likely to be a multiyear phenomenon lasting until mid-decade. The United States could benefit from Asia's rise, but there remain many challenges, including a pressing need to get its own economic house in order. Consequently, the next "Age of Globalization" could ultimately belong to Asia, reflected by a significant transfer of economic power. Indeed, it has been suggested that the next round of globalization may well be when "the West can no longer set the rules for world-wide trade," a situation being accelerated by the status of the United States as a leading debtor.[3]

The purpose of this book is to examine the rise of Asia in the twenty-first century and how that rise affects the rest of the world. In particular, we are interested in answering two interrelated questions: does Asia matter more now in the global economy than at any time in the past several centuries, and what are the economic and political as well as business implications? The short answer to the first question is that Asia does matter more in the twenty-first century in terms of its economic weight and political influence than it has for centuries. This importance is closely tied to China's growth and significance. As for the second question, the impact is and will be wide ranging and game changing. Asia now boosts an expanding cosmopolitan middle class, whose members are linked to the global communications grid and who are increasingly identifying with their counterparts elsewhere in the world. Per capita income levels are rising. Economic opportunities are spreading throughout Asia's hinterlands. At the same time, there is a new Asian economy emerging that is constructed around China's needs as an industrial workshop. Countries such as Indonesia, Thailand, and Australia, and further afield, South Africa, Sudan, and Venezuela, are drawn into a growing regional economy that orbits China. Although the point should not be overstated, there is an increasingly complementary aspect of China's relationship with other BRICs (Brazil, Russia, India, and China) and other emerging markets, such as South Africa, Turkey, and Indonesia, in terms of investment, trade, and economic policy objectives. Significantly, all of this has been extended into global economic policy making in the form of the Group of 20 (G-20) countries, a replacement for the G-7 line-up (the United States, United Kingdom, Japan, Germany, France, Italy, and Canada). Clearly China and developing Asia carry more weight, must be listened to, and represent a changing dynamic in international economic affairs.

Nowhere is Asia's rising power more evident than in the critical role China and developing Asia played in keeping the global economy from plunging into the abyss in the crisis of 2008–9. This is important as it was not the United States or Europe that rescued the global economy from the threatened depression; indeed, it was those two regions, the former in particular, that parked the planet on the brink of collapse. In its November 2009 economic update, the OECD gave China accolades for helping stabilize the economic situation. Asia's central role was also captured by Dominique Strauss-Kahn, the managing director of the International Monetary Fund (IMF), at the Asian Financial Forum in Hong Kong in January 20, 2010: "Over the past decades, Asia has become a major player in the global economy. Today, Asia is leading the world in terms of economic recovery from the crisis. And over the coming decades, the region's continued dynamism will give it an even greater role."[4] It is the region's continued dynamism that this book explores, seeking to provide substance as to what that greater role will be.

There is another important component of what this book addresses: Asia's rise is a wake-up call to the West. China and the rest of Asia represent fierce competition for global markets. Related to this is a grand experiment: China's ascendancy poses a serious challenge to those who assert that a successful capitalist system must be accompanied by political democracy. This assertion is an open question now, but its implications will be far reaching for the West and the rest of the world.

BACK TO THE PAST?

Part of Asia's transformation includes returning to the position the region held for a lengthy period of history prior to 1500. Asia was long a region of innovation, intellectual advances of new ideas about man and his place in the universe (Buddhism and Confucianism, among others), and commerce. Important developments came out of India in mathematics and astronomy. As for trade, historian Stewart Gordon in his *When Asia Was the World* observes, "Jewish traders brought sugarcane from India and began plantations along the Nile. Mango and pepper cultivation spread from India to Indonesia, where these plants become cash crops. Entrepreneurs first opened new markets, then made cheap local copies of extensive import items, such as Gujarati printed cotton cloth, Baghdad tiles, caliphate silver currency, Chinese ceramics, Damascus blades, and Chinese silk."[5]

Before the industrial revolution in the West, symbolized best by the steam engine and power loom, Asia's economies accounted for a considerably higher amount of global output. According to economic historian Angus Maddison, available data indicates that in the 18 centuries prior to 1820, the world's emerging countries (outside of Western Europe and including the Middle East, Africa, Eastern Europe, and the Americas) produced on average around 80 percent of the total output.[6] However, the force of technological innovation and developments in capital accumulation and allocation, among other things, favored the West, and by the early twentieth century, the share of the remainder of the world had declined to 40 percent. It can also be argued that once Europe got moving economically and expanded into the rest of the world, the wealth generated by its overseas ventures was an additional factor in the growing gap between the East and the West.[7] In the early twenty-first century, that trend appears to be changing, and Asian countries are clawing back global market share. While much of this gain is economic in nature, it clearly has a political component—economic clout has related political influence, something that is increasingly likely to play out in a dramatic fashion in the years ahead with Asia vis-à-vis the West.

Within the next 50 years, Asia will increasingly close the economic gap with the West and possibly even bypass the latter. Robert Fogel, director of the Center for Population Economics at the University of Chicago notes that "while the economies of the fifteen countries that were in the European Union (EU) in 2000 will continue to grow from now until 2040, they will not be able to match the surges in growth that will occur in South and East Asia. In 2040, the Chinese economy will reach $123 trillion, or nearly three times the output of the entire globe in the year 2000, despite the influence of several potential political and economic constraints. India's economy will also continue to grow."[8] Anyone watching China's economy bypass Japan's in terms of sheer size in mid-2010 must acknowledge the changing economic dynamic. Nakamoto Michiyo of the *Financial Times* wrote in August of that year that "just five years ago, Beijing was one of the biggest recipients of overseas development aid from Tokyo, which helped finance the construction of its airports and roads. Today, China has ousted Japan from a position it has held for 40 years as the second-largest economy after the U.S."[9]

Along similar lines to Fogel's projections are the following:

1. Asia is a major creditor for the United States (financing both U.S. government and private consumer debt). The giant consumer binge of the 1990s and early 2000s that bought SUVs, cheap consumer goods at Wal-Mart and Target, and new personal computers came via the courtesy of Asian central banks and thrifty Asian savers. To oversimplify, while Americans went to the mall, Asians went to work. Following the 2008–9 economic crash, China, Japan, and other Asian nations helped the U.S. government finance its massive deficits in 2008, 2009, and 2010.

2. Households throughout North America are filled with Asian-made consumer goods, ranging from autos and PCs to hammers, toys, and clothing. Any inventory of goods sold at Wal-Mart and Target is filled with Asian-made products. Asian brand names have their own followers and, like their Western counterparts, span the planet. Significantly, Asian products are not limited to cheap consumer goods but also include top-end and luxury goods and services.

3. Asia is one of the major sources for cheap labor (a comparative advantage), even for more "white-collar" services, such as medicine and financial analysis. If you are a North American—American, Canadian, or Mexican—your job or you could be off-shored to Asia.

4. Asia holds the largest portion of people on the planet, with over two billion citizens. This represents substantial demographic power, considering shrinking populations in Europe as well as large markets with increasing middle class consumers.

5. The nuclear power club in Asia is likely to grow. China, India, and Pakistan are nuclear powers, and North Korea has more than once threatened to head down that road. It is no longer inconceivable to think of a Japan with nuclear weapons.

6. People of Asian descent have spread out across the planet, adding to the various ethnic mosaics that constitute Europe, the Americas, Africa, and Australia. While they have become doctors, lawyers, financial experts, and a host of other professions, they also provide a link back to their lands of birth. Some of the larger immigrant groups have also developed their own lobby groups, helping to articulate their

views about how their new societies should be shaped, including foreign policy.

7. China is the fastest rising "new" power. Its economy could overtake the United States in terms of size within the next 50 years (possibly sooner). The mix of economic power and needs is extending China's influence into Africa, Central Asia, and Latin America. China is already developing its own set of alliances with Iran and Central Asian and African countries in order to secure its own supply chain of natural resources and friends to counterbalance the power of the United States. India also rates as a rising power, and Japan is more assertive especially as it sees a more powerful China and Korea and has growing concerns over natural resource supplies and markets.

8. Asia also has massive environmental problems, which need to be addressed. These problems include everything from a shortage of potable water to land erosion. Air pollution is endemic throughout much of the region and likely to worsen as China and India head into a consumer age that includes the widespread purchase of automobiles. Those air pollution problems end up in North America and Europe. Considering the threat poised by global warming, Asia's pollution problems are ours.

9. Although the West has long dominated global finance, Asian finance is becoming a more important factor in the world's capital flows. Some of the world's largest banks by asset size are Asian, Chinese and Japanese to be precise, but Korean and Indian banks are gaining ground and penetrating into new markets. Asian financial institutions have made considerable strides, especially since the 1997–98 economic crisis. While problems still remain (some of them potentially severe as with China), Asian financial institutions, including SWFs, are gaining in power and influence and are a spear tip into foreign economies. SWFs are broadly defined as state-owned institutions that have been given a mandate to invest a portion of a country's foreign exchange earnings into commercial assets. It is important to underscore that SWFs are a highly significant development in the process of globalization. As Richard Portes, a professor of economics at London Business School and president of the Center for Economic Policy Research, observes, "SWF's are already a major force in international capital markets. They will become increasingly important, as long as financial globalization is not reversed and emerging market countries and oil producers continue to run large balance-of-payment surpluses."[10] Singapore's Temasek is a good example of SWFs functioning as a major force in international markets. Similar institutions are on the rise in China, Korea, and elsewhere.

As the above trends demonstrate, Asia is not just moving back to the past, but it is accelerating into the future, becoming more central to the global economy. Part of that development is the embrace of green technology, something particularly evident in pollution-prone China. For a country well known for its use of domestic coal and imported oil, both of which have left their mark on the environment, the development of nonpolluting alternative energy companies is a critical step. An example of a green company being pushed along by the government, although with partial private ownership (though a Hong Kong initial public offering), is China Longyuan. In 2010 the company produced a quarter of the country's wind power, raising its generation capacity in 2006–8 by 112 percent a year.[11] For a country struggling with tremendous pollution problems, the development of alternatives to coal is a substantial step in the right direction. But China is hardly alone. One of the world leaders in alternative green energy is South Korea, which has done much in the way of energy conservation by finding more energy-efficient means of lighting in urban areas and in sustainable building technology. The path to the future is going to be lit by green technologies, and Asia is actively engaged.

VEXING POLITICAL QUESTIONS

While these trends reflect the rise of Asia, there is much that can go wrong, and politics loom large over this scenario. The economic aspect of change is a key component to be considered as it has added an element of volatility tied to fluctuating growth rates, prices, interest rates, and employment. In his *The War of the World*, British historian Naill Fergusson writes that economic volatility "with all the associated social stresses and strains" was a major factor in explaining the extreme violence of the twentieth century.[12] Certainly the interrelated financial-economic crashes in the 1930s in Europe and the United States strongly influenced political trends, much as in Asia in 1997 and Russia in 1998. The associated stresses and strains also were a major factor in shaping the structure of international relations. And this factor is very much a part of the challenge to Asia as it could undermine the region's current trajectory.

The political question raises the awkward issue of what kind of political system should be adopted—democratic or autocratic—and how that political system will interface with the rest of the world. Globalization means economic change, which stimulates social change, which in turn creates new demands on the political system. In a very broad sense, technological innovations, which lead to financial innovations, help open borders to trade, commerce, and investment and foster economic growth.

Indeed, financial globalization has accelerated the process of interconnectiveness as never before, pushing markets far closer together as well as opening the door to contagion.

The very openness that accompanies the introduction of market forces (namely liberalization of trade and investment regimes) creates a ripple effect in each society and gains supporters for greater openness as well as opponents to change. It must be remembered that not everyone wants change. The political system in all of its institutions is left to cope with change. In some cases in the developing world, political institutions were not up to the challenge. In most cases Asian political systems have proven to be adaptive, though often hard pressed to deal with new pressures. Moreover, the obvious outcome in terms of political system in Asia has more often than not been authoritarian. As Azar Gat notes in *Foreign Affairs* (2007), "authoritarian capitalist states, today exemplified by China and Russia, may represent a viable alternative path to modernity, which in turn suggests that there is nothing inevitable about liberal democracy's ultimate victory—or future domination."[13]

Along these same lines, there has been the rise of what Fareed Zakaria has called "illiberal democracy": "It has been difficult to recognize because for the last century in the West, democracy—free and fair elections—has gone hand in hand with constitutionalism—the rule of law and basic human rights. But in the rest of the world, these two concepts are coming apart. Democracy without constitutional liberalism is producing centralized regimes, the erosion of liberty, ethnic competition, conflict and war."[14] If nothing else, Zakaria and Azar, writing almost a decade apart, have captured the fact that the post-Cold War era is not a simple victory of democracy over communism but rather that alternative political arrangements remain a factor, especially in a global system marked by ongoing volatility both with political and economic dimensions.[15] And this is a difficult challenge for a rising Asia, within its own house and for its interactions with the rest of the world. It is certainly evident within the framework of Sino-American relations, touching upon everything from Internet freedom to the official Chinese government's negative reaction to James Cameron's science fiction movie *Avatar* of 2010 because of its unfavorable depiction of developers (a sensitive social issue in what was then a construction boom in which developers were often seen in alliance with party officials and bureaucrats).

Looking ahead, outside influences continue to impinge on local institutions and the societies in which they operate. This is especially the case as the newest wave of change comes in the form of what economist Alan Blinder has called "the third industrial revolution." The first industrial

revolution was the shift from agricultural to manufacturing-based economies. While this phase is largely complete (though some parts of the world
remain agricultural), the next phase was from manufacturing to services.
The latest phase is a shift within services. As Blinder notes, "because technology is constantly improving, and because transportation seems to grow
easier and cheaper over time, the boundary between what is tradable and
what is not tradable is constantly shifting—just as patterns of comparative
advantage are."[16]

Two important things to take from Blinder's observations. First, many
services are now tradable, and more will become so. This development
is hugely transforming and will be unsettling in both Asia (set to benefit)
and the rest of the world. As Blinder states, "like the previous two industrial revolutions, the Information Age will require vast and unsettling
adjustments in the way we work, the way we live, the way we educate
our children and so on."[17] Second, the transformation occurring cuts
across national borders and is very much driven by skills and geography.
While a surgeon must be near his patients, a radiologist can have x-rays
sent from thousands of miles away. A crane operator has to be in his
machine at the port, but security monitoring can be done from a distance.
All of these changes are highly transformative and socially and economically disruptive as well as having direct feedback into political systems
and the pecking order of global economics.

Taking the forces of economic change into consideration, Asian political systems have a marked penchant for order and stability. This desire
has been marked by a preference for more autocratic or authoritarian
regimes or in some cases the slow boat approach to more open political
systems such as the democratic experiments in South Korea and Taiwan.
India's democratic experiment has been the exception to the rule in Asia.
China's authoritarian system has been more the norm, hence the political
issue over how to integrate a rising Asia into a global community long
dominated by democracies in North America and Europe. The ultimate
concern is that political differences lead to political tensions, which eventually disrupt trade and commerce. This was a point of concern for
Chinese authorities in heavily censoring the Internet in 2011 after the
Jasmine revolution swept out of power a number of autocracies in the
Middle East, an abrupt and unexpected development, pushed along by
the technology of such factors as the social media like Twitter and
Facebook.[18]

Although this point should not be overstated, Asia's rising power is
clearly prompting a sharper departure as to how democracies should
respond to autocratic states like China, Russia, Iran, and Venezuela.

Evidence of the autocrats gathering to challenge democracies include the creation of the Shanghai Cooperation Organization (including China, Russia, and the Central Asian states); Russia's strongarm politics vis-à-vis the countries on its borders, including the use of oil and gas as tools of influence; and the coziness of China with such regimes as Sudan, Venezuela, and Iran. Those, like neo-conservative Robert Kagan, who see what has been called the "autocratic revival" as a threat believe that the United States and other liberal democracies should forget the possibility of global convergence and cooperation. Rather, they should reinforce links among themselves, possibly through a formal "league of democracies." Additionally, the democracies should prepare for increasing rivalry and conflict. Along these lines, U.S. policy should be guided by containment rather than engagement, military rivalry rather than arms control, and balance of power rather than concert of power.[19] Consequently, the political element remains very much a central factor in the rise of Asia and the further integration or not of economic relations.

Going forward, it will be increasingly more difficult to separate politics and economics in global relations. In many regards, 2008–9 is a point of departure in the post-Cold War era; it is a time when the last pretense of a dominant U.S. unipolar idea was put to rest. The country that has gained the most is China, which has been relatively insulated from the economic crisis. Roger Altman, CEO of Evercore Partners and the U.S. deputy secretary of the treasury in 1993–94 notes that "much of the world is turning a historic corner and heading into a period in which the role of the state will be larger and that of the private sector will be smaller. As it does, the United States' global power, as well as the appeal of U.S.-style democracy is eroding . . . historical forces—and the crash of 2008—will carry the world away from a unipolar system regardless."[20] The biggest winners, accordingly, are China and Asia, but they are going to have to work hard to maintain their gains and even harder to make further advances.

OUTLINE OF THE BOOK

The book is divided into nine chapters, including the introduction and conclusion. Chapter 2 is historical and deals with Asia's decline and its struggle to catch up economically in the second half of the twentieth century and into the early twenty-first. Chapter 3 examines the reasons behind China's rise, which is essential in order to understand the shape of the new Asia that is emerging. Chapter 4 discusses the emergence of a regional Asian economy, which is constructed around China as the dominant economic power. Chapter 5 covers the further linkages of China in the world via the BRIC countries and examines the complementary nature of these countries' joint development. Although this should not be overstated, the growing commonality of interests and synchronization of economic policies is a new factor on the international stage, and Asia is playing a key role.

In chapter 6 the focus is on the set of challenges facing Asia. Simply stated, China's great rush to industrialize has left in its wake substantial environmental degradation. Similar problems are evident in India, Indonesia, and Thailand. At the same time, the economic changes occurring in the United States are demanding structural changes in China, which is still heavily dependent on top-down investment and export-driven industries. Risks also loom in the investment of Asia's vast foreign exchange reserves as well as in outward investment of its companies.

Chapter 7 discusses the political echoes of Asia's trajectory. China's political system is authoritarian, while India is the world's largest democracy. Japan, South Korea, and Taiwan exercise meaningful elections, while limits exist in other countries such as Vietnam, Burma, and North Korea. The experimentation with differing political systems represents a tough challenge of balancing societal need for political stability and order with human rights and liberties, a situation increasingly complicated by the Internet and travel. Handling these political challenges represents one of the key elements to how Asia will navigate its future, especially as to how it interacts with the rest of the world.

Chapter 8 thematically follows from chapter 7: how does the West respond to the rise of Asia. This chapter covers everything from the Western belief that liberal democracy is the end result of history to increasingly fierce competition over markets and natural resources in Latin America, the Middle East, and Africa. It also includes the challenges of foreign investment, both entering and coming out of Asia. While the United States and Europe are down economically at the close of the first decade of the twenty-first century, they are hardly out. Indeed, both economic blocs represent considerable wealth, industry, and productivity. The rise of Asia sits as a major challenge to Washington and Brussels, with issues ranging from currency, trade patents, and intellectual rights to human rights, containment of the spread of weapons of mass destruction, and the handling of terrorism. The political dimension remains a significant pivot upon which the economic components will turn, and in some ways this could be the most difficult hurdle for the creation of what some have called "the Asian century."

The conclusion takes a look at where Asia is likely to be in 2030. Is there going to be a Greater Asian Co-Prosperity Sphere (a China-centric

Asian version of the European Union), or is Asia going to be a battle zone between contending empires and states, with China having fragmented into warring states? Will Asia morph into competing blocs, economically, politically, and militarily? Will the current trajectories lead to a concert of nations synchronizing global economic policies for the betterment of the global system?

The twentieth century began with a global economy dominated by financial capitalism, with London and New York functioning as the major hubs. That dominance lasted until 1914, with the next several decades through 1945 being defined by a struggle between democratic capitalism, fascism with an emphasis on state capitalism and a limited private sector, and communism in which the role of the state and party ruled supreme with no allowance for competitors. From 1945 to 1992, the struggle morphed into one between democratic capitalism and communism. In 1989 the Berlin Wall came down, and democratic capitalism appeared to have won the great contest. Capitalism and reintegration into the global economy was the norm from Albania and Latvia to Vietnam and India. But the era of unchallenged democratic capitalism slowly came to an end as the main driver in the system, the Anglo-American economies, experimented with a high-octane form of financial capitalism, which ultimately came unglued in 2008–9 under a tsunami of debt, greed, hubris, and bad business decisions, as well as an overemphasis on the consumer fueled by foreign savers. In 2008–9 the global economy reached a watershed. The rise of nondemocratic capitalist states, the autocrats, and Asia are taking the world in a new direction, one still not entirely formed but defined by different views of the interplay between politics and economics. In many regards, the clock has been turned back to the pre-1914 era, a period of financial capitalism ending and uncertainty looming. If nothing else, the world ahead is going to be defined by the rise of Asia, the central importance of China in that mix, and the ability of Americans and Europeans to reinvent themselves in a world in which Western norms no longer fully determine the ebb and flow of business.

Chapter 2

THE GREAT DIVERGENCE

The rise of Asia in the twenty-first century is not occurring in a vacuum. It is part of a long historical experience that encompasses the rise and fall of empires, significant technological breakthroughs, and the development of what were to become well-defined civilizations. Yet at some point Asia faltered in its development (at least in an economic and military sense), and this faltering left it at a disadvantage when it clashed with a vigorous capitalist-driven West. In a very broad sense, Asia went from what some of have argued was a level of superiority or parity with the West to a Great Divergence from which it was to struggle to overcome, most notably in the twentieth century.

It is the purpose of this chapter to briefly examine the Great Divergence with the West by focusing on the experience of China, Japan, India, Indonesia, and Korea. We contend that Europe's long wave of globalization, beginning with a concerted effort at the end of the fifteenth century, was to contribute to Asia's temporary slippage in the international pecking order and forced the latter to seriously reconsider its development strategies. One dimension of this reconsideration was the importance of Asia's financial development, in particular, the ability to raise and to prudently allocate capital as well as the related aspects of enhancing competition, investing in human resources and strengthening the legal environment. The West's ability to take advantage of this process was a major factor in its expansion out of the Atlantic and around the world. If nothing else, Asia's "falling behind" Europe in economic and military terms was to provide a very strong catalyst for future leaders and their populations to catch up and bypass the West. We would caution readers looking for a more extensive and in-depth and historical treatment of Asian history to consult other sources as we have sought only to provide a very basic historical overview.[1]

THE GREAT DIVERGENCE

There is a considerable debate over how and why Europe emerged as the home of the world's first global powers. The turning point probably came around 1500 when Europe's productivity (especially in the area of agriculture) and population began to surge. This was initially reflected by the rise of Spain and Portugal as world powers, followed by the Dutch, English, and French. By the late eighteenth and early nineteenth centuries, Europe's development of modern weapons, improving naval technology, expansion into the Americas, and exploitation of native peoples and resources gave it an edge over what it found in Africa, the Middle East, and Asia. Europe also appears to have created more effective institutions for mobilizing large sums of capital willing to wait a relatively long time for returns.[2]

Europe was to develop a powerful financial structure that provided badly needed capital for the great expeditions and trade missions that were soon to pull together the first global economic system. The financial infrastructure came from humble beginnings in the Italian city-states and the trade fairs in Champagne and the Low Countries, eventually morphing into the bourses of Bruges and Antwerp and then spreading to Amsterdam and London. In a sense trade and finance developed hand-in-glove, fostering an entrepreneurial business culture that drove Europeans from their own lands and into the larger world in search of economic gain. The capital generated by Europe's merchants also made a ready pool of capital for the continent's monarchs to finance armies, create bureaucracies, and enforce the dominance of the political center over regional challengers.

While many of the reasons for Europe's rise to the apex of the global economy are of importance, there are other reasons specific to Asian civilizations. But it is important to underscore that both China and India possessed well-defined great civilization traditions that had influenced the sociopolitical and economic development of their neighbors in South, Southeast, and East Asia. Between them, China and India produced and refined Hinduism, Confucianism, and Buddhism; made a lasting impact on the cuisines of Southeast Asia; and produced technological advances such as gunpowder and rockets. In addition, Asian goods, such as fine silks and spices, were well-known and highly desired goods in the West.

Yet Asia's great powers were not up to the task of dealing with the waves of Europeans, who descended upon them in fleets of ships, both for trade and war.[3] Europe's technological and economic innovations changed the paradigm between East and West from one of infrequent interactions largely based on trade and occasional war to a relationship in which the Europeans had a global reach and national interests that allowed them to interject themselves into the Asian world as never before. This meant that when the Europeans came, they did not leave—at least until the twentieth century. Also, there was a profound transformation in Asia from being a fragmented group of independent kingdoms and empires with modest links to the global economy to a series of colonies and dependencies, tied to the international economy via European intermediaries either in trade or finance. This situation does not suggest that local Asian elites were entirely hapless natives, prone to being the lackeys of Western capitalists. Indeed, there were some exceptions to the Western advance: Japan, Afghanistan (more an issue of overall ungovernability as opposed to organized resistance), and Thailand. Although these countries were in a clear minority, Japan by the early twentieth century adapted enough Western ideas and practices to become an imperial power in its own right. It should also be noted that China's decline was partially of Asian design: while Western powers picked away at the Xing dynasty, the Sino-Japanese War of 1894–95 witnessed a Westernized Japanese military crush Chinese forces on both land and sea. Even in China and India, local forces resisted the West.

A TALE OF THREE COUNTRIES

The appearance of a strong Western presence in Asia hit different countries in different ways. This difference was evident in some of the larger states and empires, as reflected by the experiences of India, Indonesia, China, Japan, and Korea.

India

India's interaction with the West has a long history. The land to the west of India represented trade and, more often than not, conquering or raiding armies, such as those of the Persians, Greeks (under Alexander the Great), and Arabs. Contact to the east was limited by geography, massive mountain ranges limiting communications between India and China, though there was a moderate degree of trade and cultural exchange. In contrast, there was much greater contact with Southeast Asia because of the relative ease of communications via water. The West, however, was to remain a challenge.

Arab traders started showing up in the 700s A.D., but militant Islam came in several waves, the most permanent arriving in 1192. Although the Muslims remained powerful in the following years, parts of India remained independent under Hindu resistance. However, in 1527, the Mughal dynasty emerged as the major power in India. The Mughals imposed a higher degree of unity to India; built lasting cultural landmarks in the Taj Mahal, the Pearl Mosque, and the Red Fort; and proved able in defending the land frontier from the west against any new threats (such as the Afghans). Where the Mughals failed was with the seaborne empires of the Europeans.

The Portuguese arrived in the Indian Ocean at the end of the fifteenth century. A nation with strong trading traditions, they founded a number of small enclaves, the most important of which was Goa (1510). The Portuguese were drawn to India because of that country's pivotal role in the East-West trade. The Indian coastal regions were geared for trade, with the littoral kingdoms exporting cotton and silk cloth, wheat, beans, pepper, and indigo and importing horses, ivory, and bullion. This was ideal for the Portuguese who came to trade (pepper being one of the most important commodities and in heavy demand throughout much of Europe) and who were not deeply interested in conquest.[4] Moreover, shortly after the arrival of the Portuguese, the Mughals rose to power, with Babur, the founder of the dynasty, very focused on conquest and in control of a strong military machine.

The Portuguese, however, were not the only Europeans to come to India. In 1610 the British made their entry into India, chasing off a Portuguese naval squadron. In 1613 the East India Company established an outpost at Surat from which the British would expand and eventually push out its European rivals to control all of India. By 1615 the Portuguese were largely eclipsed by the British, Dutch, and French, though it was the first mentioned who would win the subcontinent.

The Indians were unprepared for the British. In particular, the Mughals looked upon the British and their East India Company as just another group of European traders, who were driven by greed and who lacked any real sophistication in the ways of India. As historian Percival Spear notes, "India thought she had their measure and regarded them (northern Europeans) as pawns in the never-ending games of politics and commerce. . . . India had most to do with the northern Europeans and to her they seemed to be heavy, not shrewd, and dull, and in no context dangerous."[5] History was to show just the opposite, especially with the East India Company.

The East India Company was created in 1600 as a specially chartered British corporation, vested by Queen Elizabeth I, who gave it a royal monopoly to develop trade with India. Along these lines, it was an exceedingly powerful institution, representing British commercial interests, backed by the Crown and empowered with both diplomatic and military capabilities.[6] Consequently, the more traditionally minded Mughals came up against what was to be one of the cutting-edge creations of the Western capitalism, the East India Company, a well-honed corporate entity geared to gain control of trade and willing to crush all rivals, even local states.

Another factor in India's weak response to the British was the decline of the Mughals. While the sixteenth and seventeenth centuries were a period in which the Mughals brought India to one of its high points, the eighteenth century witnessed their decline. The last Great Mughal ruler Aurungzebe died in 1707, leaving his three sons to fight over the empire. Sadly for India, this fighting left the Mughal Empire in a weakened state just as the Europeans began to assert themselves. Of the next eight Great Mughals after Aurangzeb, whose combined reigns covered only 52 years to 1759, four were murdered, one was deposed, and only three died peacefully on the throne.[7] While Mughal leaders were busy killing each other, India was also hit in 1738 by an invasion by Nadir Shah, a Turk who had taken power in Persia. Nadir Shah's army crushed a weak Mughal force and sacked Delhi.

The Mughal decline was terminal but gradual. Mughal authority was increasingly challenged by the rise of new kingdoms and by the Europeans, in particular the British and their East India Company, which made inroads with the penetration of trade and the development of alliances with some of the upstarts. The French, however, remained a challenge. By the Battle of Plessey in 1757, India's destiny had reached a crossroads. With the Mughals on the sidelines and with an alliance with the French in hand, the young Nawab Siraj-ud-Dowlah of Bengal made his move to replace the old dynasty. Plessey, however, was to be the day of Robert Clive, the British leader who routed a combined French and Indian army. The result was to shift the position of the British from being traders to governors over India's affairs by incorporating their first major area of jurisdiction of the Indian subcontinent in Bengal.[8]

Following Plessey, Mughal power declined in a more precipitous fashion. By 1858 the last Mughal emperor, Bahadur Shah II, was deposed after he surprisingly was adopted (somewhat reluctantly) as the symbolic figurehead of the Great Mutiny in 1857. He was to die in exile in neighboring Burma in 1862. At the time British control was extensive, holding sway throughout most of present-day India, Pakistan, Sri Lanka, and Bangladesh. In many regards, the British takeover of India was a major historical coup. After all, the British came from a small island off the coast of Europe and their numbers were never great compared with the millions of Indians. The British, however, were well organized, with their authority first centering on the East India Company and over time, in a highly effective and organized system called the Raj (which represented the authority of the British Crown). The Raj functioned through divide-and-conquer politics, fielded an army of locals (with British officers), and created a lasting civil service. All of this, of course, would have an impact on the shape of India's economy and the thinking of its national elite once independence was achieved.

China

Although India and Indonesia were well on their way to becoming European possessions by 1800, Qing China was still very much seen as a power. China had a long tradition of being one of the major civilizations on the planet, and its innovative people gave us cast iron, the compass, gunpowder, paper, printing with movable type, windmills, navigation equipment of all kinds, paper money, porcelain, and silk spinning, weaving and dyeing. Following the Manchu conquest in 1644, the Qing dynasty provided a higher degree of military security, actively promoted land clearance, and oversaw the introduction of new crops. It also offered tax incentives for people to move west, promoted the commercialization of the handicraft producing system, and assumed management of water and irrigation facilities.

China's economy was largely driven by agriculture. Economic expansion was relatively vigorous during the eighteenth century and into the next, but it was ultimately constrained by concerns over population growth vis-à-vis the ability of the land to sustain people. As economic historian Philip Richardson observes, "the economic expansion was also paralleled by the maintenance of the social stability which was the overriding aim of the ruling Confucian political economy."[9] Industrialization was negligible and with the emphasis on stability, some of the more entrepreneurial elements of the population failed to find the same outlets as their Western counterparts. Although trade flourished at times in China, it was ancillary to the agriculture, which provided the state's lifeblood.[10] By the early 1800s, the Qing political economy was internally struggling, faced by the limits of growth, corruption, and a ruling class disinclined to provide an activist approach to a creeping crisis. The result was that when the aggressive Westerners appeared, China was already falling behind Europe economically and was ill prepared to meet the economic, political, and military challenges of the future.

China's decline at the hands of the West is well documented. Although China's ruling class of Mandarins sought to keep the British and other Europeans at arm's length in Canton's designated trading area, far to the south of Beijing, the imperial capital, the Opium War of 1840 radically changed circumstances. In what started out as an effort by the Chinese authorities to curb a nasty trade in narcotics conducted by the British (from their colonial base in India), the Qing dynasty suffered a humiliating military defeat and was forced to open five ports to foreign commerce, provide an indemnity, and cede Hong Kong.[11]

The issue of trade remains a point of contention as to how China was to progress and how it responded to the seaborne European challenge. China's losing out to the West probably came from the decision by the authorities during the Ming dynasty to cease all seaborne voyages and to embrace isolationism. During the early Ming years, in particular from 1405 to 1433, seven large Chinese expeditions set out to explore and to bring under the Chinese tributary system the vast periphery of the Indian Ocean. These were fleets of hundreds of ships and several thousand men. Considering the distances the fleets sailed (out to Africa), the Ming voyages reflected that Chinese ocean-going technology was equal to, and perhaps superior to, European seafaring at the time. If nothing else, the voyages indicated to other countries in the region that China was the major power in the neighborhood, capable of projecting its power beyond its usual zone of influence.

The obvious question that comes out of the Ming dynasty's major seagoing voyages is why did they stop? And, what if they had continued? Would China have rounded the Cape of Good Hope before Vasco da Gama, allowing the Chinese to discover Europe? The decision to discontinue the voyages and end China's sea-going power was due to the very pronounced centralization of Chinese power in the emperor and the court, and related to a struggle in the Imperial Court between the Confucian courtiers (who favored isolation) and the palace eunuchs (who were pro-sea power). The Confucians won, and China embarked upon a policy of isolationism. By 1500 it was made an imperial offense for a Chinese to go to sea with more than two masts without special permission. In 1525 another ruling authorized officials to destroy the larger classes of ships. These decisions made certain that the European entry into the Indian Ocean and Asia's waters was free of a contending Chinese naval and economic power.

It cannot be denied that China during the Ming dynasty opted for isolationism. While some of this can be laid in the lap of the Confucians at the Imperial Court, there are other factors for this shift. First and foremost, the main security threats to China usually came from land: the Mongols and others were constantly testing the frontier in the north. Having a large navy did not really help fend off Mongol and other invaders on the land frontier. In addition, improvements in the internal canal system in China made transport on those routes easier and safer than sea routes, which were often infested by pirates. All the same, China opted to impose isolation. In turn, this isolation fed Chinese thinking that regarded the outside world as an abstraction as to what was really important: life within the Middle Kingdom. Hence China from the Ming to Qing dynasties was comparatively but entirely isolationist. Moreover, it was not open to new ideas from the outside, allowing it to lose its technological advantages over the West.[12] By the Opium War in 1840, Western power was much greater than Chinese in terms of military strength.

The outcome of events for China in the years ahead was largely negative. More defeats at the hands of the West followed, while internal problems mounted—grain blockages (1830s), tax-resistance riots (1840s), and a number of rebellions, the most widespread and damaging being the Taipings. Despite efforts to assimilate foreign thinking, the efforts encountered ongoing resistance from Confucian hardliners who clung to the view that China remained the Middle Kingdom around which all other countries and peoples orbited. By 1900 China was a deeply troubled country, the Qing dynasty in severe decline, and Western dominance a fact. The political center was in a downward and terminal spiral from which there was no recovery. Disorder and chaos became the rule, not the exception. In 1911 a revolution swept away the Qing dynasty, replacing it with a weak republic that never fully consolidated its power over the warlords and eventually the Japanese in the 1930s. For many Chinese the modern era was associated with foreign exploitation, political instability, and vast societal upheaval.

Japan

Japan's experience differed from that of India, Indonesia, and China. Although Japan's economy was largely agrarian and foreign trade was tightly controlled, the Western approach was met by a forceful, yet pragmatic reaction. In many regards, Japan was better equipped for modernization because premodern Japan had already started to abandon Confucian influences and because much of the national leadership came from military backgrounds that gave these leaders a quicker comprehension of the danger represented by Western military superiority.[13] Perhaps more significantly, Japan benefited from the existence of sophisticated proto-banks and financial markets, an entrepreneurial merchant class (especially in the free cities and regional domains), and one of the highest literacy rates outside of Europe. It is important to underscore that there was no dramatic, discontinuous transformation from feudal backwardness to twentieth-century industrialization; rather the processes of change were already well in place when the Europeans arrived.[14]

In the sixteenth century Portuguese and Spanish missionaries sought to convert the Japanese (and small numbers did become Christian), creating considerable trepidation among the ruling elite. In 1638 forces of the Shogun (the ruling entity) massacred Christian converts, foreign missionaries were expelled, and all foreign books were banned. All contact with Westerners was limited to a small enclave of Dutch merchants in Nagasaki. It is important to clarify that despite the suppression of foreign influence in Japan, foreign learning still continued in the form of Rangaku, Dutch learning (that outside knowledge allowed to be introduced by this handful of Europeans). Nagasaki became the main point of contact between the West and Japan. In 1720 the ban on Western books was relaxed, and the Tokugawa shogunate quietly made some reforms to improve agriculture.

Two other factors benefited Japan: first, despite the official opprobrium on foreign contact, there was a robust contraband trade with China and Korea by the Western domains on the Japan Sea, and second, agricultural productivity was quite high by the 1880s. The second of these factors provided a foundation for improving education and industry as well as to bolster a middle class.

Unlike China, Japan did not regard itself as the center of the world. Although Japan's neo-Confucians maintained control over the country, Dutch learning spread. In addition, a powerful and sophisticated merchant class arose in coastal cities such as Osaka. Although the merchants had lower social standing than samurai, the warrior elite; peasants; and artisans, their wealth gave them growing influence. And they were well aware that the world outside of Japan was changing and that as long as their country was isolated, it was effectively cut off from technological knowledge. The Opium War thus was a wake-up call. According to Ian Buruma, "news of the disastrous Opium Wars in the 1840s came as a shock, for it not only proved how backward China had become, it showed Japan's own vulnerability."[15]

Japan also profited from the more military frame of mind among its elite. Although neo-Confucianism was strongly entrenched and provided the basis of a world view, the samurai class was more open to practical applications of what the West could provide—better weapons.

Consequently, although Japan's elite was careful as to what was imported in terms of ideas, it allowed firearms to become part of the weaponry of any aspiring political leader. This explains how and why firearms were introduced into a country that was supposedly hermetically sealed from the outside world. Simply stated, firearms were a practical application of foreign technology, a trend that only gained momentum with China's defeat in the Opium War. This presence of foreign technology also meant that a debate was already in motion and various elements of Westerniza-tion were evident in Tokogawa Japan, well before the arrival of Commo-dore Perry and the Black Ships that constituted the U.S. action to "open" Japan to the outside world in 1853–54.

The debate on how to modernize and deal with the foreign threat also captured the core issues for the reformers involved in the Meiji Restoration in 1868 that swept away the Tokogawa Shogunate and replaced it with a new government dominated by conservative reformers. Japan, in fact, quickly sent out a number of fact-finding missions to Europe and the United States. Unlike the Chinese, who had a dilemma arising from their regarding China as the center of global civilization, the Japanese had ear-lier borrowed ideas from China, and having observed the victory of Western arms, they were flexible in looking to alternative strategies. Along these lines, Japanese leadership was impressed with the British path to political stability: careful and gradual reforms, building upon tradition and avoiding the destructive revolutionary tendencies of the French. There was also a certain commonality with Germany, as both nations shared similarities in their recent problems and objectives: restoration of the mon-archy, political centralization and unification, the promotion of popular education, the securing of frontiers, recognition abroad, and the develop-ment of commerce and industry.

The result of Japan's approach to the Western challenge was radically different from the rest of Asia. While India and Indonesia became outright colonies of Western nations and China was an informal empire, Japan emerged as the first modern Asian industrial and imperial power. Instead of a downward spiral of economic divergence, Japan became a market-oriented economy with a leadership driven by a strong desire to catch up with the West. The key elements that defined the Japanese model encom-passed a pivotal function for the state, concentration of private economic power in the hands of a small number of business groups (*zaibatsu*), a group of large banks that worked hand in glove with the state, an emphasis on exports, and a political system geared for maintaining control, though willing to allow some concessions to opening up participation in the political system.

ASIA'S EVOLVING PLACE IN THE WORLD

During the nineteenth and twentieth centuries, Asia evolved along two distinct tracks: one of eclipse and one of convergence. Although this is a very broad generalization, China became a combination of zones of foreign influence, and India became an outright colony of the British. Japan was the exception to this pattern and as such deserves an explanation. Consequently, the long colonial period had a major influence on Asia, especially in the development of a world view in the aftermath of colonialism. In particular, the following features were evident across a wide spectrum: 1) there was little development without outside interference; 2) trade opened the door to outside control (very strongly felt in India and China); 3) foreign ideas in some areas were necessary to throw off foreign rule and regain and maintain independence; and 4) political order was difficult to maintain in changing societies (more so for China and Korea than for Japan and parts of Southeast Asia).

Although China was not officially a colony, it was dominated by the major powers, including Japan and the United States. The Chinese government (such as it was following the 1911 revolution that toppled the Qing dynasty) was forced to deal with foreign enclaves, extraterritoriality, and unfair treaties. Hong Kong was under direct British control, Taiwan was lost to Japan in the Sino-Japanese War of 1894–95, the Germans took the Shantung Peninsula, and considerable concessions were made to the Russians in Manchuria. Even the Americans took advantage of the situation via trade rights and extraterritoriality. Certainly in the cases of India, Indonesia, and China, trade had been one of the forces opening the door to outside intervention and control.

Yet for all of the negatives associated with Western domination introduced by trade, Japan embarked upon a radically different path than its neighbors. The Japanese were quick to recognize the unfair nature of the global system dominated by the West but were equally fast in understanding that foreign ideas and technology could be used to reduce outside control. Indeed, Japan was able to harness the Western learning and largely overhaul the economy and through that, society. While China, India, Indonesia, and Korea were pushed further apart from convergence with the West (from a power standpoint based on economic and military capabilities), Japan moved closer to the Western powers. The Sino-Japanese War clearly emphasized Japan was the regional Asian power. However, the Russo-Japanese War (1904–5) in which the Asian country defeated the Tsarist Empire left little doubt that Tokyo's effort to join the ranks as an imperialist power had been successful. It was also the first time in modern history that an Asian power defeated a Western power.

Japan's rise as a world power was not without challenges. The Japanese government faced samurai rebellions and assassinations of officials in the beginning and peasant riots as the industrialization process took root. There was also some degree of political volatility as the authorities sought to steer the country through the advent of political parties, extending voter rights and maintaining a balance between military power and other societal needs. In a sense political order was critical to maintain change in Japan. Make no mistake, the modernization process was top-down, with the Meiji reformers keenly aware of the stakes if either factional or popular discontent were able to derail reforms.

The Japanese experience was driven by the pressing need to catch up with the West. This drive was underpinned by a deep sense of nationalism that also embraced a strong sense that the West had victimized Asia. And Japan's rising power was duly noted by the rest of Asia. It was not surprising that many Indians, Chinese, and other Asians traveled to Japan beginning at the start of the twentieth century to witness an Asian country emerging as capable of challenging the West.

By the late 1930s, Japan's posture had increasingly turned militant, and its ideas of empire more focused on its neighbors, China and Korea. The latter was of particular importance to Japanese national security considering its geopolitical location as a peninsula thrust at the middle of Japan. Japan's conquest and incorporation of Korea was at the root of the wars against China and Russia. At the same time, this situation hardly left the Koreans content. Under direct Japanese rule since 1910, they were forced to speak Japanese, develop an industrial economy geared to the benefit of Japan, and lacked any political freedoms, let alone the ability to have a separate Korean identity. Simply stated, Japanese imperialism was harsh, setting the stage for a legacy of ill will in the postcolonial period.

The linkage between economics and politics came into sharp focus when Japan's aspirations for a larger Asian-Pacific empire brought it at loggerheads with the United States, one of its major trade partners. As the United States increasingly gravitated to the side of China, Japan found itself threatened by U.S. economic threats, supported by those of Europe and their Asian colonies—locations of key resources required to keep the Japanese economy running. By 1939, when Europe plunged into war, conflict between the United States and Japan was not far behind. The ensuing world conflict was to bring an end to European dominance of the region, reshape Japan's role as a global player, and elevate the United States as the key power, a situation destined to last through the end of the twentieth century.

THE POST-WORLD WAR II SHIFT

Following World War II, most of Asia was an economic backwater. The regional economic dynamo, Japan, had lost the war and was occupied by the United States. Its once powerful industrial infrastructure had been bombed into useless rubble. Korea was divided between a communist North and a Western-leaning South. Although some of Japan's colonial industrial infrastructure survived in Korea, the looming threat of war eclipsed hope of sustainable economic growth. China was also finishing one conflict—World War II—and gearing up for a bloody civil war between the Nationalists and Communists. In Southeast Asia Europe's colonial embrace was loosening, and new nationalistic forces were competing for control. India was also restive, and the days of the British Raj were numbered. After considerable agitation led by M. Gandhi and others, the British decided to depart. India emerged as an independent nation in 1947.

A central theme running through almost every country in the region, with the exception of Japan (which had already experienced it), was a political awakening in which nationalism was rising, sometimes leading to conflict with communist forces and at other times to be commandeered by the Communists as in China, North Korea, Vietnam, Laos, and Cambodia. Political concerns overrode economic concerns. In addition, the international environment was uncertain as the United States and the Soviet Union were gradually shifting from allies into adversaries and as the global economy was unsettled between reconstruction, decolonialization, and the creation of new international organizations such as Bretton Woods, the International Monetary Fund, and the World Bank.

While much of Asia was rocked by political problems during the 1950s through the 1970s—the Korean War, the Vietnam War, the Cultural Revolution, political succession in China, and the rise and fall of Sukarno in Indonesia—Japan began the gradual process of economic reconstruction. That process was considerably helped by a substantial curtailment in military expenditures and by the protection of the U.S. nuclear umbrella and troops. Historian R.L. Sims writes that the emphasis placed on the economy "provided a nationally and internationally acceptable outlet for Japanese nationalism."[16] The Korean War (1950–53) also helped the Japanese economy as the Asian nation functioned as a backup base for U.S. and UN forces.

During the 1950s and 1960s, a combination of factors helped elevate the Japanese economy: close coordination between the government, the ruling Liberal Democratic Party (LDP), and the business sector; a talented and skilled population with a strong work ethic; initial U.S. assistance in economic reconstruction, which led to all-new industrial plants; a strategy based on export growth; and a willingness on the part of the population to make personal sacrifices for the national good. The government's role was to provide stability and guide the public and private sectors into a coordinated effort, much as a country would be mobilized for war.

From being a defeated imperial power, Japan steadily rose to become Asia's leading economic heavyweight. Real GDP growth rates of close to 10 percent were achieved in the 1956 to 1973 period. By 1970 Japan had achieved a production level twice that of China, three times that of Africa, and twice that of Latin America. In 1972 gross national product stood at an impressive $290 billion, a substantial uptick from $1.5 billion in 1945.

While Japan moved toward an embrace of international markets, Asia's other giants moved in the other direction toward greater self-sufficiency based on state-led heavy industrialization. In China and India there was a lingering suspicion about trade (considering how it had opened the door to foreign domination) and suspicion of capitalism. In China, the Communists under Mao Zedong sought to totally restructure the economy, putting agriculture into collectives and throwing scarce resources into the development of heavy industry. At the same time, Mao's desire for power guaranteed ongoing political upheaval, purges among the leadership ranks, and a highly unstable economic policy environment. The result was a dysfunctional economy, and China's retreat from the global economy. The Great Leap Forward (1958–62) was designed as an alternative model of development from the Soviet Union's. It accelerated the collectivization of agriculture from small units to large communal ones and emphasized industrial production. Part of the Great Leap Forward was the infamous Backyard Furnace campaign in which Mao stated that China would double steel output and catch up with the United Kingdom in terms of steel output in 15 years. Consequently, small steel furnaces were made in the back yards of communes throughout China, with people using every type of fuel they could to power these furnaces. This meant that millions of peasants scurried about looking for coal—and anything else that would burn. They also used everything they could find that was made of steel and iron, turning pots and pans and important farm tools into steel girders. The only problem was that the steel girders were often of very poor quality. One result was a massive famine that killed millions. Lumps are poor substitutes for hoes. When Mao came under attack for the failure of such policies, he briefly retreated only to return again in force with the launching of the Cultural Revolution. At the height of the Cultural Revolution in the mid-1960s, China even withdrew a large number of its ambassadors as the country's focus narrowed to political survival at home, with workers and students under Mao's guidance bringing the country to a standstill. When Mao died in 1976, the Chinese economy was largely agricultural, underdeveloped industrially, struggling to feed itself, and inward looking.

Asia's other giant India embarked upon a moderately different path, but one nonetheless dominated by a suspicion of international trade and the need to become more self-sufficient, though the political situation was radically different in that the parliamentary system of rule was well established. Jawaharlal Nehru, who became the country's first prime minister in 1949, faced an enormous task. The country over which Nehru headed was poor, struggled to feed itself, and had a rudimentary industrial infrastructure. In addition, in 1947 former British India split into what would eventually become three separate political units: India, Pakistan, and Bangladesh (initially part of Pakistan). The split between the predominantly Hindu India (with a large Muslim minority) and Muslim Pakistan left the country with a major trauma, as thousands were killed in religious violence and as Nehru's government was faced with assimilating 10 to 15 million refugees. Adding further to the challenges for the newly independent India was the division of Kashmir, the related military threat from Pakistan, and the integration of the princely states and foreign enclaves (mainly Portuguese).

Nehru's role at the helm of the new India was critical in determining the country's economic path. What shaped the Indian leader's world view? Heavily influenced by Fabian socialism, Nehru was committed to a coordinated program of planned development in which the state was to play the leading role.[17] He was impressed by elements of Chinese cooperative farming after a trip to the People's Republic in 1954 and found inspiration from Stalin's Soviet Union in its ability to industrialize and resist Hitler. Nehru also had a disdain for business, an attitude that would not help the development of India's private sector.[18] All the same, it would be wrong to mistake Nehru for a Communist. As political scientist Ranbir Vohra observes of Nehru: "he was at best a democrat-socialist who was anxious to develop rapidly and increase its wealth so that poverty could be eliminated and living standards raised."[19]

Nehru also inherited some strong positives from the British. Despite the enormous challenges facing him and the ruling Congress Party, the country had a high-minded, highly ethical elitist civil service (this would change as corruption wormed its way into the growing ranks), a professional and apolitical military, and a well educated and experienced political class. Moreover, there was a broad consensus within the ruling Congress Party and other mainstream political parties for the need to create and maintain a united and prosperous India.

What was to evolve from this complex set of factors was a mixed economy in which the state dominated national development through a bureaucratic regulatory mechanism that would be called the License Raj. Private sector companies were allowed, especially in the consumer sector, while a clear preference was given to public sector company development in heavy industries. Reflections of this developmental strategy were the nationalization of the insurance sector and the infamous budget of 1957–58 (which substantially raised taxes on businesses and helped bury the Indian stock market for decades). The net result of the Nehru era, which would extend into the 1980s, was an economy that looked largely inward, that was dominated by a massive bureaucratic tangle that hindered (but did not kill) the private sector, that looked upon foreign investment with suspicion, and that set the country on a track of slow, yet steady economic growth. By the 1980s many within India would begin to question the Hindu path to development, especially when compared to what was happening in the rest of Asia.

THE NEW ASIA RISING

By the late 1970s, Japan was now a major economic player in international markets. It was also increasingly looked upon as a model for other Asian countries, many struggling to move beyond political issues and focus on economic development. Japan offered an example of success. In a very simplistic sense, its development model in the aftermath of the World War II was one of government-guided, relationship-driven finance geared toward finding competitive export sectors. For various reasons Singapore, Taiwan, South Korea, and Hong Kong emerged as the first group of Asian "dragons" or "tigers" to follow Japan (and elements of its model) into a higher level of economic development. Although smaller than Japan, the four economies were similar in that they lacked natural resources but had comparatively well-educated populations capable and willing to learn new skills. Taiwan and Korea had both been Japanese colonies, a factor that perhaps helped them adopt the system of close government-business cooperation. In addition, Korea and Taiwan benefited from a close political and military relationship with the United States.

The security factor also played a role in Singapore and Hong Kong. Both were cities, surrounded by potential enemies. This threat increased the sense of urgency about the need for economic success relative to elevating their populations' per capita income and making their commercial enterprises more competitive. As Korea, Taiwan, Singapore, and Hong Kong developed, they also became more attractive to foreign investors. Investment came in two forms: direct investment by large multinational corporations and portfolio investment via institutional investors and small investors (through mutual funds and American Depository Receptors). The multinational corporations increasingly found that setting up shop in this handful of Asian countries made strategic sense. These countries offered cheap, yet relatively well-educated and motivated work forces, geographical proximity to potential growth markets (like China), adequate infrastructure, and usually a high degree of political stability. Hong Kong and Singapore also offered two of the best harbors in the world.

Korea's development was probably one of the most stunning. In 1960 South Korea had an average per capita income of $80, putting it roughly at the same level as Ghana and Sudan and a bit behind India. Natural resources were scarce, and the national infrastructure was still recovering from the Korean War (1950–53). Private cars were a novelty, and electricity and running water were seen as luxuries. At the same time, the World Bank's Asian up and comers were Burma and the Philippines. The World Bank, in fact, was not optimistic about South Korea's prospects, regarding it as destined to remain a perennial mendicant. South Korea, however, made significant progress in the 1960s and 1970s, becoming one of the world's more industrialized economies by the 1980s.

A second wave of tiger economies emerged in the 1980s, encompassing Malaysia, Thailand, and Indonesia. Each country had adopted export-oriented economic policies, benefited from the U.S. economic boom, and had strong governments that were able to focus largely on policy matters. Real GDP rates were to pick up considerably. (See table 2.1) A third wave of tiger development came with China, which began the economic reform process in 1978 but which gradually moved to a faster pace, especially in the early 1990s. A fourth wave appeared to be forming in the mid-1990s that consisted of the Philippines, India, Vietnam, Pakistan, and Burma.[20]

As globalization made inroads into Asia and capital markets were relaxed, foreign investment rushed in. While China was one of the major beneficiaries, the rest of the region was very much on the investment map. Indeed, the amount of capital flowing into non-Japan Asia was considerably larger than that flowing into Latin America, the Middle East, and Africa combined.

Table 2.1
Asian Real GDP Growth (%)

Country	1980–1990 (%)	1990–1998 (%)
China	10.2	11.1
Hong Kong	6.9	4.4
India	5.8	6.1
Indonesia	6.1	5.8
Korea	9.4	6.2
Malaysia	5.3	7.7
Myanmar (Burma)	0.6	6.3
Philippines	1.0	3.3
Singapore	6.6	8.0
Thailand	7.6	7.4
Vietnam	4.6	8.6

Source: World Bank, *World Development Report 1999/2000: Entering the 21st Century* (New York: Oxford University Press, 2000), pp. 250–251.

While countries such as Malaysia, Thailand, and Indonesia attracted foreign investment, it was China that increasingly stole the show as the 1990s progressed. Three key reasons dominated foreign investment decisions about China: the sheer size of the potential China market dwarfed the rest of Asia (and Latin America and other emerging markets); the Chinese government was actively seeking to attract foreign investors with a wide range of incentives; and China was moving to further open its economy by joining the World Trade Organization (WTO). Another factor was China's relative political stability. Gone were the days of the chaotic Cultural Revolution of the 1960s or the democratic fervor of the late 1980s. China was clearly focused on its economic development. Indeed, China's great transformation, beginning in the late 1970s, was to change the dynamic between East and West.

CONCLUSION

Over a period of several centuries, Asia's economies went from parity (in some cases superiority) to divergence with the West. This phase was marked by a long period of political decline, with the notable exception of Japan. At the same time, the heavy involvement with the West was to create subtle changes in the way Asian governments approached development, placing an emphasis on exports to pull up the local economy. Consequently, by the time Asia reached the second half of the twentieth century, the stage was set for a shift from the long trajectory of divergence, which also entailed a weakness in political power vis-à-vis the West, to the other direction—economic convergence. Beginning in the 1980s, calls for the twenty-first century to be the Asian century reflected the hope that not only was convergence in motion but that the region could actually surpass the West. After all, the Asian export-led economic model had resulted in rapid paces of expansion, rising levels of per capita income, and a growing middle class. These developments would only accelerate in the years to come, despite the economic stumble of the 1997–98 economic crisis. Coming a little later to the development game, China would increasingly come to represent the major force in Asia's rise, the subject of the next chapter.

Chapter 3

THE RISE OF CHINA

China in 1949 emerged from a long period of conflict, first against Japan beginning in the 1930s and 1940s and then a brutish civil war between the Communists and Nationalists. The Communists under "the Great Helmsman," Mao Zedong, founded the People's Republic and aggressively moved to pull the Chinese economy out of the global system, control all interchange with the world, and reorder the domestic socioeconomic and political landscapes. Despite a modicum of trade, China underwent a long period of being more inward looking and only selectively engaged with the global economy. By the global economic crisis of 2008–9, China was a critical economic locomotive keeping the Great Recession from turning into a new Great Depression. By 2010 China had bypassed Japan to become the world's second largest economy after the United States. Now its goods sit on the shelves of stores from Africa and the Middle East to Europe and North America, and it is one of the largest buyers of commodities in Australia and Brazil.

It is the purpose of this chapter to examine what happened to change China from its inward-looking and often disruptive experimentation with Maoism to its becoming a major economic power in the late twentieth century. The real turning point came in 1978, which marked the beginning of a long period of dynamic economic expansion. What is significant is that China embraced a development strategy, "market-Leninist" (also called the Beijing Consensus), that provided it with the tools to overhaul what had been an inward-looking economy. China then turned into an investment-guided and export-driven machine. This system can be defined as the adoption of quasi-market economic policies implemented under the exclusive political control of the Chinese Communist Party (CCP). According to Joshua Cooper Ramo, the former *Time Magazine* editor, who coined the term "Beijing Consensus" in 2004, China's political economy implied strong central control, complemented by economic prosperity. But whether we call it market-Leninism or Beijing Consensus, the combination of political control in a changing society, combined with a gradual marketization of economic life, has made China an amazing success story in terms of improving the standard of living and elevating China back into the ranks of great powers.

This is really a remarkable experiment. Many scholars and politicians in the democratic Western countries would argue that it is impossible to have meaningful economic growth and prosperity over a sustained period of time unless it is accompanied by political democracy. They might excuse the obvious exception of Singapore as too tiny a case to matter. But what are we to make of China, which has had one of the fastest growth rates in the world for more than 10 years? Approximately 400 million people have emerged from dire poverty to the lower middle classes or middle classes in that time in China. (Of course, many millions remain desperately poor as well). And yet the authorities have not relaxed their hold on the nation's political or social institutions in a meaningful way during this entire period. Chinese officials would argue that one size does not fit all, that their history and political culture is unique, and that theirs is a distinctly Chinese or Confucian way of doing things.

Perhaps we are witnessing just a temporary state of affairs. If so, then maybe the Chinese middle classes will demand greater political rights over time. Should that come to pass, then the Chinese system will adapt or it may falter. But we are not there yet. If nothing else, the Chinese case teaches us not to be so quick to lump all economically successful states together. Perhaps there may be meaningfully different strategies to economic development other than the Western model.

In essence, the Chinese citizen has surrendered his or her political rights (at least in a liberal Western sense) for the opportunity to become more affluent or, at the very least, to determine what economic endeavor to pursue. This reflects an approach to development that places the obtainment of economic objectives over political change (the end objective being a more open political system). Indeed, the improvement of the country's economic standing and the massive transformation of personal incomes are meant to reinforce political order and stability. While the trade-offs between political and economic freedoms have not provided a perfect system, China has clearly been successful in pulling a vast number of its population out of poverty and in elevating its economy into a world class power, whose volatility is of critical importance to the rest of Asia and the world. China is also displaying an alternative approach to development, which has a ready echo in other parts of the world, notably Africa and Asia.

Much of the credit for China's departure from inward-looking Maoist collectivism should be credited to Deng Xiao-ping, who became the nations' key political figure from 1978 until his death in 1997. Armed with such pragmatic maxims as "it does not matter if the cat is black or white, as long it catches mice, it is a good cat," Deng pushed his country along the lines of a gradual opening of the economy, strong economic growth and engagement in the global economic system. This combination functioned as an important firewall to the economic crisis that struck Asia in the 1997–98. To a significant degree, the 1997–98 crisis demonstrated the growing significance of China in the regional economy. Further, the subsequent 2007–8 global economic crisis demonstrated China's arrival as a major international economic player of an equal weight with the United States, Europe, and Japan. This was best demonstrated in the important role played by China in buying U.S. debt in the form of Treasury bonds, which were needed to help finance the U.S. large fiscal deficit. China's financial support was also critical to helping crisis-ridden Greece and Portugal in 2010 and 2011 by buying bonds and/or investing in the economy. Although China continues to face many significant challenges including environmental pollution, widespread corruption, and income inequalities, its rise to world prominence has been one of the most important developments of the late twentieth and early twenty-first centuries.

DENG XIAO-PING'S SURPRISING ROAD TO SUCCESS

By the time that Deng Xiao-ping came on the international public stage in 1978, he was 74 years old, short and rotund.[1] His apparently jolly face disguised his incredibly difficult path to power. Born in 1904 in Sichuan Province in China's rugged interior, he joined the Communist Party while studying in France (1920–25). He was a veteran of the Long March and joined the Party Central Committee in 1945. By 1956 he was a member of the Politburo Standing Committee in which he worked closely with Liu Shaoqi, who came to power in the aftermath of Mao's disastrous Great Leap Forward. Mao's eclipse was brief, and during the Cultural Revolution, Deng's pragmatic nature in economic policies made him an easy target for the more ideologically driven figures surrounding the Great Helmsman and his ultra-left Gang of Four (including Mao's wife Jiang Qing).

It is important to underscore that prior to Deng's rise to power, China was one of the leading opponents to globalization. Not only was China caught in a Cold War with the United States and its allies, it also maintained chilly relations with the Soviet Union and the Warsaw Pact, both developments leaving Beijing defiantly opposed to what it perceived as Western and Soviet efforts to integrate the world into one or the other of competing global systems. As long-time Asian hand William Overholt notes of China prior its reforms, "it opposed the global political order and the major global institutions such as the IMF and World Bank. It believed that global disorder was a good thing, and under Mao Zedong it actively promoted disorder throughout the world, including the promotion of insurgencies in most of China's neighbors, in much of Africa and Latin America, and even in our universities."[2] Along these lines, the Cultural Revolution (1966–76), with its Red Guards, was a rejection of tradition, bureaucratic governance, the older generation, and anything that smacked of the outside world (and by implication, the West and capitalism).

The Red Guards attacked Deng as the "Number two Capitalist Roader" (behind Liu). The ultra-left clique around Mao brought considerable chaos to China. The disruption of the mid- and late 1960s left China adrift. By the 1970s China had reached an economic plateau. The Maoist policy of "hard struggle and self-reliance," though admired by some as a superior model for development for the Third World, offered diminishing returns to the Chinese people.[3] Despite considerable potential and some actual gains in some sectors, the country's politics neutralized what could have been achieved. China had an industrial base capable of steel production, light industry producing consumer goods, and substantial oil and coal reserves to fuel those industries. The population was still largely rural, but much better organized, healthier, and educated than in the past. At the same time, the disastrous and ideologically driven push for economic self-sufficiency left China isolated, and its agricultural production severely limited which in turn contained the upside of growth. Moreover, for all the country's industrial base, the ideological tint left economic planners reluctant to pursue anything that smacked of consumerism—to the detriment of the average Chinese citizen.

Deng survived China's upheaval by being sent to work in a rural tractor factory. In the aftermath of the Cultural Revolution, Zhou Enlai, second behind Mao, pushed to reinstate Deng as premier deputy in 1973. With Zhou's support Deng soon launched the Four Modernizations, a government agenda that focused on strengthening agriculture, industry, technology, and defense, as well as stimulating badly needed economic growth, all seen as critical in order for China to catch up with the West.

Zhou died in January 1976, and Deng was purged once again by the Gang of Four. However, when Mao died in September 1976, Deng quietly came back to power, backed by the bureaucracy, military, and most of the party, all tired of the incessant ideological ferment that weakened the country. Mao's picked successor, Hua Guofeng, was easily pushed aside, and the Gang of Four were arrested and put on trial.

Deng's approach to the economy was pragmatic, placing an emphasis on economic betterment and incentives, both of which had capitalist undercurrents. From the Four Modernizations came other economic reforms, including a relaxation of price controls, more say for local officials and state-owned enterprises (SOEs) managers in decision making and the creation of Special Economic Zones (SEZs) and township village enterprises (TVEs) in the 1980s. The SEZs significantly gave local authorities the right to negotiate with foreign companies. This was a radical step. Deng's more pragmatic approach also opened the door to greater trade with the West. China was stepping back into the global economy (a development helped by a Sino-American rapprochement in the early-1970s). With Deng at the helm, China went back to work. In both the rural and urban parts of China, the standard of living rose, and the annual average rates of growth pushed upward to 10 percent in agricultural and industrial output. At the same time, China became self-sufficient in grain production.

By the late 1980s, an outcome of China's economic success was greater demand by a more prosperous population for an extension of freedoms into the political realm. Initially led by students and intellectuals and partially inspired by the changes in the Soviet Union, a liberalization and anticorruption movement gained momentum. At the same time, China was hit by a surge in inflation, something that hit urban dwellers, including workers, some of whom were attracted to protests. In 1989 this mix of forces resulted in demonstrations for a more open political system in Beijing's Tiananmen Square in 1989. It was deeply feared among party elders that political liberalization could quickly spin out of control and the CCP would be ousted by an angry population, much in the same fashion as various dynasties. The matter was further complicated by a more liberal wing of the party, led by General Secretary Zhao Ziyang, who was locked in a battle with party conservatives. Zhao failed to carry the day, and martial law was declared, allowing the use of troops against large-scale demonstrations in the capital.

Party conservatives quickly blamed Deng's experiment with a mixed economy for the mass demonstrations. Deng was briefly forced to retreat in the aftermath of the suppression of China's democratic movement, but in his famous 1992 tour of southern China, economic reform and fast growth were back in vogue. He also benefited from the economic acumen of Zhu Rongji, who was plucked from his position as mayor of Shanghai in 1991 and given free reign to push economic reforms.[4] The fact that Zhu was younger than Deng and worked well with President Jiang Zemin (despite some worries over rivalries between the two), helped instill vigor and continuity to the economic reform process.

Deng died in 1997, but the economic development process he put in motion continued into the next century. His main legacy was the transformation of China from being an inward-looking agriculturally dominated economy into an industrial "socialist market" country.[5] He argued (and no one dared to dissent too much) that Asia's largest country was in the primary stage for socialism and that the CCP's duty was to perfect "socialism with Chinese characteristics." This translated into the state playing an important role in directing the economy while promoting the development of a private sector. For this program to succeed, the state has to maintain a technocratic bureaucracy, has to have the ability (via the government-controlled banks) to allocate capital to key sectors, and has to allow market incentives (profits). It also emphasized exports and sought to attract foreign direct investment. The reform process was imposed from the top, was gradualistic in nature, was focused on upgrading the standard of living and on rapid growth; additionally, the leadership kept tight control of the country's political life.[6] The CCP, led by Deng and his immediate successor, Jiang Zemin (president 1993–2003), allowed people to make economic decisions but clearly not political ones.

The fundamental structure of China's political economy was put into place in the Deng and Jiang years. Although the political system was Leninist and clearly autocratic, it increasingly placed an emphasis on consensus among the leadership elites. Equally important, the party was keenly aware of the need to maintain legitimacy in the eyes of the public. This took economic policymaking down the path of being strongly pro-growth, with an eye to job creation and the establishment of a more affluent society. The persistent problem of official corruption also forced public policy from the political center to periodically crack down on wrongdoers, some of them high-ranking officials.

Significantly, China's links to the outside world were to take off in the 1990s, even after the political stink of the human rights crackdown following Tiananmen Square. The West and Japan continued to trade and invest in China, investments being drawn by cheap labor and incentives. Although foreign direct investment inflows to China stayed under $10 billion in 1990 and 1991, they were to regain momentum in 1992 and by mid-decade topped $40 billion.[7] To the Chinese political elite, the Tiananmen crackdown meant that chaos was averted and stability maintained. This was in sharp contrast to the unraveling of the Soviet Union and Warsaw Pact, which unraveling was accompanied by considerable political turmoil and economic shock. While the Soviet Union collapsed in 1992, the CCP was presiding over one of the world's most stunning and far-reaching economic transformations. The CCP's decision not to pursue economic shock treatment or attempt political liberalization left them still very much in control while their counterparts in East Germany, the Soviet Union, and Romania went into the trash can of history. Moreover, China's embrace of globalization was only to accelerate a transformation that was to be highly successful on the economic side.

By the early 1990s a dualistic China emerged, which was to take the country into the next century. The Janus-like nature of the political economy was marked by the sometimes repressive political system, constructed around a well-marked elite, backed by a security apparatus (including the powerful People's Liberation Army or PLA), willing and able to use police surveillance, intimidation, and coercion. But this control was matched by a social and economic revolution that is pulling a large proportion of humanity out of poverty over a relatively short period of time. It also created a very different civil society than before; gone was the seemingly arbitrary violence and ideological rigidity of the Maoist era and in was a social order that was, within limits, given a green light to be more pragmatic and geared toward consumption. Traditional Confucian values of study, hard work, and hierarchy (key to social order) were encouraged. Additionally, there was encouragement to embrace the rest of the world through globalization.

The CCP also moved to be more inclusive, a development that brought into the party capitalists, an outcome of progrowth policies. This policy was the work of Jiang Zenin, who suggested in 2001 that private entrepreneurs be allowed to join the CCP. This group had been banned in 1989 following the Tiananmen Square demonstrations. Despite opposition to private entrepreneurs or "red capitalists" joining, Jiang argued they were a new social stratum making important contributions to the country's development and modernization and hence deserving of a place in the ruling party.[8] This inclusion created an odd mix with big-time capitalists joining the ranks of Communist Party officials. However, it was clear the reform process was to establish a system by which China enjoyed the rewards of economic development without having to accommodate the political consequences.

GLOBALIZATION, GROWTH, AND THE ASIAN CONTEXT

Any discussion about China's rise must be seen in how the country approached the issue of globalization and how it handled the Asian economic crisis of 1997–98. The term "globalization" was first used by Chinese officialdom in 1996 by then Foreign Minister Qian Qichen at the United Nations. It was a significant signal that China acknowledged that economic affairs were playing an increasing role in post-Cold War international relations. By that time China was in the midst of another growth spurt and was attracting billions of dollars of foreign direct investment. But globalization was observed as a force limited to advances in science and technology. In a sense globalization was a neutral force to be defined largely in economic terms. As political scientists Yong Deng and Thomas Moore aptly observe, "when globalization first entered Beijing's diplomatic lexicon, officials described it as a trend driven by advances in science and technology that were producing increased cross-national flows of capital, goods and know-how. The emphasis was on the technological drivers underlying this realm in official Chinese analysis although the term was soon understood elsewhere in the world to include social, cultural, political, and security dimensions."[9]

In this context China approached the 1997–98 Asian economic crisis, an event that clearly had economic as well as political dimensions. By the early 1990s, the considerable success in much of Asia, in particular in Korea, Singapore, Hong Kong, Taiwan, Malaysia, Thailand, and Indonesia, was not lost on China's leadership. Even India, the lumbering democracy next door, was implementing new market-based economic reforms. If there had been any doubts over Deng's policies and those of his successor Jiang Zemin, it was difficult to argue with the rest of Asia's success and the take-off in China's exports. Between 1978 and 1996, China's total exports expanded from $9.5 billion to $151 billion, a fifteen-fold increase. At the same time, Chinese disposable incomes rose, and Chinese consumers gradually began to develop more sophisticated tastes, including for imported goods. For most major multinational companies, the changes occurring in China could not be ignored. Despite concerns over the lack of transparency, official corruption, the creaky state of the banking system, copyright infringements, and the problematic nature of the state-owned companies (which often received subsidies or were protected by tariffs), the threat of being left out of China was a key force in the country's investment boom during the 1990s and its continuation into the 2000s.

China's economic surge cannot be seen in isolation. The extended surge in Asia's economic powers clearly had a political element, adding a degree of swagger in relations with the West. This was most evident in the rise of the idea of "Asian values," a counterpoint to Western liberal-democratic capitalism. A popular idea among leaders in Malaysia, Singapore, and Indonesia, Asian values essentially advocated that Asian countries possessed a unique set of institutions and political ideologies, largely influenced (but not entirely) by Confucianism, that emphasized family, corporation, and nation. In this system there was a sacrificing of personal freedoms for the greater good in the form of social stability and economic prosperity. Combined with a strong work ethic and thrift, Asian societies were able to pursue academic and technological excellence, a pursuit that meant they would overcome the more democratic (and less goal-focused) West. And there were substantial advances in GDP size, in real GDP per capita gains, and in global market share. The idea of Asia economically converging with the West, with the implication of catching up, was a heady concoction and at times bordered on hubris. Malaysia's Prime Minister Mohammad Mahathir and Singapore's Lee Kwan Yew emerged as two of the most articulate spokesmen for Asian values, something that was used to counter criticism for their own quasi-authoritarian use of power while in office.

In 1997–98 Asia's great capitalist leap forward came to an abrupt and bruising halt. The combination of a massive inflow of foreign investment, a fulsome (though unbalanced) embrace of globalization, liberalization of capital markets (except in China and India), weak local regulatory institutions, and real estate bubbles, compounded by overvalued currencies, eventually lead to a region-wide implosion. This crisis was ignited by the Thai government's ill-fated decision in July 1997 to devalue its currency after months of depleting foreign exchanges reserves in an effort to defend the baht in international foreign currency markets. Like someone casting a stone in a pond, the shockwaves rippled outward, overwhelming Asia's financial markets and threatening the global financial system.

As the crisis hit, the great rush of foreign capital that had earlier flowed in, now flowed out with a vengeance. Hot money not linked to foreign direct investment projects offered a pillar of sand in time of crisis. Thailand, Indonesia, and Korea were ultimately forced to seek aid from the IMF, while the better-managed economies of Malaysia, Hong Kong, Singapore, and Taiwan came under severe pressure. China, however, was able to weather the storm as its latecomer status, and capital controls left it less exposed to the vicissitudes of international hot money. Moreover, it did not devalue its currency, something that it could have done to improve its competitive export advantage. China emerged as a concerned Asian power and partner, its reputation greatly enhanced by what many regarded as cool and prudent behavior. In contrast, Japan (with its wobbly banks) was a point of deep concern for policymakers throughout the rest of Asia and in Washington. In a realpolitik sense, the Asian financial crisis of 1997–98 was Japan's loss and China's gain; the former was a point of concern, while the latter was helpful and supportive.

The Asian financial crisis dashed hopes for the speedy rise of the region over the West. Arrogance was replaced with a profound sense of frustration, bitterness, and sadness. More significantly, the crisis raised serious questions about the bank-centered model of development that in many cases elevated business cronies over common sense. The Asian crisis left a profound impression on local policymakers and business leaders, many of whom vowed never to be caught in such circumstances again. Although most countries were able to retain social cohesiveness and political stability, the downfall of Indonesia's long-standing dictator Suharto, who was forced to resign in a popular backlash against economic upheaval and pervasive official corruption (some of the worst coming from the president's family) left an impression on China's leadership. In many regards Suharto's New Order was based on an unspoken yet critical contract with the population to have the right to economic freedom while leaving the political realm to the Suharto elite. When official corruption increasingly impeded the economic freedom part of the contract and Suharto family cronies crowded out aspiring entrepreneurs, the crisis galvanized an angry public to end the Suharto administration's rule, something taken to heart by the CCP. Suharto had, after all, been in power since the mid-1960s.

Asia's rebound from 1997–98 was to be dynamic and broad based. An important lesson was learned: as Asia was much more integrated with global markets, the penalties for wrong-headed policy decisions were much more rapid and exacting. This realization meant that the banks had to adopt more risk management techniques, expand into other Asian markets, and provide greater transparency and disclosure. At the same time, Asia's cash-hungry companies were forced to clean up their books, especially if they wanted foreign money.[10] As we will see, China was not immune to these trends.

By 2005 considerable economic changes had occurred throughout Asia, many of them positive. At a very basic level, for the region defined by the Asian Development Bank as "developing Asia," which included East Asia's two giants China and India as well as smaller economies like Bangladesh, Cambodia, and Nepal, per capita GDP at 2000 constant prices rose from $424 to $1,030 between 1990 and 2005. The annual growth rate was 6 percent, "a pace with few parallels in history."[11] Equally important to Asia's development was the decline in extreme poverty.

According to the Asian Development Bank, the incidence of extreme poverty declined from 34.6 percent to 18 percent between 1990 and 2005. Poverty levels are more concentrated in South Asia than in East and Southeast Asia. Indeed the decline in the number of extreme poor from 945 million is generally due to the achievement of China and Vietnam.[12] China had embarked upon one of the most substantial economic transformations in modern history.

REDEFINING CHINA

While Deng was a radical reformer, his successors Jiang Zemin and Hu Jintao (2003–12) were more moderate in their redefinition of China. All the same, Jiang and Hu adhered to remaking China into a world power, albeit at a more gradual pace aimed at maintaining the broad characteristics of market-Leninism. A high point for Jiang came in November 2001 when China joined the World Trade Organization (WTO). This was the product of a long negotiation process and was to have long-term consequences for China and the world. China's leadership regarded this membership as an important signal that the country was a vital part of the global economy. Being in the WTO meant that China was part of the club that included the United States, Canada, Germany, and Japan, among others, who could no longer discriminate against Chinese goods. It also made China more open to investment, with an inflow of foreign capital from the United States, Europe, and Japan as well as other developing countries such as India and Singapore. Jiang also saw the peaceful return of Macau (1999) and Hong Kong (1997) to Chinese rule, removing what were long regarded as imperialist stains on China's past glory and standing in the world.

Equally significant was what happened in 2003. China achieved an important political watershed: its second bloodless turnover of power from Jiang to Hu. While Jiang's rise to the presidency was fraught with tough factional infighting with a background of Tiananmen Square turmoil, Hu's rise to the presidency was a peaceful affair. Although Jiang initially retained some influence, Hu and his premier Wen Jinbao increasingly became the dominant forces in keeping China on the path of market-Leninism. At the same time, the ruling party was forced to recognize that it needed to be more responsive, accountable, and participatory in order to counter growing public discontent with corruption and to achieve a merging of interest between party members and powerful state-owned companies.

The apparent smoothness of the political process was evident in 2008 when the National People's Congress voted on second terms for Hu and

Wen as president and premier, respectively. This election reflected that China's leadership in the post-Deng years had evolved into a more collective mode, with the general secretary of the party, in this case President Hu, being the first among equals. At the same time, Hu injected into the party constitution his "scientific outlook on development," a theory of Chinese socialism that incorporates sustainable development, social welfare, and the creation of a "harmonious society."[13]

China's economic success was evident in other ways. It had earned solid investment grade ratings from international rating agencies (Moody's, Standard & Poor's, and Fitch), amassed over $1 trillion in foreign exchange reserves by 2007, and created a growing fleet of large, internationally savvy "national champion" companies such as China National Offshore Oil Company (CNOOC), PetroChina, and Minmetals. (There is more on these companies later.) In May 2007, Moody's Investors Service complemented China for its prudent external debt management, strong export performance and pragmatic reform, and WTO liberalization policies. But the process of dynamic change did not stop. Even through the 2007–8 global economic downturn, China's economy, pumped up by a stimulus program of close to $600 billion, bucked global trends and expanded by over 10 percent in 2008 and 2009. At the end of 2010, its foreign exchange reserves stood at close to $3 trillion, well beyond any other country's foreign exchange reserves on the planet.

DEMOGRAPHIC CHALLENGES

China in the early twenty-first century faces a choice. It can either climb up to the next level of development into the ranks of the more affluent societies (defined by very large middle classes) with related leadership responsibilities in terms of the global economy, or it can shy away from leadership responsibilities while seeking any possible gains in markets at the expense of others. Because of these choices, China faces a number of major challenges that will define the development path ahead.

One of the most significant issues is demographics. In 2010 China was a nation of 1.33 billion people, making it the world's most populous country. In a relatively short period of time, it has realized tremendous gains in its populations' standard of living. Since the 1950s China's population has dramatically increased its life expectancy from 35 years to 72 years. Even since 1990 the average lifespan rose by 2.8 years. Improvements in public health have also been marked by the elimination of small pox, diphtheria, and polio. As a consequence of the eradication of these diseases, China has reduced the child mortality rate, with deaths of children under age five declining from 12 percent to 8.5 percent since 1990, according to government data. Certainly the greater reliability of food supply and the end of ongoing political upheaval have combined with strong economic growth to improve the lot of most Chinese, especially when compared to their counterparts at the end of the civil war in 1949.

Despite these positive changes, China's population picture faces two major problems: an overall decline in population size and a shortage of women. China's population growth rates have been declining since the mid-1980s and are projected to decline further in the coming decades. In fact, demographers believe that India will overtake China in terms of population within ten to fifteen years. China's "one-child policy" is a key reason for this population decline. In fact, according to UN projections (UN Report 2010), Chinese population growth is projected to turn negative from 2035 onwards. Not surprisingly, China's total fertility rate (number of children per woman of child-bearing age) is declining and is now below some developed countries including the United States, the United Kingdom, and France. It fell below the replacement level of 2.1 children per woman during the period 1990–95, was stable during the period 1995–2010, and is expected to increase slightly during the period 2010–30.

The gender gap is also high in China, especially at lower age groups. According to UN Population Division Data (2010), in 2010 there are 1.2 males per female in China in the 0–14 age group. The overall 2010 male-female ratio for China is 1.079. This ratio is attributed mainly to the preference for a male child, and this preference leads to the willingness of families to use abortions and increasing use of technology to detect early in pregnancy the sex of the baby. It is easy to imagine that a gender imbalance of this magnitude could lead to social dislocation and episodes of instability as these "Young Emperors" reach the age of maturity. An estimated 20 to 30 million Chinese men will not be able to find wives. This should be a serious social problem.

It also follows that if the population growth rate is slowing, so is the growth rate of the labor force. In the past ten years, more than 16 million internal migrants had come to the cities and supplied abundant labor for the nations' booming factories and service industries. But this internal migration has slowed. In fact, the United Nations predicts that total labor force growth will be close to zero in the period 2015–20. Data from the Asian Development Bank also points to a shift from high to low fertility rates and population growth to a gradual loss in surplus labor occurring in China after 2015.[14] Consequently, the era of young and cheap rural labor to the cities is coming to an end. This impending labor shortage raises serious questions as to China's long-standing comparative advantage in terms of low labor costs and raises the issue of where do China's labor-intensive companies go to find cheap workers. Some Chinese companies have begun to move operations into the country's interior, and there is a growing discussion of looking further afield to Africa and Latin America for cost-competitive or surplus labor.

In the meantime, more than 700 million people or 54 percent of the total population still live in rural areas. This puts pressure on the authorities to find new ways to stimulate employment in both the countryside and urban areas. The worst case scenario is that agricultural production continues to improve, becoming less labor intensive and more mechanized and hence forcing more workers from the land. This, in turn, could stimulate greater pressure on urban areas in terms of housing and work with a spillover into food prices.

Another dimension of the demographic issue is an aging population that is increasing. The size of the country's population aged 60 and over is expected to increase dramatically from an estimated 200 million people in 2015 to over 300 million in 2030. In Shanghai alone, one in five people, is a senior. That ratio is projected to rise to 1 in 3 by 2020.[15] The number of one-child families, which are also on a continued rise, only underscores the challenge of supporting the growing numbers of elderly Chinese. And China is not known for its long-term health-care medicine and sunset living facilities.

We argued earlier in this chapter that China is embarked on a grand experiment. It has attained great economic success since the 1980s while retaining a strict authoritarian political structure. Central to this unlikely (to western eyes) mix was fast growth that relied on a cheap and willing labor force. But an aging labor force will compel changes in this economic model. It may also make commanding political authority more difficult. An aging population will force national reallocations of resources and priorities as more funds flow to health care and pensions. Money that would otherwise go to investment and production might soon be spent on rising demands for benefits and services. So, a declining labor supply and increased public and private spending could result in a new economic growth model for China. Japan's economic stagnation, partly related to the aging of its population, might be an extreme example of what China has to look forward to.[16]

A CHANGING CHINESE ECONOMIC LANDSCAPE

China's economy has emerged as one of the largest in the world, a key factor in its emergence as a locomotive for global growth in the late 1990s and early 2000s. In 2010 China's economy bypassed Japan's as the second largest in the world, a remarkable performance. With an average growth rate of 9.4 percent per year in real terms, GDP has increased twelve fold since 1979. Chinese trade with the rest of the world has risen by a factor of 30 times. This increase has meant that China has made substantial inroads into world trade, becoming one of the major trade partners of the United States, Japan, and Europe as well as Australia, Latin America, and the Middle East. This is actually quite startling. Total trade (exports plus imports) amounts to 75 percent of China's GDP, which compares with 37 percent for the United Kingdom and just 20 percent for the United States.[17] As China has been opened to foreign investment, it has constructed a highly competitive industrial infrastructure, with a flood of major foreign companies setting up factories there.

The 2008–11 financial crisis in much of the world has been less damaging to China, which has partly shielded itself with a closed capital account and a largely nontradable currency. In 2009 net exports did fall and the decline represented a loss of 3.9 percent of GDP growth. Imports fell too, and this fall represented lower import volumes and a drop in residential building investment. But the story quickly changed. The Chinese government announced a substantial stimulus package (as did most Western governments), and consequently the trade balance has narrowed as China focuses more on domestic infrastructure investment. Imports and exports have recovered. Further, the Chinese government's fiscal and monetary policy stance up until the financial crisis had a tightening bias to counter an overheating economy. As a consequence, the Chinese economy seems poised to record strong growth again over the medium term. Yet, the changes occurring in the global economy, especially in the United States (which is de-emphasizing the consumer and leverage), portend changes to come in China's economy. Failure to make changes will complicate China's global role as a key trade partner, but it will also affect the finely tuned Chinese balance between the country's socioeconomic and political systems.

China's consumption patterns are also changing rapidly. China is still a poor country: in 2008 GDP per capital was only $6000 on a purchasing power parity (PPP) basis, and half that when measured at international prices. However, household income has been growing rapidly (at 10 percent on average since the 1980s) and has accelerated even further in the past decade. The expected upward trajectory of income growth suggests that there is significant potential for consumption demand to continue to grow rapidly.

Some of the areas with the greatest growth potential include the following:

1. Consumer durables. China is at a point in 2010 where demand for durable goods is surging as income in urban areas is growing. Demand for motor vehicles, for example, is soaring as China's auto market outgrew that of the United States in 2009. If China follows Korea and Japan's path, then Chinese motor vehicle ownership, which is just 30 per 1000 people in 2008, could boom to 600 per 1000 by 2030.

2. Stronger demand from rural areas. More than half of the Chinese population lives in rural areas, where the penetration of consumer goods is low. Although almost every Chinese urban family owns a washing machine, a refrigerator, and an air conditioner, fewer than half of their rural counterparts enjoy such luxuries. But as infrastructure bottlenecks are removed and income increases, the demand for consumer durables from the rural areas will increase substantially. This will be most evident in central and western China.

3. The service sector. China's service sector currently represents only 40 percent of GDP. However, although food is still the biggest expenditure item for Chinese consumers, as is normally the case in a developing economy, household demand for services should start to increase with income improvements. This includes travel and entertainment, which offer potentially huge markets. If health care was to be included under the services sector, demand for this product is going to grow considering the nature of the country's demographics.

4. Savings rate reductions. China's household savings rate is about 22 percent of GDP, one of the highest in the world. Reasons for this rate include the underdevelopment of China's financial markets, the limited availability of formal credit, and most importantly, the weakness of the social safety net. People save to pay for basic health care services, to care for elderly parents, and other medical needs. Political leaders have asserted that they intend to develop and expand the coverage of a social security system. Such a system would reduce the need for precautionary savings for health care and retirement, thereby boosting household consumption. In fact, in urban areas the propensity to save has been dropping since the mid-1990s as a social security system has begun to emerge. The weakness of a financial services system has also meant a lack of ready capital from the state-owned banks for small and medium-sized businesses, something that has encouraged the development of an unofficial and unregulated informal banking sector, sometimes referred to as the gray market.

HONG KONG AND SHANGHAI AND THE NEXT WAVE

China has also benefited from the return of Hong Kong to its control as a Special Administrative Region (SAR) and the development of Shanghai into an important financial center. Indeed, these two major financial, trade and shipping centers are now competing for primacy, with Shanghai seemingly on the ascension and Hong Kong seemingly on a slight decline.

China is developing Shanghai into an international financial center in accordance with the country's economic strength and the growing international status of the renminbi. Meanwhile, Hong Kong's role as a gateway for products entering and leaving China is becoming less significant amid China's rapid expansion of its port and airport facilities as well as improvement of its trade services. Moreover, Hong Kong's middleman role for cross-strait economic exchanges looks set to diminish as direct Taiwan-China links develop. That said, throughout its history Hong Kong has been a highly resilient economy that has adapted quickly to change. We think that this will remain the case.

At present, Hong Kong continues to maintain its leading edge as a value-added service platform (particularly as a key south China-international logistics center and financial capital). It also remains a gateway for Chinese enterprises looking to international markets. It has the best airport in China (and perhaps all of Asia) and world class port logistics and infrastructure, freedom of capital flows, a range of world-class financial and professional services, and a sound and transparent legal system. In addition, new opportunities are emerging for Hong Kong in the Chinese market:

1. Closer economic integration with the Guangdong and Pearl River Delta (PRD)
2. Financial cooperation and capital market development
3. Market deregulation under the Closer Economic and Partnership Agreement (CEPA)
4. Cross-border infrastructure links

Hong Kong also remains a vital bridge for the Chinese mainland to the Association of Southeast Asian Nations (ASEAN) countries. Furthermore, Hong Kong's long-time role as a middleman facilitating trade flows, transportation, tourism, and financial ties and investment between Taiwan and China will be enhanced as cross-strait links continue to develop.

Going forward, the Chinese government has pledged to restructure the economy toward knowledge-based, high value-added activities. To that end Hong Kong's existing strengths in financial services, trading, logistics, and tourism have been identified as the major contributors to jobs and growth in the future. Also, the government has identified six key emerging industries for development both in Hong Kong and on the mainland: education, medical services, testing and certification, the environment, innovation and technology, and cultural and creative industries. This development would certainly fit some of the more pressing challenges facing China: the need to develop the service sector, grow the domestic market, and provide health care for the aging.

The booming city of Shanghai will also be central to this vision of the future. Shanghai's leap into the twenty-first century can only be described as impressive. For a lengthy period in the first part of the twentieth century, Shanghai was one of East Asia's financial hubs. The political turmoil of the Second Sino-Japanese War in the mid-1930s, World War II, and the Chinese civil war and revolution ended Shanghai's fortunes as a financial center. There was no room for the city's money men under Mao. While the city benefited from the export revolution during the 1980s, both as a port and home to industry, it was the expansion of its financial services that pushed it back up the ranks as a key international urban center.

The Shanghai Stock Exchange (SEE) was established in 1990, and within a decade it became the preeminent stock exchange in mainland China in terms of listed companies and number of shares listed. According to the World Federation of Exchanges, the SEE's market capitalization stood at $2.7 trillion in 2009, with 870 listed companies. This placed it behind the Tokyo Stock Exchange's market capitalization of $3.3 trillion and 2,335 listed companies but well ahead of India's Bombay Stock Exchange with $1.3 trillion market capitalization and 4,955 listed companies.[18]

The development of the SEE went hand in hand with the creation of its home, Pudong, an eastern district of Shanghai. Created about the same time from a nondescript patch of land along the Yangtze River Delta, Pudong is now regarded as the mainland's major financial and commercial hub and rival to Hong Kong. Many international corporations that are doing business in China have come to Pudong. Its skyline contains the Oriental Pearl Tower (the third tallest tower in the world), which symbolizes China's arrival as a modern global economy.

Shanghai has emerged as the largest city in China with over 20 million residents. Its suburbs are dotted with factories as far as the eye cans see. Its skyline still is an ongoing visual challenge, considering the frequent changes as new skyscrapers vie for prominence. For many China observers, Shanghai is the greatest symbol of the new China of growth and prosperity but also of terrible pollution and inadequate infrastructure. But most notably, Shanghai is modern urban China in microcosm, and a stark symbol of the progress that China is finally enjoying.

CHINA HAS ARRIVED

In 2010 David Lampton, dean of faculty and director of China Studies at Johns Hopkins School of Advanced International Studies, wrote, "The speed of China's emergence, as a great power has been unsettling, but the country has become a positive and virtually indispensable element in the global economy, woven into a web of interdependent relationships that connect it to many nations, including the United States."[19]

Perhaps the crowning moment of arrival came in 2008 when China hosted the summer Olympics. This was a highly symbolic event as the Olympics highlighted China's successful push into the ranks of the world's largest economies. As one reporter noted, "China used the Olympics as a global platform to introduce itself as a rising, modern power—and largely succeeded in dazzling the world."[20] China's effort included spending $40 billion to build subways and ultramodern venues such as the Water Cube and Bird's Nest. One result of the successful running of the Olympics was that it bolstered China's pride in its achievements, something that helped reinforce the legitimacy of the CCP.

While China's 2008 hosting of the Olympics was a critical moment of arrival and instilled greater pride in the country, Beijing's response to the global economic crisis in 2007–8 marked another critical turning point— the return of Asia's largest country as a global power. The troubles that commenced in the U.S. subprime mortgage market in 2007 spread throughout the world in 2008. In the carnage of a near financial collapse in the United States and Europe that claimed such august institutions as Bear Stearns, Lehman Brothers, and Northern Rock, China emerged as the sole economic power not taken down by a combination of greed, excessive leverage, and interconnectedness. China's banks had largely sidestepped what would become the toxic waste of subprime synthetic financial instruments, and Beijing was able to respond positively to the global crisis.

As noted earlier, with the U.S. economy heading into its worst crisis since the 1930s and with Europe soon to follow, China was able to implement a massive $584 billion stimulus package, much of the money being pumped into infrastructure via the country's banks. Although this inflow of money helped create a property bubble and concerns became more manifest about the predominant role of state companies at the expense of the private sector and innovation, China's economy bucked the downward trend in 2009. Real GDP in 2009 for China was 9.1 percent, compared to −5.2 percent for Japan, −2.6 percent for the United States, and −4.1 percent for the Euro Area. In many ways China became the critical force that kept the global economy from tumbling into a depression as it continued to buy goods and bonds from the United States (being for a period the largest buyer of U.S. Treasury bonds), to absorb Europe's exports, and to provide some degree of leadership in Asia.

The crisis in Western capitalism eroded U.S. power and elevated China's. Asia's largest country gained important stature because it emerged from the Lehman shocks as one of the most competitive economies upon which the United States, Europe, and Japan were to varying degrees dependent for their well-being. At the same time, the development of China during the 1990s and 2000s as a major buyer of commodities underscored a growing centrality of Beijing in global economic affairs. As an IMF report in October 2010 stated, "China's strong and sustained growth over the past several years has served as a linchpin for global trade, benefiting exporter of commodities (for example, Australia, Indonesia, New Zealand) and capital goods (for example Germany, Japan, some NIEs [Newly Industrialized Economies])."[21]

One component of China's newfound economic power is the emergence of powerful national champion companies, SOEs backed by the government and increasingly aligned with members of the CCP. National champions, large modern corporations that are meant to compete with the world's leading firms based in the high-income economies, gained greater weight as part of China's business revolution of the 2000s. The creation of what has been referred to as a national team differed from the Anglo-American approaches to private enterprise, liberalization, and globalization. It also differed from the industrial policies of the former Soviet Union and Eastern Europe. In many regards the national team concept reflected a more statist form of capitalism, something along the lines of past policies of Japan and France. In this concept the investment rate remained high, being helped by a gradual increase in the productivity performance of the economy.

By 2008 it was estimated that China has selected around 150 national champions, cutting across a number of sectors but concentrated in such sectors as metals and mining and industrial production and banking. Some of the best-known companies are Chinalco, Minmetals, Beijing

Automobile Industry Corporation, and PetroChina. Backed by the state and led by the CCP members, the national champions became much more evident in the first decade of the twenty-first century as they expanded at a rapid pace and gained privileged access to stock market listings and bank finance. One academic study observed in 2009 that "over the past decade their assets, sales, and R&D expenditure grew on average at a staggering 25 percent a year. Their profits grew even faster—at around 40 percent a year."[22] The same study also noted that national champions have been at the forefront of China's internationalization efforts, accounting for 40 percent of the country's total overseas foreign direct investment in 2007.

China's strong arm of state capitalism benefited from the economic and financial crisis among the Western developed economies in the 2007–11 period. In particular, China's companies were not hit as hard by the temporary collapse in the global financial markets as their Western counterparts nor did the Chinese economy go through a bruising recession. What these factors meant was that China's banks, measured by market capitalization, became four of the world's ten largest (in 2009).[23] At the same time, China's industrial companies climbed the ranks of the top 100 businesses in the Fortune 500, with PetroChina becoming the largest company (by market value).[24]

Additional economic muscle was evident in the creation of sovereign wealth funds (SWFs). While many countries have one such company, China has a number: SAFE Investment Company (founded in 1997), China Investment Corporation (2007), and the National Social Security Fund (2000). The Hong Kong Monetary Authority Investment Portfolio is also a significant SWF. Considering the size of China's foreign exchange reserves (over $2 trillion in 2010), the multicontinental reach of its national champions, and SWFs' financial clout, China's rise is one of the most obvious developments in the twenty-first century.

But China's rise is not limited to national champion multinationals, foreign exchange reserves, and SWFs. It also encompasses technology, space exploration, and an ability to wage cyberwar. China has poured and will continue to pour considerable resources into its space program. It has already stated that it wants to put a human on the Moon, and in 2003 put its first human into orbit around the Earth. More orbit missions followed in 2005 and 2008. China also is planning to create its own space station. In sharp contrast to the U.S. space program, China's program does not face financial constraints evident in the United States in the wake of the Great Recession.

The combination of the market-Leninist system, avoiding the risks inherent in runaway financial capitalism (and instead still making real products), and taking to heart the lessons of Asia's 1997–98 economic crisis, China has been able to return to the ranks of the great powers in the late twentieth century, with an even greater push into that status in the early twenty-first century. While part of China's rise can be attributed to the West's stupidity and arrogance, much of the credit is China's. As we will see in later chapters, China's great capitalist leap forward has many problems and cannot be taken for granted. China can still slip; it can travel down the same road as the Qing dynasty in the late nineteenth by tinkering with reforms when it should be making major overhauls. Yet, China has come a long distance since 1949 and, for that matter, 1978. A special *Economist* report on Sino-American relations in October 2009 caught some of the moment of China's rise: "But suggestions of a 'G2' hints at a remarkable shift in the two countries relative strengths: they are now seen as near-equals whose co-operation is vital to solving the world's problems, from finance to climate change and nuclear proliferation."[25]

CONCLUSION

The rise of China in the late twentieth and twenty-first centuries is clearly a seminal event in history. It represents the long difficult return of China to the commanding heights of the global economy, and with that return it exerts a pull on the rest of Asia and parts of emerging markets that raises these latter up the development rung. This process has been challenging and is hardly complete. It has also been unsettling for some of China's neighbors and its trade partners. Simply stated, China's rise in a competitive world has not come without ruffling some feathers, especially in Europe, Japan, and the United States. At the same time, China's development process and its interlinkages with other emerging market countries need to be better understood and are the subject of the next chapter. Equally important, China's spectacular rise has its own set of problems, ranging from official corruption and questions over the state role in the economy (and conversely the role of the private sector), to pollution and political development. Those problems will also be examined in later chapters. But despite substantial problems, China has achieved a central role in the unfolding drama of global economic development, finance, and business.

Chapter 4

CONSTRUCTING THE NEW ASIAN ECONOMY

In the early twenty-first century there is a new Asian economy forming. Centered around China, it is driven by a robust trade in raw materials and manufactured goods and increasing capital flows and the deepening of local consumer markets. This new Asian economy includes South Korea, Indonesia, Thailand, Burma, Singapore, and Vietnam. It also encompasses India and Japan, two countries that are heavily engaged with China but that have long-standing rivalries with it and are developing their own regional linkages. India, in particular, has gained attention for being highly complementary to China as part of "Chindia" due to what some have perceived as the two countries' growing diplomatic and economic convergence. A little further afield, Australia, Papua New Guinea, and New Zealand are important components to the new Asian economy (especially for commodities). Part of the excitement over Asia's emergence as a "global economic powerhouse" was captured in 2010 by Anoop Singh, the director of the IMF's Asia and Pacific Department: "Based on expected trends, within five years Asia's economy (including Australia and New Zealand) will be about 50 percent larger than it is today (in purchasing power parity terms), account for more than a third of global output, and be comparable in size to the economies of the United States and Europe. By 2030, Asian GDP will exceed that of the Group of Seven major industrial economies (G-7)."[1]

The strong pull from the Chinese economy is redefining the region's place in the global economy. It is also leading to considerable examination as to what coming into China's orbit means and how that interfaces with national interests, be it of South Korea, Indonesia, or Japan. China is not the only game in town as many countries are willing to expand trade and investment relations with other partners, something that Japan, India, and Vietnam have demonstrated a notable willingness to explore both through bilateral and multilateral trade arrangements. Many Asian countries are also increasingly seeking to protect some of their industries from China as local businesses are raising concerns of being swamped by cheaper Chinese goods. While a more integrated Asian economy has considerable upside potential, the heavy weight of China could function as a double-edged sword. Any major economic downturn in China will have an impact in the rest of the region. Nonetheless, Asia has evolved into a de facto regional economy, increasingly bound together, a trend likely to continue as the century progresses.

HESITANT STEPS TO A REGIONAL ASIAN ECONOMY

The European Union (EU) and North American Free Trade Agreement (NAFTA) represent two of the most comprehensive efforts to build regional trade blocs. The European effort started in the 1950s when a small elite of policymakers centered around Jean Monnet, Robert Schuman, and Alcide De Gasperi decided that an economic union would prevent future wars by facilitating trade and growth and provide a better foundation for global competition. It would also provide a solid foundation for a more pan-European identity as opposed to the highly destructive recent history of out-of-control nationalism that led to two world wars. The effort started with a core of countries—Belgium, Italy, France, the Netherlands, Luxembourg, and West Germany. The first step was the European Coal and Steel Community, which was superseded in 1957 by the Treaty of Rome which gave birth to the Common Market, later to be called the European Economic Community (EEC). The EEC eventually became the European Union, absorbing some 27 countries, including most of Western Europe and a swath of the Balkans as well as Malta and Cyprus.

The EU created a European regional economy, with a common currency (the euro), a market for goods, and an unprecedented degree of labor mobility. Despite the EU's troubles in the early twenty-first century, the creation of the regional economy brought a high level of prosperity and generally peaceful development to over 350 million people for over 50 years—not a shabby track record by any standard. Not all members adopted the euro, with the notable exceptions being the United Kingdom, Sweden, and Denmark. Additionally, the EU's political authority is limited despite the existence of a permanent president of the European Council and an elected European parliament.

While the North American Free Trade Agreement's experiment in developing a regional economy was not as grandiose as that of the EU (as it lacks a political component, having nothing like the European Parliament), it has solidified into an economic bloc of the United States, Canada, and Mexico. The agreement came into force in January 1994 and helped to more than triple trade and investment between the three countries. A number of other trade agreements were extended elements of NAFTA to parts of the Caribbean and most of Central America (in 2004 the United States entered into the Central America Free Trade Agreement or CAFTA).

In contrast to the EU and NAFTA, the development of regional trade in Asia has been a slower process. Asia's approach to a regional trade bloc in modern history was associated with the Greater East Asia Co-Prosperity Sphere. Unfortunately this concept came out of Imperial Japan in the 1930s and envisioned the creation of a self-sufficient bloc of Asian countries. Japan, of course, was the leader of this Asian bloc, which also intended to end Western colonialism. This idea became unattractive once many of the occupied countries found Japanese imperialism little different from that of the West. Tokyo's policy of regional economic integration under its flag was not helped by the brutal war with China which started in the mid-1930s and continued until 1945. The resurgence of Western power, in particular the United States and its occupation of Japan, killed the idea of the Greater East Asian Co-Prosperity Sphere.

Asian regional trade also failed to develop in the postwar era as China was wracked by civil war, followed by a communist victory that led to its withdrawal from the global economy. India also unplugged from the global economy because of the more socialist orientation of the Nehru government and a suspicion of trade and foreign investment (which many Indian policymakers regarded as a major cause of their loss of independence at the hands of the British). Furthermore, the Cold War climate did little to help incubate regional trade as reflected by the Korean War (1950–53), the Sino-American. tensions over Taiwan (1954 and 1958), and the wars in Indochina. Adding to the disruption of trade was Indonesia's confrontation of Malaysia and a number of insurgencies in Burma, the Philippines, and Thailand. With the exception of Japan, which was very much under the protective wing of the United States, the bulk of mainland Asia was not at the heart of global economic development and regional trade was diminished.

The early steps toward encouraging regional trade came in Southeast Asia. In 1967 Indonesia, Malaysia, the Philippines, Singapore, and Thailand formed the Association of Southeast Asian Nations (ASEAN) with the purpose of developing cooperation and trade. This was a bloc backed by the United States, with an eye to communist North Vietnam and the eventual fall of South Vietnam, Cambodia, and Laos to communist forces. ASEAN was to gain greater momentum with the economic takeoff of Singapore, Malaysia, Thailand, and Indonesia in the 1980s, the end of the Cold War (which allowed Vietnam, Laos, Burma, and Cambodia to join), and the economic transformation of China and India (which brought about a return of the two giants into regional trade in the 1980s and 1990s).

One consequence of the changing international environment was a greater effort to develop stronger economic relationships within Asia. After all, the Cold War was over, the newly freed countries of Eastern Europe were looking to become members of the European Union, and NAFTA was forming. In response to all of these events, Malaysia's Prime Minister Mohammed Mahathir proposed the formation of the East Asian Economic Group (EAEG), a body that would encompass ASEAN members, China, Japan, South Korea, Hong Kong, Taiwan, and Vietnam. EAEG was soon changed into the East Asian Economic Caucus (EAEC) as the EAEG fell victim to U.S. hostility. Washington had a marked preference for the Asia Pacific Economic Council or APEC, which was established in 1989 with strong U.S. and Australian support. China also opposed the EAEG, insisting that its members had to be sovereign states, a view clearly aimed at Taiwan and Hong Kong. Considering the U.S. stance, Japan and South Korea backed away from the EAEG and supported APEC instead.

APEC was created to create a more broadly defined Asia Pacific regional economy, based on the promotion of free trade and economic cooperation throughout the region that stretched from the Pacific shores of South America to East Asia and Australia and New Zealand. This broader-based approach was exemplified by APEC membership being extended to such nonmainland Asian countries as Canada, Mexico, Chile, Peru, and Papua New Guinea. An offshoot of APEC was the Trans-Pacific Strategic Economic Partnership (TPP), which has four members, Chile, New Zealand, Brunei, and Singapore, and possible additional members of the United States, Australia, Peru, Vietnam, Canada, the Philippines, and Japan. The TPP's goal is to create a multilateral trade agreement in order to integrate Asian-Pacific economies.

The mix of more Asian-centric trade blocs and larger Asia Pacific trade blocs led to an ongoing chain of executive meetings and declarations and helped push the idea of further trade liberalization within well-defined blocs. However, it did not result in anything of the same scope and scale as the EU or NAFTA. Consequently, the push for a more regional Asian economy evolved along three tracks: an emphasis on Asian institutions (as well defined as within the region, chiefly mainland Asia), a crisscross matrix of free trade and preferential trade agreements between Asian countries, and a more broadly defined Asia Pacific zone. Although Japan was long a supporter of multilateral approaches and multilateral financial institutions like the IMF and World Bank, it moved to bilateral trade when in 2002 it signed with Singapore a free trade agreement (FTA), which was followed by similar agreements with South Korea, Malaysia, the Philippines, and Thailand. China also embarked down this path. In 2002 it entered into a comprehensive framework agreement with ASEAN and another agreement with South Asian countries. South Korea added a FTA with Singapore in 2004. The result of all of these FTAs was the ad hoc creation of a regional Asian economy. As one observer observed in 2005, "a de facto economic zone has in effect been created in the area of trade and investment based on market principles, despite the political, social and historical differences among the countries in the region."[2] While this economic unity should not be overstated, the idea of a more defined Asian economic zone gradually formed in the early 2000s, and the possibility for further integration was considerable.

Consequently, the "new Asian economy" as of the early twenty-first century is broadly defined as China-driven, although balanced by Japan (still an economic power in its own right) and more and more by India. The more industrialized East Asia (with its core of China-Japan-Korea), supplemented by Singapore, Thailand, Malaysia, Indonesia, the Philippines, and increasingly Vietnam, is linking up with the South Asian countries of India and Pakistan. China, Japan, Singapore, Korea, and India provide investment and offer some of the most advanced markets, helping to stimulate a flow of commodities and goods. Much of Southeast Asia also functions as part of the conveyor belt for Japanese, Taiwanese, and Indian manufacturing companies, sending end products to Europe, Australia, the Middle East, Latin America, and North America. Helping to undergird the growing linkages between such diverse countries as China and Pakistan or Japan and Thailand is an array of free trade agreements. These FTAs are steadily reshaping Asia and gradually pushing the region into a very loose type of free trade zone stretching from Pakistan to Korea.

While it lacks a European Union-like structure and any administrative capital like Brussels, the emerging Asian economy does have the Asian Development Bank (based in Manila) and the Chiang Mai Initiative (CMI). While the Asian Development Bank is a multilateral development bank with members from outside the region and the CMI does not embrace all of Asia, both function as a financial and developmental support mechanism for greater Asian economic unity. In this regard the CMI is notable as it is a regional financial arrangement that came into existence in 2000 between the ASEAN countries and China, Japan, and Korea (the +3). Under the auspices of the ASEAN +3, the CMI was created to establish a network of bilateral swap agreements among members to provide liquidity support to countries experiencing balance of payments difficulties.

The vision of a more cohesive Asian economy was well articulated by Min Zhu, a special Advisor to the IMF's managing director and a former deputy governor of the People's Bank of China (the central bank). In an interview in June 2010, Zhu stated, "The center of growth is moving from the West to Asia, and in particular emerging Asia. I think that's a pattern that will continue for at least the next five years, which will change the whole global economic structure."[3] The following reasons are why Zhu reached this conclusion:

- Asia's role in world trade is growing, but in the 2008–9 crisis, trade flows to the advanced economies fell dramatically and were balanced by a strengthening in interregional trade flows. This trend of interregional trade will continue. Advanced economies are experiencing a weak recovery, while Asia's is strong, resulting in a multilevel and multispeed recovery (to the advantage of Asia).

- Advanced economies still suffer from difficult fiscal situations, while Asian economies are on much firmer ground, helping the sustainability of the recovery. The outcome: "we can expect global assets to relocate, with Asia attracting more capital."[4]

- Asia's strong economic growth in 2010, the emergence of a yuan-based bond market (called dim sum bonds) in Hong Kong, and the deepening of regional trade and investment ties as well as Europe's sovereign crisis (2010–11) appear to underscore Zhu's vision. And Zhu is hardly alone in believing in this vision for Asia's economic future.

THE RISE OF INDIA AND ITS PLACE IN THE NEW ASIAN ECONOMY

One part of the Asian regional economy that appears to be lagging is South Asia. While steps toward a de facto economic zone materialized between East Asia and Southeast Asia, South Asia was noticeably absent from the party. But integrative forces are now in motion. While the rise of China has already been discussed, the significance of India and the creation of South Asian regional trade linkages are important. South Asia is a region that encompasses Bhutan, Bangladesh, India, Nepal, Pakistan, and Sri Lanka. This group of countries have had a disappointing developmental track record; from 1950 to 1980 the region witnessed near stagnation in per capita incomes and low levels of economic expansion.[5] South Asia was also regarded as one of the world's least integrated regions in the world as late as the early 2000s. As late as 2010, the Asian Development Bank observed: "Limited participation in Asia's production networks, exacerbated by high protection and elevated trade costs, has hampered South Asia's integration with the vibrant economies of developing Asia. Even for India, deeper regional integration and further efforts at trade facilitation are crucial to fully leverage the potential of closer economic ties and network trade with East Asia and Southeast Asia."[6] Yet, India's shift in economic strategies starting in the 1980s and the dramatic increase in growth has been an important force in stimulating a more regional South Asian economy, though the China factor has clearly dominated outside of India.

India has two faces. One is that of a lumbering elephant and the other is that of a sleek tiger. Prior to the 1980s, India was the former with 3.5 percent real GDP growth (1965–81) (sometimes referred to as the Hindu rate of growth). The situation changed in the period 1981–87 as growth accelerated to 5.1 percent and then to 6.0 percent during 1987–2004.[7] Real GDP in the period 2005–8 averaged about 8.0 percent. Although trade was not the dominant factor, it did play a role in pushing India's economic machine to becoming a far more significant factor in regional and global economies, a fact that points to the liberalization of trade in South Asia's giant (and the neighborhood). Along these lines, a World Bank study notes, "This acceleration in growth has taken place in an environment of declining trade barriers in the entire region."[8]

Why did India shift economic gears starting in the 1980s? Part of the reason was that the country's leadership became increasingly aware that India was economically falling behind many of its neighbors. Much of Southeast Asia was enjoying strong growth, experiencing upward swings in per capita income, and capturing export markets. Even China, India's longtime rival, was making strides by embracing export-based growth, while the Soviet Union's collapse pointed to the cul-de-sac of communism. Reforms were hesitantly started in the 1980s, but Prime Minister Rajiv Gandhi's assassination in 1987 slowed the process. What functioned as a critical catalyst was a balance of payments crisis in 1991 that was caused in large part by the first Gulf War, which forced up oil prices and damaged India's remittance flows (highly important to the country's capital flows). In many regards, the difficult decisions about reform were pushed to the fore, and India found itself embarking upon a new economic path that included trade liberalization and a downsizing of bureaucratic red tape. India also benefited from the great push toward globalization that was occurring in the West and rapidly spreading into Asia and other parts of the world.

What helped propel India along the tiger path of development was a number of factors that included a work force able to compete in a world economy driven by globalization (English-speaking, educated, and comparatively cheap), technology (some of it homegrown), and innovation. In particular, India was and continues to be able to capitalize on the expansion of the global services industry that demands an educated and in many cases specialized work force. This need has certainly been the case in high tech and pharmaceuticals but has also extended into financial services and animation. One observer writes of the off-shoring financial analyst jobs to India that "cost is an undeniable factor in why managers are moving more research to India . . . the cost of an analyst with less than three years experience in the United States is $140,000, compared with $40,000 in India."[9]

An important foundation for India's thrust into the tech services sector was the creation of the Indian Institutes of Technology (IITs). Established in the late 1950s, with the last being added in 2002, the IITs were given the mission of training scientists and engineers for the newly independent India. The seven schools, located throughout the country, took advantage of U.S., German, and Soviet assistance and came to be the foundation of India's high tech industry. The IITs produce highly sought after graduates, and by international standards, they compete at the same level as Stanford and Cambridge.[10] Many IIT graduates have gone to the United States, with many heading to Silicon Valley.

Another important factor that helped elevate India is the existence of a robust and entrepreneurial business class. While India is attracting foreign direct investment and Western multinationals, it is also producing its own set up multinational companies such as Vedanta, Wipro, Dr. Reddy, Tata Motors, and Reliance. This rise of Indian multinationals was profoundly evident in 2006 when Mittal Steel, owned and run by an Indian living in London (Lakshmi Mittal), bought Europe's largest steel company, Arcelor. This came after the French chief executive officer, Guy Dolle, had sniffed that Mittal planned to pay for the acquisition in "monkey money" and "we make perfume, Mittal makes eau de cologne."[11] Mittal certainly had the last laugh over Dolle, and his company and others increasingly became part of the greater Asian economy.

There are two other factors helping bolster India's competitive advantage: first, the South Asian country is the world's largest democracy, and second, it has a relatively well-trained and nonpolitical military, an important part of the New Delhi consensus. Although India's political life is complicated by corruption, by religious-ethnic differences (mainly among Hindus, Muslims, and Sikhs), and sometimes by ramshackle multiparty ruling coalitions, the country's political system has managed to uphold an electoral system that provides the foundation for much of the give and take of parliamentary politics. It can be said that such a system allows an escape valve for public frustrations as Indians have the option, which they have used more than once, to "throw the rascals out." Unlike its neighbors (in particular Pakistan and Sri Lanka), India has not been subject to military coups or civil wars, nor has it undergone mass starvation like that which hit China in the aftermath of the Great Leap Forward in the 1950s. As *Business Week*'s Niranjan Rajadhyaksha notes, "a working democracy and a free press have kept the country free of ridiculous social experiments."[12] Even when Indira Gandhi declared the Indian Emergency (1975–77) and the country flirted with a more authoritarian mode of rule—with the prime minister granting herself extraordinary powers and pursuing a substantial crackdown on civil liberties (such as forced sterilizations) and on political opposition—India steered back to elective politics in 1977.

The combination of the above factors has helped create an India that is of far greater consequence in the regional and global economies than at any time prior. One critical difference between India and its continental rival China is that the South Asian economy is still largely driven by demand from its 1.2 billion people rather than exports. Whereas China's development has become in many ways lock stepped with the fate of the U.S. consumer, India's development remains comparatively more inward looking—at least in the medium term. At the same time, India is not standing still: it is a major source of demand with higher spending on infrastructure, adopted measures for its significant rural population, and possesses an expanding middle class.[13] Moreover, India has initiated a new set of trade and investment relations. Ironically, these relations are not so much in South Asia but in Southeast Asia. In 2005 India and ASEAN signed a trade agreement that provided an opening for the growth of trade between this region and South Asia's largest economy.

India's economic leap forward has not occurred without problems. The process of taking India from a poverty-stricken and inward-oriented economy is hardly over. For all of the hype about India as a land of investment potential, the results are disappointing. According to the United Nations Conference on Trade and Development, India's foreign direct investment (FDI) in 2001 was $3 billion; by 2004 it was $6 billion. Over the same period, China's FDI went from $47 billion to $62 billion and

Singapore's from $15 billion to $21 billion. Other challenges include the lack of sufficient infrastructure in the form of modern roads, railroads, highways, airports, and water facilities as well as reliable electrical grids. The last mentioned includes a growing gap between power supply and demand. While corruption and red tape have complicated building more power plants, the situation is also hindered by a weak regulatory framework, land acquisition problems, stretched capacity of domestic construction companies, and scarcity of equipment. Without power India will be unable to further develop its industrial-manufacturing base, badly needed to absorb a growing shift of people from the countryside to the city.

Water is another issue. Fresh drinking water can be hard to find, even for a growing middle class in some of the more affluent parts of the country. According to Pramit Mitra at the Center for Strategic and International Studies, "the water crisis, decades in the making, is getting worse just as India's economy is making impressive strides. A soaring population, rapid urbanization, and a thirsty farm belt are all putting enormous strains on India's anemic water infrastructure."[14]

Related to the shortness of drinking water is the problem of adequately removing sewage. Although India has a comprehensive regulatory and institutional framework as well as technical guidelines to handle various types of hazardous waste, there are several gaps. In the nation's capital city, New Delhi, some 45 percent of the population is not connected to the public sewage system, and it is estimated that more than 77 million Indians, roughly two-thirds of the population, lack adequate sanitation.[15] The following description of the Yamuna River, which runs through New Delhi and functions as the primary source of drinking water as well as being the principal drain for the city's waste, captures some of the sordid nature of the dilemma: "Coursing through the capital, the river becomes a noxious black thread. Clumps of raw sewage float on top. Methane gas gurgles on the surface."[16]

The issue of urbanization in these two Asian giants is particularly fascinating. By 2025 China is expected to add 400 million people to its urban population, a number that will account for 64 percent of the total population, and by the same year, India is expected to add 215 million to its cities, whose populations will account for 38 percent of the total. Never before in history have two of the largest nations in the world urbanized at the same time and at such a pace. In India urban GDP is projected by the McKinsey Global Institute to grow at a rate of 6 percent a year from 2005 to 2025, while China will see growth of 7.3 percent. The number of urban households with true discretionary spending power in India could increase sevenfold, to 89 million households in 2025. In China there are

55 million middle class households today, and that number could quadruple by 2025. From a business perspective, this significant increase in per capita urban incomes and middle-income households offers the potential of vibrant new markets to serve. In both countries demand for transportation, communications, housing and utilities, food, and health care services will be massive.

Other problems confronting India include the rise of disease, official corruption, and unclear law pertaining to land ownership. According to the World Bank, 21 percent of communicable diseases in India are water related. That includes diarrhea and mosquito-borne diseases (like dengue fever and chikungunya). Rounding out the picture are malaria and TB as well as a growing problem with HIV/AIDS. India also faces an educational challenge: in much of the country's more remote and poorer areas, school buildings are often in a state of disrepair, blackboards are scarce, and teachers poorly paid and stretched. In many regards, there is a dangerous disconnect between the perception of India as a knowledge platform par excellence and the still significant agricultural roots of its population. The Amy Kazmin of the *Financial Times* observed in 2010 that "its estimated 4 million English-speaking software engineers and call-centre workers—as well as talented scientists and investment bankers—create an aura of an emerging knowledge superpower, brimming with untapped talent waiting to be absorbed. In reality, however, about 50 percent of the population still lives in rural areas and works in agriculture."[17] This large rural population, of course, raises concerns about the sustainability of India's push into the global services market and a broader-gauged economic growth pattern.

Despite these many challenges, India is increasingly carrying greater weight in the new Asian economy. One of the key reasons for this is demographic. Over the next 30 years, India will become the world's most populous country. According to the World Bank, India's population will expand even as the annual growth rate declines from 1.7 percent to 1.3 percent as projected for the period 2004–20. The issue is that India's population numbers are more dynamics when compared to China's—the latter is rapidly aging and has a median age of 32.7 years. This assumes greater importance considering that more than half of the 1.09 billion Indians are under the age of 24.9 years. As Sumit Ganguly and Manjeet S. Pardesi write, "India's youthful population is expected to provide not only an expanding market and working-age population, but also to generate innovation and promote more rapid growth."[18]

The rise of India has also meant a growing push by the South Asian giant into the rest of the larger Asian regional economy. Unilateral trade policies were introduced in the late 1980s and gained momentum on a more systematic basis in the 1990s. The easy advances came in the expansion of Indian and other South Asian exports to the rest of the world, leaving South Asian markets relatively protected. As one World Bank study noted in 2006, "South Asian countries have maintained a higher level of protection within the region than with the rest of the world. Restrictive policies within the region have neutralized the beneficial effects of common cultural affinity, common geography, and the 'gravitational' pull of proximity on movement of goods and people within the region."[19]

Although the South Asian Association for Regional Cooperation (SAARC) was founded in 1985 with the mandate to create economic, social, technological, and cultural regional self-reliance, the trade part of the initiative lagged behind. The founding members of Bangladesh, Bhutan, India, the Maldives, Nepal, Pakistan, and Sri Lanka often found more to disagree about than agree. This was certainly the case between India and Pakistan that fought three wars (1947, 1965, and 1971). Trade between the two largest nations in South Asia is minimal and usually routed through Singapore, Dubai, and Sri Lanka (with which both countries have a FTA). There are also some lingering concerns about India's vastly larger and upwardly mobile economy, which equaled three-quarters of South Asia's GDP. This changed in the early 2000s because most of the countries have undertaken some degree of trade liberalization, setting the stage for the creation of the South Asian Free Trade Agreement (SAFTA) in 2004 (went into effect in 2006) and because of the growing pull of China. Sri Lanka did not join SAFTA but embarked upon its own free trade agreement with India.

Considering the slowness to open local economies up to foreign investment, lingering pressures to protect certain sectors, and ongoing political tensions between India and Pakistan and political upheaval in Nepal and Afghanistan, a strong South Asian regional economy failed to emerge. As of 2008 intraregional trade accounted for a diminutive 5 percent of total merchandise trade.[20] This number has not varied much over the last couple of decades. Another issue is the wariness of the smaller countries toward India, which in the past has not hesitated to remind them of its power. Despite this failure for a strong regional South Asian economy to emerge, what liberalization that did occur in individual countries ironically opened the door to a larger pan-Asian economy, driven more by China.

Since the early 2000s China's economic involvement in South Asia has increased. Trade between SAARC and China has expanded from $13 billion in 2000 to $50 billion in 2008 and was estimated to be heading to over

$70 billion for 2010. This increased trade is evident in a number of ways. In Nepal China's three leading airlines, China Eastern, China Southern, and Air China, operate passenger flights to Nepal's capital Kathmandu. The two countries also signed an agreement in May 2010 under which the larger country would provide duty-free access to 361 Nepali products. China is also helping on a number of infrastructure projects.[21] At the same time, China has emerged in the first decade of the twenty-first century as Bangladesh's major trading partner, displacing its traditional partner, India. The Sino-Bangladeshi relationship also encompasses China's selling the South Asian country considerable military hardware, being offered oil exploration rights, and the Chinese naval gaining access to the Bangladeshi Chittagong port.

Pakistan has also been pulled into the East Asian-driven regional economy, largely due to China. Annual trade increased from less than $2 billion in 2002 to $6.9 billion in 2009.[22] While the United States retained its position as Pakistan's number one trade partner, China surpassed the EU as a major partner, exporting goods worth $5.5 billion to the South Asian economy and importing $1.3 billion worth of products. There is a strong likelihood that China will emerge as Pakistan's leading trade partner in the not-too-distant future. To that end Beijing has pledged trade concessions to Pakistan that the South Asian economy is not receiving from the United States and the EU. Rounding out this picture, China has made substantial increases in investments in port development, roads, railways, telecommunications, hydro and thermal power, mining, electronics, and nuclear energy. While China clearly regards Pakistan as an important geopolitical and economic partner, a more fulsome embrace is prevented by security concerns, namely the Pakistani Taliban. There have been a number of incidents of Chinese workers coming under attack by local radical Islamists.

BECKONING CHINDIA

The most essential relationship in pulling South Asia closer to the rest of Asia is that between India and China, with 40 percent of the world's people between them. Until 1900 these two giants comprised one-half of the world economy. Today, this deepening relationship is leading to what some have called Chindia, the converging and complementary nature of two of Asia's largest economies. The actual term was coined in 2005 by Jairam Ramesh, a former Indian politician and journalist, who hailed the signing of the 2005 Strategic and Cooperative Partnership for Peace and Prosperity between China and India as a landmark event. That agreement set the stage for a transformation in the relationship between Beijing and New Delhi that was to herald a new economic frontier, helped along by growing diplomatic ties. In a simple sense, in the early twenty-first century China and India were finally recognizing the convergence of national interests. According to *Business Week's* Pete Engardio, "in a practical sense, the yin and yang of these two immense work forces already are converging. . . . Thanks to the Internet and plunging telecom costs, multinationals are having their goods built in China with software and circuitry designed in India."[23]

The potential power, both economic and political, of a China-India combination would be enormous. It would include over $3 trillion in foreign exchange reserves, some of the world's largest and competitive companies (across a wide range of sectors), and close to half of the world's population. The combination of the two economies would also represent a massive market for everything from capital services and insurance to food and energy products. A real Chindia would represent a very different configuration of the geopolitical landscape, considering that a large swath of the Eurasian landmass would be given heavier weight in the affairs of neighboring regions such as Central Asia, the Middle East, and Africa. Supporting this argument of expanding networks of investment, production, commerce, and trade is the rising tide of two-way trade. Total Sino-Indian trade has risen from a tiny $332 million in 1992 to $60 billion in 2010. Moreover, there has been a substantial reduction in trade costs between China and India (in tariff equivalent terms, trade costs fell from 117 percent in 1990 to 44.3 percent in 2008).[24]

In 2010 China was India's second-largest trade partner, and India was China's tenth. The same year saw one of the largest contracts ever between the two countries when India's Reliance Power ordered $10 billion worth of power generation equipment from Shanghai Electric in a deal financed by Chinese banks. Investment between the two countries has witnessed an upswing in the first decade of the twenty-first century. Shalendra D. Sharma, author of *China and India in the Age of Globalization* (2009), notes, "Since 2005, trade in services—particularly in construction, engineering, education, entertainment, financial services, information technology (IT) services, transport, tourism, and health—have seen robust growth. Chinese and Indian companies, including major players such as Huawei and Infosays, have made significant cross-border investments."[25] Another touch in the growing closeness was the Indian decision in 2010 to introduce Mandarin Chinese into Indian secondary schools' curriculum, a step that New Delhi regarded as a part of a "confidence-building" strategy.[26]

While there is much to herald in Chindia, the discussion of a powerful new economic combination is premature. It is true that India and China complement each other. China's large and diverse manufacturing base and India's advanced IT industry do provide an outlet for synergies between the two countries' economies. At the same time, China is protective of its own high tech industry, excluding Indian higher value-added products from its domestic markets. The same argument extends to Indian pharmaceutical exports. The financial service sectors in both countries have very limited exposure to each other, and India remains concerned about its Himalayan border with China as well as Beijing's plans for water diversion. Indian concerns have also been stoked by China's economic penetration in South Asia. Traditionally South Asia was dominated by India as the local economic and military power. Through the first decade of the twenty-first century, Chinese penetration in the economies of Sri Lanka, Nepal, and Bangladesh have not gone unnoticed. The same could be said for Chinese growing closeness with Pakistan, India's arch rival in the region. Add to these concerns the considerable clout China has in Burma including naval-basing rights and a road system stretching from Yunnan Province into the Burmese highlands, and India has some sense of trepidation regarding its neighbor.

China regards India as an important strategic partner in the development of a regional Asian economy (which means the exclusion of non-Asian actors). At the same time, China has had few qualms about upgrading its military relationships with a number of South Asian countries, in particular Pakistan. It is also a keen competitor on the energy front vis-à-vis India. China imports roughly 40 percent of its energy needs, India 75 percent. Chinese companies have aggressively sought to find new sources of energy around the world, locking in long-term agreements with Sudan, Nigeria, Angola, Burma, and Russia; Indian companies have put into place similar arrangements with Russia, Kazakhstan, Iran, Sudan, and Libya. Sharma observes, "In their quest for energy security, China and India are engaged in a fierce competition with geostrategic implications."[27] The conclusion one can draw from this energy race is that the most likely future scenario is an intensification of competition in Africa, Central Asia, and Latin America.

The importance of Sino-Indian relations will continue and most likely grow. There is a compelling motivation for deepening some form of Chindia. This motivation was part of the reason for China's premier Wen Jiabao to visit India in December 2010. As *Wall Street Journal* reporters Jeremy Page and Tom Wright write, "the concern for China now is that India—with the region's third-biggest economy, and second-biggest armed forces—is being drawn into a loose strategic alliance with the U.S. and its Asian partners to counterbalance Beijing's growing economic and military might."[28]

The December 2010 visit of Premier Wen Jinbao was treated with considerable fanfare by the Indian government, but there was no move on what Beijing really wanted—a free trade agreement. Instead, China was treated as a friend, albeit one that needs to be watched and its motives carefully scrutinized. The words of Indian foreign secretary Nirupama Rao earlier in the same month underscore the nature of the relationship: "The view that China and India are rivals to me is an over-generalization as well as an over-simplification of a complex relationship."[29] A translation of this statement is that Indian and Chinese national interests have a common goal in developing a regional economy in which the two countries play a growing and central role but that the relationship is one of nuances that capture China's great power aspirations, Indian sensitivities to such aspirations, and India's own great power dreams, all balanced by other economic and political actors in the form of the United States, Japan, and ASEAN.

THE LIMITS OF CHINESE ECONOMIC DOMINATION

China's explosive growth of trade and investment throughout Asia—South Asia, Southeast Asia, and East Asia—cannot be ignored. It is a major thread that is providing a more interwoven Asian regional economy. While we have discussed China's penetration of South Asia, Chinese companies and officials are also busy in Burma, Cambodia, and Indonesia. In Cambodia in 2010, the Bank of China provided a five-year $500 million equipment and servicing contract with Huawei Technologies, one of China's largest telecoms company. The loan, the largest such financing project of its kind in Cambodia, underscores the growing influence of China and its companies in the small Southeast Asian economy. Yet China's growing profile has raised concerns about its impact on local economies. In most cases the trading relationship is strongly in favor of China. Add to this imbalance the occasional Chinese less-than-subtle reminder that they have become a major power, other Asian countries are willing to deal with China but with a degree of caution. As Tim Johnston of the *Financial Times* wrote in 2010, "in Vietnam, Chinese plans to mine bauxite have run into heavy public criticism; in Cambodia, farmers and fishermen worry that their land and water are being bought up; even in Burma, which has few other friends, China's growing stature and self-confidence are being watched with a degree of trepidation."[30]

Southeast Asia is an important element in any regional Asian economy. It has 600 million people and a regional GDP of $1.5 trillion. While China is a major force in Southeast Asia, the region has other suitors. Kishore Mahbubani, professor at the National University of Singapore observes that "ASEAN is going through one of its sweetest moments in its history because it has four suitors interested in it. It could be a battlefield if the competition is military, but if its economic it will be wonderful for Southeast Asia."[31] This competition is clearly evident in the more aggressive interest in Southeast Asia as a place to do business on the part of U.S., Indian, European, and Japanese companies. Such competition has a healthy aspect to it from the perspective that too much dependence on a single economy, like China's, can be unhealthy. While China has had a tremendous trade record in expansion since 1978, a downturn in that economy cannot be ruled out, a development that would most likely have a negative impact on the global economy.

Another factor that puts a brake on the creation of a more cohesive Asian regional economy in the orbit of China is the lack of a regional financial market. Asia does have a number of well-established stock markets: Hong Kong, Shanghai, Tokyo, Osaka, Mumbi, and Singapore. Billions of dollars, yen, euros, and yuan pour through these markets on a regular basis. China is also developing a yuan bond market in Hong Kong, which has tremendous potential. In 2010 this market, sometimes referred to as the dim sum market, enjoyed a takeoff as large multinational corporations, including the U.S. heavy machinery company Caterpillar, issued debt in yuan 1 billion denominated bonds for the first time. This was a significant development as it opened the door for demand for yuan-denominated assets. At the same time, China's financial system lacks transparency and disclosure, the state plays a major role in the running of the banks, and the currency is not fully convertible.

Although Asia's financial markets are relatively sophisticated, they lack a degree of integration necessary to service the region's needs, much as London and New York do. This is a critical factor. In a 2010 report Standard & Poor's observed that: "given the region's scope and diversity, it would be unrealistic and unproductive to expect it to come together as some kind of tight-knit union of national financial markets in a one-size-fits-all manner."[32] The rating agency went on to note that "the deeper, more liquid, and more interlinked the region's capital markets become, the sooner the region's economies will be able to make the transition from emerging to established market status and achieve the sustained growth that will enhance quality of life across the region." What can be hoped for is "an alliance of national financial markets, preserving some differences but standardizing and harmonizing a rage of enabling financial practices and legislative frameworks." In many ways Asia is marching in the right direction, and the dim sum markets holds considerable potential, but a lot more needs to be done to make a functional fulsome regional economy, backed by a comprehensive financial system.

The vision of a more cohesive Asian economy is not likely to fade because of apprehension and resistance to Chinese dominance. Integration will continue because it makes economic sense. If millions of Indians, Thais, and Koreans can improve their standard of living by exporting products to China or by servicing Japanese tourist, the regional glue becomes stronger. If Chinese, Japanese, and Singaporean companies can take advantage of free trade agreements and make greater profits in other Asian markets, the incentive to advance further into regional integration continues. One indication of this is that in 2010 companies based in China and Hong Kong announced 44 acquisitions in Japan worth a combined $438 million, the largest deal count in a decade.[33] These acquisitions occurred despite a tense maritime dispute between Japan and China that brought relations to a new low. And Japanese companies remain interested in the Chinese market and thus far have proven resilient in riding through the sometimes contentious relationship between Asia's two largest economies.

So, what are the most likely scenarios for further Asian regional integration? One possibility is that China and Japan will work together in developing a common political space in East Asia, much like the role of France and Germany in Europe's integration process. Another scenario involves China taking on a more aggressive leadership role in regional integration. If China emerges as the region's engine of growth, it could take the lead in monetary and trade integration issues. A third scenario is to widen the group to ASEAN +6 by including Australia, New Zealand, and India, although we suspect that this move would introduce too many competing voices. Perhaps the most realistic scenario might be one of muddling through, at least for the foreseeable future. Former Japanese Prime Minister Yasuo Fukuda promoted this approach, as had his father, the former prime minister Takeo Fukuda who spoke of the Fakuda doctrine of Asia for Asians. This promoted policy dialogue in the region as a way of promoting understanding over time.[34]

As a practical matter, in 2011 those expressing views about fiscal and monetary integration in the region are restricted to a small number of intellectuals. But we suspect that this number will grow as the efficiencies associated with further integration become more obvious.

CONCLUSION

In the aftermath of World War II, there was no Asian regional economy. In the first decade of the twenty-first century, there is a de facto Asian regional economy, and the process of integration is accelerating. Although the fuller integration of the Asian economy has a number of challenges, a patchwork of bilateral and multilateral agreements is promoting the idea of greater regional trade, the development of more sophisticated interregional financial systems, and to some degree common goals. The ability of Asia to form a more intimate set of institutions along the lines of the European Union does not have a high level of expectation. The possibility of a NAFTA-like arrangement would be more likely, though even that is years away. Part of the issue is how to handle China as it is the powerful new economy and as its efforts to assert its will have the opposite impact on forging a more cohesive Asian regional market. In fact, the more aggressive China becomes, the more it runs the risk of creating coalitions to counterbalance Beijing's power, something that undermines a regional integration process. Consequently, we are left with an Asia geared to greater interregional trade and investment, complimented by some degree of financial coordination. Yet, the pace is constrained by concerns over the end game of policymakers in Beijing.

Chapter 5

THE SUPPORTING CAST: BRICs AND BEYOND

It is difficult to exclude the emerging markets factor from the rise of Asia. Africa, Latin America, the Middle East, and Central Asia are large factors in supporting Asia's rise. They offer a wide range of essential commodities as well as growing markets and strategic partners. At the same time, this so-called supporting cast of countries is not a subservient collection of Chinese or Asian satraps; countries such as Brazil, Russia, and India (which with China make up the so-called BRICs) and others such as South Africa, Turkey, and Indonesia have well-defined national interests and are becoming more active players on both regional and global stages. Russia and Turkey, in particular, have been great powers in the past, a factor that provides a lens through which their foreign policies and economic growth trends are perceived. The challenge for this group of countries is to manage their way through a changing global economic environment, leveraging off the strengths of each other. At the same time, the fortunes of the BRICs are becoming more closely woven with that of Asia, a development that includes China but also Japan, India, and South Korea. Simply stated, it has become a more complex world, and the matrix of relationships reflects a more south-south hemisphere-driven world than the past north-south one that dominated much of the last three centuries.

A DIFFERENT WORLD ORDER

The concept of the BRICs is usually attributed to a senior economist at Goldman Sachs, Jim O'Neill (now head of Goldman Sachs Asset Management), who in 2001 wrote "The World Needs Better Economic BRICs." The fundamental spark for the BRIC idea was 9/11. O'Neill later noted that "around the horror of that event, the underlying message was that globalization was going to continue and thrive. It was going to have to be on a more complex basis, and it wouldn't effectively be about the Americanization of the world."[1] O'Neill's simple premise was that Brazil, Russia, India, and China were large, significant countries with considerable resources that would embrace productivity changes to further develop their global trade and globalization. One of the more intriguing items to be pulled from the historical grab bag is that development patterns changed somewhat over the last 30 years, with the reintegration of two of the world's largest countries (in terms of geographic and population sizes), China and India. More specifically, the entire BRIC idea is based on the rise of China and India as manufacturing- and high tech-powered economies, working with the commodity-based giants of Russia and Brazil (though the Latin country does have an expanding industrial base).

O'Neill's original study was followed in 2003 by another from two other Goldman Sachs economists, Dominic Wilson and Roopa Purushothaman. The latter used demographic projections and a model of capital accumulation and productivity growth to reach the following conclusion: "The results are startling. If things go right, in less than 40 years, the BRICs economies together could be larger than the G6 in US dollar terms. By 2025 they could account for over half the size of the G6. Of the current G6, only the US and Japan may be among the six largest economies in US dollar terms in 2050."[2] Later added to the BRICs were the Next Eleven: Bangladesh, Egypt, Iran, Indonesia, Mexico, Nigeria, Pakistan, South Africa, Turkey, Philippines, and Vietnam. These countries were also selected by their size, demographics, and economic growth rates.

In the first decade of the twenty-first century, the BRIC idea gained traction, both from multinational corporations and the countries designated as BRICs. For the former the idea of large markets containing a little under half of the world's population with rising per capita incomes was attractive. At the same time, the BRICs began to have a little more coordinated economic policy line, especially when operating within the G-20 group of nations. While there was not a clear-cut alignment of national interests between Brazil, Russia, India, and China, in 2009 at Yekaterinburg, Russia, the four countries did hold their first summit meeting from which they issued a hazy declaration favoring an equitable, democratic and multipolar world order. Considering that Russia and China are identified as having autocratic governments, the reference to democracy was regarded as lip service to Brazil and India. At the same time, the stated preference for a multipolar world was clearly pointed at the waning, yet remaining superpower, the United States. Considering this meeting came in the aftermath of the 2008 financial meltdown that deeply wounded the U.S. economy, the signal was clear: a new order was being formulated, something that took into account the decline of U.S. power.

Although the BRIC idea had been around for a while, the economic turmoil of the 2008–11 period brought the group into better focus. The combination of Brazil, Russia, India, and China (the last one in particular) was a major force in the global economic recovery. In the OECD's November 2009 Update, the starring role was given to China. Although Russia's experience was more challenging in the downturn (due to its excessive dependence on oil and other commodities), China, India, and Brazil did not fall into a problematic debt crisis and economic freefall. Instead, they proved more resilient than many expected. According to Jorgen Elmeskov, the OECD's chief economist, "the non-OECD countries weren't affected by asset-price meltdowns as much and up to the downturn ran sensible economic policies."[3] As already noted in an earlier chapter, China continued to expand its economy during the downturn and was the key motor of growth. Brazil, India, and Russia were able to bounce back quickly in 2009 and 2010, indicating that their growth trajectories were not simple flash in the pans. And there is something to be said for sensible economic policies. Those policies allowed a number of the major non-OECD countries to maneuver through one of the most difficult economic downturns since the 1930s, a downturn that had been just as devastating to the nonindustrialized world as to the industrialized.

The BRIC idea has some strong points and a number of weak ones, most notably the absence of strong judicial systems in any of the BRIC countries. But the mere idea that China, Brazil, India, and Russia would actually begin a process of summits indicates that there is a structural transformation occurring in international relations, both mirrors of U.S. decline and of globalization (but without a Western stamp). However, the current combination has made considerable strides in the size of its members' economies and certainly in the cases of Brazil, China, and India, there has been some real progress in terms of economic diversification and social improvements. The BRIC idea has also helped push the idea that the largest and more critical emerging market countries deserve a place in governmental forums deciding global policy, a development evident in the shift from the G-7 (the United States, United Kingdom, Canada, Germany, France, Italy, and Japan) to the G-8 (adding Russia) to the G-20 (which since its inauguration in 1999 includes Brazil, China, and India). All these developments need to be understood in the context of Asia's rise as well as how the influence of this new alignment has limitations.

Russia as a BRIC

While we have discussed India in the prior chapter and China before that, it is worthwhile to briefly discuss how Brazil and Russia have changed and why they are considered BRICs. Becoming a BRIC did not occur overnight. All four countries had a bumpy ride on the development highway in achieving their emerging market superstar status. There were important changes that had to occur in each case to make a break with the past; even while questions linger over the sustainability of the BRIC status. Equally important, there are dissimilarities between the four countries that could limit a deeper coordination of policies. Russia is probably the weakest link in the BRIC order when one considers its dismal demographics, heavy dependence on commodity exports, and geostrategic challenges. Still, it is considered a BRIC, so let us briefly explore its voyage into that status.

At the end of the Cold War, the Soviet Union fragmented with Russia emerging as the largest single political and economic entity. The newly formed Russian Federation in 1992 was considerably smaller than the old Soviet Union, especially considering the loss of the Baltic, Central Asian, Caucasian states; Ukraine; and Belarus. Moscow did, however, keep control of Siberia with its vast tracks of land and abundant natural resources. Indeed, Siberia's oil, natural gas, gold, and other minerals have become an important component in Asia's supply chain. This relationship is a natural extension of Russia's sharing borders with China and Mongolia as well as having a Pacific coastline that provides it easy access to Korea and Japan.

Russia emerged from a Soviet Union that was a vast centrally planned economy that was increasingly unable to compete in the dawning high tech industrial revolution that commenced in the 1980s. Equally important, the Soviet economy had become highly dysfunctional, with grandly announced targets falling prey to bargaining between factory managers, bureaucrats, and local and national political leaders. Statistical cover-ups became commonplace. When Mikhail Gorbachev belatedly sought to reform the system, it collapsed, an unexpected and traumatic event for those that lived through it.

In 1992 a new Russian economy painfully emerged from the old. The process was marked by boom-bust cycles (the most dramatic being in 1997–98), a rapid and opaque privatization of state enterprises, the creation of an unstable and poorly regulated banking system, and in the 1990s the rise of the oligarchs, a small group of well-connected businessmen. While the last-mentioned group was to become the dynamic force behind Russia's capitalist revolution during the Yeltsin presidencies, it came to dominate where the country was heading. The problem was that the oligarchs had emerged at a time when the old system failed, and this failure meant that they presided over a vacuum without effective laws and a state so badly weakened it could not enforce laws that were on the books.[4] The result was the destruction of the old communist system, concentration of wealth into the hands of a few, and a rising level of lawlessness. For many Russians the new capitalist order was a socioeconomic disaster—personal security was questionable, the employment picture tenuous, and prospects for the future dark. By 1999, when President Boris Yeltsin left office, there were serious questions as to where Russia was heading and who was in control.

Russia took a very different direction in the first decade of the twenty-first century that helped it obtain BRIC status. Two important things happened. First, Vladimir Putin, who succeeded Yeltsin and had the support of the country's security apparatus, broke the power of the oligarchs, concentrated economic power back into the state, and curtailed the rough-and-tumble nature of Russian democracy (such as it was). Elections were held, but the results were controlled. Second, international energy prices made a spectacular rise, something Russia took advantage of because of its substantial natural gas and oil reserves. In turn, these developments meant a return to strong economic growth, an increase in foreign exchange reserves, and a higher degree of social stability. Russia established its own sovereign wealth fund and through its state champions (as some of the earlier privatization process was reversed) began to invest outside of Russia. A stronger, more confident Russia was back, and its strength was reflected by a tougher stance on energy and other issues with Ukraine, Belarus, and Georgia (including a short war in 2008). Russia's role as an energy producer clearly added to the country's return as a power as Moscow has sought to maximize its advantages as a major oil and gas producer especially vis-à-vis the European Union (which has made much noise over energy independence but is limited in what it can do).[5] This Russian influence was evident in the EU's flaccid response to Moscow's Georgian War in 2008.

Russia also played an important role in China's future development as an energy supplier, which is what O'Neill had in mind when he created the idea of the BRICs, with China as a manufacturer and Russia as a supplier of commodities. The East Siberia-Pacific Ocean (EPSO) oil pipeline was put into operation in December 2009 and was designed to pump up to 1.6 million barrels of crude per day from Siberia to Russia's Far East and then on to Japan, China, and the rest of the Asia Pacific region. Russia's sale of oil to China was a slow process because of intense competition from Japan for Russian crude and Moscow's security issues with China over Siberia—underpopulated, yet so full of natural resources. Trade between the two countries was over $50 billion in 2010 and included the export of Russian commodities and electrical products and Chinese exports of cars and other consumer goods.

The Sino-Russian relationship is important, with both states maintaining high-level visits such as that of Putin's successor President Dmitri Medvedev's September 2010 trip to China to attend the ceremony marking the opening of the Chinese section of the first oil pipeline between the two countries. Russia is also a member of a Chinese-initiated regional organization, the Shanghai Cooperation Organization, which was formed from the earlier Shanghai Five founded in 1996. This group includes China, Russia, Kazakhstan, Turkmenistan, Uzbekistan, and Tajikistan. The purpose is to provide better regional cooperation between these countries, but it also serves to be a counterpoint to U.S. and European influence in the region. The group also remains an autocrat's club, being highly suspicious of any such movements akin to those that ousted authoritarian leaders in Georgia and Ukraine.

Russia-China relations might be classified as quite warm as of 2011. As noted, there had been territorial disputes between the two powers, particularly over Siberia, but this conflict was largely resolved in 2005. Any outstanding disputes today over borders are dormant. Both countries work to prevent intervention in their internal affairs and to take advantage of complementary interests concerning energy supply (Russia) and demand (China). Russia is China's leading source of advanced military equipment and technology. China exports manufactured goods to Russia. In addition, both countries are United Nations Security Council members, and they have coordinated their approach on several international security issues including blocking sanctions against Iran, Burma, and Zimbabwe. Both countries share fears about Islamic extremism, the regional drug trade, human trafficking, and organized crime. Both nations seek stability, China because it wants to focus its resources on domestic economic development and Russia because regional instability can feed instability back home. China is a natural trade partner for Russia, and the two countries share similar autocratic political systems. Additionally, both countries have their differences with the United States.

Where does this leave Russia as a BRIC in the rise of Asia? Russia remains a member of the supporting cast for China's and Asia's economic juggernaut—but only to a point. Despite its similarities with China, Russia still needs a hedge against China. The Asian country has a far larger population, one of the biggest economies on the planet, and through the 1990s and into the early twenty-first century, an enormous appetite for a wide range of commodities. Russia's Siberia is underpopulated, has many commodities in demand south of the border, and is perceived by many Russians as vulnerable. A possible future scenario has China marching north and seizing Siberia with the objective of carving out living space for its population and gaining control of key natural resources. While this scenario sounds much like a science fiction plot, Russia started a program in 2007 to attract Russian exiles back to the homeland, with a particular focus on repopulating Siberia.

Russia also received a lesson as to the structural weaknesses of its economy in 2008–9. The financial crisis in the West was felt severely in Russia as the global economic downturn demonstrated a very high dependence on oil and gas and other commodities. When commodity prices fell, so did Russia's GDP. In 2009 Russia's GDP shrank by 7.9 percent before rebounding to 4 percent in 2010. Russia's economic growth was comparatively weaker than China's over the same period, no doubt a factor acknowledged in Moscow.

How is Russia to hedge its strategic bet with China? Trade between Russia and the other two BRICs, India and Brazil, is important, but only around $10 billion compared to the $50 billion plus trade between China and Russia. Despite Russia's efforts to step up relations with New Delhi and Brasilia, Beijing is of far larger consequence. This concerns Moscow, and it should.[6] Consequently, Russia continues to work to integrate its economy with China and the rest of Asia, but it hedges by playing the United States, Europe, India, and Japan against Beijing. In this context the EU remains an important trade partner, though it has less to offer politically and militarily, especially following the 2009–11 sovereign debt crisis that hit the region. Russia is left with a complicated geostrategic game as it must balance a declining Europe in the west and a rising Asia in the east. It also confronts a militant wing of Islam in the Caucuses, with a legacy of problems stemming from its control of Chechnya. All of these problems point back to the challenge from a China that is growing economically and becoming more willing to use its power to get what it wants. China and Russia are BRICs, but the relationship remains fluid and conditioned by past rivalries and differing national interests. Russia may recognize China's economic might, but it has little interest in being part of a Beijing-led alliance.

Brazil's Rise

For a long time the common refrain about Brazil, Latin America's largest country, has been that it is the country of the future and will always be. Throughout the past century, there were periods of impressive economic expansion, often dubbed economic miracles. Yet, the economic miracles usually ran out of steam, and crises erupted, some of them ending in debt defaults. For a number of reasons–inept leadership, poor economic decisions and strategies, and a heavy dependence on volatile commodity prices—Brazil's developmental track record was uneven. Latin America's giant left its great expectations unmet. That does not discount some important infrastructural advances, the creation of a substantial agro-industrial and manufacturing base, and the emergence of a broad-based national consensus about the need to advance along a capitalistic system conditioned by a healthy dose of social democracy.

Following the debt crisis that rocked Brazil and most of Latin America in the 1980s, Brazil benefited from the two terms of President Fernando Henrique Cardoso, who implemented a number of key reforms designed to stabilize the economy from excessive external debt and inflation. During this period Brazil reaffirmed its place as the world's largest producer of sugar and concentrated orange juice and the largest exporter of soy, cattle meat, and tobacco. Warner Baer, a noted economist on Brazil, writes that "in 2005, after more than five decades at industrialization, Brazil was producing 2.4 million motor vehicles, 33 million tons of steel, 34.4 million tons of cement, 5.9 million television sets, 23.3 cellular phones and 4.8 million refrigerators yearly. The country's paved road network increased from 36,000 kilometers in 1960 to about 190,000 kilometers in 2006. Brazil had 90,700 megawatts of installed electric power capacity in 2004, and over 60 percent of its exports consisted of industrial products."[7] At the same time, Brazil's major companies expanded outside of the country and became active as global players. These companies included Vale, a major global mining enterprise; Embraer, the world's fourth largest aerospace company; Gerdau, a large iron and steel company with operations in North America; and the state-owned Petrobras, the world's fourth largest energy company.

In the early twenty-first century, Brazil is clearly the economic powerhouse of Latin America. It has a population of 190 million, making it the fifth largest in the world in terms of population. It covers 47 percent of South America and possesses a wealth of raw materials, including iron ore, manganese, bauxite, copper, lead, zinc, nickel, tungsten, tin, uranium, industrial diamonds, and gem stones. Additionally, it has large reserves of oil and gas, more than enough to sustain itself. Starting with the Plano Real Stabilization Plan during the Franco administration (1992–94) under then Finance Minister Cardoso and continuing under Cardoso's back-to-back presidencies (1994–2002) and Luis Inacio Lula da Silva (2002–10), Brazilians were finally able to harness their resources and produce the long-awaited economic miracle. Significantly, inflation, long a problem for the country, was brought under control. At the same time, Brazil's external debt was reduced in a meaningful fashion to the point that the U.S.-induced global financial crisis failed to spark an economic crisis. In the past the economic-financial problems of advanced economies often dried up global liquidity and resulted in an external debt crisis.

Another important factor for Brazil is that it is one of the world's largest democracies. Although not on the same scale as India's experiment with pluralistic government, Brazil maintains an elective form of government, has seen a rotation of parties in office (from both the left and right), and allows a relatively high degree of press freedom. Since the military returned to the barracks in 1988, it has left the running of the government to the civilian authorities. The success of Brazil's democratic experience was highlighted in 2002 when da Silva became president. In his election Brazilians witnessed the triumph of a peasant's son as proof that Brazil was not just a land of the privileged and powerful but an inclusive democracy with room for all views and voices, even at the top.[8] To his credit Lula opposed changing the constitution to allow him an opportunity to run for a third term and publicly stated, "the alternation of power is an important measure of a full democracy."[9]

The Brazil that looks forward into the twenty-first century is far more cosmopolitan and economically more powerful than it was at the close of the last century. President da Silva helped elevate his country into the ranks of the G-20 and BRICs, making Brasilia's view important in many deliberations of global economic policy. At the same time, Brazil has considerable challenges: a fractious set of political parties that complicate coalition building, rigid labor laws, high crimes rates, a bloated pension system, high taxes, and substantial socioeconomic inequalities. While Brazil is able to project its power into the larger world, these challenges demand a heavy focus at home. This entire picture raises the question as to how much is Brazil part of a supporting cast for the rise of Asia, and China in particular?

Asia factors significantly into Brazil's global outlook for a number of reasons. One of the larger minorities in the country is of Japanese descent; these people's forefathers immigrated in 1908 aboard the *Kasato Maru* to work in the coffee industry. In 2011 the Brazilian-Japanese minority remains a distinctive and successful group in the country, providing a human link to Asia, which has long been supplemented by trade and investment. Annual Japanese-Brazilian trade has been around $10 billion, but it was estimated that in 2010 Japanese individuals accumulated more than $73 billion in Brazilian investments.[10] A large part of the attraction for Japanese investors with Brazil is the relative value of the South American country (strong economic growth, expanding companies, and positive demographics) vis-à-vis their own (weak or stagnant growth, struggling domestic companies, zero or negative interest rates, and negative demographics).

But Japan is not the story for the rise of Asia in Brazil. China dominates that tale. This Asian country's involvement in Brazil has surged in the first decade of the twenty-first century. Chinese companies have aggressively been purchasing Brazilian real estate, buying up farmland and iron mines, and gaining contracts to help develop major infrastructure projects that range from utilities to ports. In 2010 Chinese investment worldwide rose from $5.5 billion in 2004 to $56.5 billion in 2009. In Brazil alone, Chinese companies are expected to invest over $10 billion in 2011, with one of the most significant projects being the $989 million investment by China's State Grid, the world's largest utility company.[11] Also, Chinese banks have lent $10 billion to Petrobras, the Brazilian national oil company, and $1.23 billion to Vale, the iron ore miner. Chinese officials now predict that total investment by Chinese companies in Brazil will reach $100 billion by 2013, something that will make the Asian country the biggest foreign direct investor.[12] Also in 2010 China pushed aside the United States as Brazil's major trade partner. Additionally, classes in Mandarin Chinese are becoming increasingly popular.

China's rise to power is also reflected in Brazil's rise to power. The Latin American country's political and economic stability over the past decade has made it a more attractive partner for China, especially as the Asian country is looking for places to invest and diversify outside of the financially troubled United States and Europe. In many cases there is a convergence of national interests, which has been helped along by a series of meetings by former President da Silva and China's President Wu Jintao and other high-ranking officials. China's concerns about U.S. fiscal irresponsibility and financial scandals no doubt made it sympathetic to President da Silva's comments in 2009 upon the visit of the United Kingdom's Prime Minister Gordon Brown. In what was clearly a stab at the Americans and British, the Brazilian leader stated, "This crisis was fostered and boosted by irrational behavior of some people that are white, blue-eyed. Before the crisis they looked like they knew everything about economics, and they have demonstrated they know nothing about economics."[13]

China also represents a challenge for Brazil. That challenge comes in a number of ways. One is the strategic challenge of China's growing influence in Latin America. Brazil has sought to project itself as the major power in the region. This projection has not entailed intervening with troops and strong-arming its neighbors, but Brasilia's influence is duly noted throughout South America and the Caribbean. At the same time, other less democratic poles of power have emerged as in the case of Venezuela's populista strongman Hugo Chavez, who has sought to develop a like-minded cadre of left-leaning autocratic states in Bolivia, Nicaragua, and Ecuador. China's willingness to foster its influence in these countries by military and trade missions and investment has not always been appreciated by Brazil.

Along the same lines, China's muscular push into Africa, in particular the Portuguese-speaking countries, has put Brazilian and Chinese companies in direct competition in places such as Angola and Mozambique. Brazil's own demand for resources has pushed companies from Latin America's giant to Africa, with imports from Africa rising from $3 billion in 2000 to $18.5 billion in 2008.[14] Brazil's African line-up includes oil imported from Algeria and Nigeria and food exports to Egypt and South Africa. Trade relations have also expanded in Morocco, Libya, and Cameroon, while embassy representation throughout Africa has increased. President da Silva himself had actively engaged Africa, making eight trips and visiting around 20 countries during his tenure which concluded in January 2011.

Another point of concern about China's push into Brazil is whether it is good for the country's business. One view is that China's surge of involvement in Brazil is a net gain. According to Eduardo Centola of South Africa's Standard Bank, "China's interest in Brazil has gone from looking for assets in resources to infrastructure. Its aim is to create a stronger middle class so Brazil becomes a stronger customer and partner for China."[15] Yet, many Brazilians remain concerned that China's state-owned companies, backed by cheap loans from state-owned banks, operate with unfair advantages in regard to their Brazilian counterparts. Additionally, Chinese investment often does little to generate new employment opportunities. Roberto Giannetti da Fonseca, head of international relations and trade at Sao Paulo business group FIESPI, observed, "The Chinese investment is welcome, but not with much enthusiasm because it is creating hardly any jobs and not having much impact on increasing our exports."[16]

There is also an ideological difference between Brazil and China. Brazil represents a democratic country that is increasingly successful in dealing with poverty and other development issues. This assessment is by no means to argue that Brazil has eradicated much of the structural problems that mark its socioeconomic inequalities, but it is on a comparative basis successful, especially when it postures thus in Africa, where its track record has some degree of appeal. In particular, the Brazilian program of reducing poverty through social welfare payments that are conditional on school attendance or visits to clinics has generated interest in a number of African countries. In a sense Brazil offers a soft sell for democratic government, backed by concern over poverty reduction, a sharp contrast to China's more muscular approach and willingness to deal with any regime, including those with odious human rights records such as Sudan.

China and Asia's rise represents a challenge for Brazil. There is no single right approach to dealing with the thorny issues of China's surge into global markets. While Brazil is willing to be part of a supporting cast for Asia, it also has its own core interests, which include developing its economic relationships in Latin America and Africa. Moreover, it has little interest in becoming an outpost for a greater Chinese empire built around commodities extraction and a market for Chinese goods to the detriment of its own manufacturing base. This dual nature of Brazil's policies vis-à-vis China is evident in its currency policy. Brazil is not comfortable with China's currency, which it regards as artificially weak and harmful to the real. Brazilian manufacturers, in particular, feel the brunt of the strong real-weak remimbi exchange. At the same time, the Latin American country's commodity exporters are reluctant to do something that will irritate China, their major market. But Brazil is not without clout in this matter. Economist William Cline writes that "China may be more sensitive to what the other emerging market countries think about its currency. It undermines their moral high ground when it's Brazil criticizing them instead of the U.S."[17] Brazil, like Russia, is an important partner for China, but the relationship will require considerable attention from both sides to manage it so that both feel the benefits.

The BRIC idea has not ended with the four countries. In January 2011 China issued an invitation to South Africa to join the BRICs. The Chinese government indicated that it believed South Africa's accession would "promote the development of BRIC and enhance co-operation between emerging economies."[18] While this invitation was something strongly desired by South Africa, it also made a signal that the BRICs saw that their bloc could expand in terms of numbers as well as influence. By adding South Africa, probably the strongest African power, to the mix, the BRIC alignment cut across Latin America and Eurasia as well as Africa, giving a little more heft to the claims of growing power in the south.

BEYOND BRICs: THE AFRICAN SCRAMBLE

Asia's emerging global reach is also notable in Africa. Although the other BRICs are heavily involved in Africa, it is China that heads the pack. This is evident in a number of ways. The value of trade between Africa and

China expanded from $4.1 billion in 1992 to $107 billion in 2008, making the Asian country the continent's second-largest trade partner after the United States.[19] Largely focused on oil, natural gas, and other mineral resources, China has expanded its net of relationships both in terms of countries with which it is doing business and the type of products that it seeks. As journalist John Ghazvinian observed in 2006, "even beyond these statistics, the scale and ferocity of China's entry into Africa has been breathtaking. China has started construction on a new railway in Nigeria and a new port for Gabon, has paved most of the roads in Rwanda, and is building roads, bridges, power stations, schools, and cellular-phone networks in at least a dozen African nations. . . . In tiny Lesotho, nearly half the supermarkets are owned and run by Chinese, who also operate textile factories in the country."[20] It should also be noted that China paid for and Chinese companies built Lesotho's parliament building.

China's entry into Africa was initially led by ideological concerns.[21] Those concerns were encapsulated in the desire to spread revolution around the world by the Chinese Communist Party under the guidance of Mao Zedong. In regard to Africa, Beijing's policies centered upon supporting African liberation movements against European colonial governments and upon independence providing assistance against the forces of imperialism (namely the West and later the Soviet Union). In addition, China offered to help in economic development projects. Considering the financial and military limitations facing China and the better opportunities to stir up trouble closer to home (Southeast Asia), Africa was hardly a priority. The disruption of China's political and economic affairs during the Cultural Revolution in the 1960s also undercut any major efforts in Africa. China's profile rose marginally during the 1970s when it became involved in building a railroad connecting Tanzania and Zambia. The railroad was started in 1970 and financed by an interest-free loan of $500 million from China. Despite that and ongoing trade ties to Africa, it was energy that would bring the Chinese surge.

One of the most attractive plays for China in Africa is to help develop the region's oil and natural gas capacity. In 1993 China officially crossed the line from being a net exporter of oil to being a net importer. As China's industrial development ramped up so did its demand for oil. By 2005 China drove past Japan to become the world's second largest oil importer, behind only the United States. While China's hunger for energy took its state-owned companies to neighboring countries such as Burma and Indonesia and to Middle Eastern countries (such as Iran), it eventually brought it to Africa. With comparatively less explored reserves and sweeter crude than Latin America, Africa has become the key supplier of the future. By the late 2000s, Angola, Sudan, and other suppliers in Sub-Saharan Africa came to provide 25 percent of China's crude oil imports.[22] There is also a geostrategic dimension to China's African involvement. As China is geostrategically generally excluded from the Middle East (a situation reinforced by the U.S. invasion of Iraq), Africa thus became the center of China's movement into the international extractive industry economies.[23]

China demonstrated its newfound commitment to Africa by launching its New Asian African Strategic Partnership (NAASP), which was followed by a major China-Africa summit in 2006. The latter was attended by more than forty African heads of state, and $5 billion in new loans and credits were dished out to African countries. This money was especially good news to African countries as these loans were not made conditional on transparency and disclosure regulations pushed by the West and did not depend on any linkages to human right. One observer noted, "In terms of sheer scale and ambition, the summit dwarfed anything Britain, France, or the United States had achieved—or even attempted—for Africa in the past."[24]

China's energy push has been most notable in Angola and Sudan, two of the newer oil countries. Angola, a former Portuguese colony and home to a lengthy civil war ending in 2002, emerged during the late 1990s as a major oil producer, ultimately vying with Nigeria for being the number one crude oil producer in Africa. China made a concentrated push into Angola, willing and able to use cheap Chinese bank loans and other forms of official aid (offering a $9 billion loan for infrastructure projects) to shove aside the competition. In 2010 Sinopec (China Petroleum & Chemical Corp) spent $2.5 billion to acquire a stake in Angolan oil field (Block 18). Angola's economy is highly dependent on oil, and the two major foreign powers involved in the emerging African economy are China and the United States. Those two countries consume some 90 percent of Angolan oil. China's other major African oil adventure is Sudan, where it invested an estimated $6 billion.

China is not alone in the deepening of trade and investment linkages with Africa. Indian, Japanese, and Korean companies are increasingly active in Africa, in many cases competing with each other and European, Latin American, and North American companies. This competition is reflected by Indian mining companies such as Vendanta playing a role in resuscitating the mining industry in Zambia or the Tata conglomerate opening the Taj Cape Town Hotel in South Africa or selling buses in Ghana and Benin. It is also reflected by South Korea's KOGAS (Korea Gas Corporation) signing an agreement with Mozambique's Hydocarbon

Company to explore for and maximize the use of natural gas in the South African country.

India's growing involvement in Africa and other parts of the supporting cast is worth a few additional words. While we have already noted India's growing ties to Southeast Asia, China and Japan, Africa is not without its own significance. African exports to India grew from $3.1 billion in 2000 to $12.7 billion in 2006 and were above $15 billion in 2010. Africa's imports from India also grew from $2.2 billion to $9.5 billion and were above $10 billion by 2010. Indian investment has been largely guided by oil and mining, but services and manufacturing are on the rise. For example, Vendanta's investment in the Zambian copper industry has helped revive that country's exports and standing as one of the largest copper producers in the world.

THE SWORD OF NATIONAL INTERESTS

While there is much to bind the BRICs together, there are also points of potential friction as these countries become more widely accepted players in the international system. They face a wide range of issues like environmental pollution, transnational crime, cross-border disease, and worrisome geopolitical tensions in the Middle East, parts of Africa, and North Korea. The question is does this wide range of issues provide a platform for the BRICs to develop a more common front, or is it easier to maintain individual positions and play the other countries off against each other? Alternatively, it may be easier just to blame the advanced economies for the world's ills. Considering Asia's growing economic and military might and its rising political aspirations (restructuring the leadership of such international organizations as the International Monetary Fund and United Nations), there are plenty of issues upon which either to flounder or to establish a common front.

The challenge in forming a common BRIC front is substantial, let alone the idea of observing the birth of a China-led emerging markets bloc. China's clear push into Africa and Latin America in fact has increasingly caused reassessments about the nature of the relationship with an eye to who benefits. While Chinese trade and investment are welcome, there are concerns about who gains the most from the relationship, how workers are paid as well as their working conditions, and what all of this involvement does to national balance of payments. If all of the gains are on the Chinese side of the ledger, the terms of the relationship cannot be taken for granted.

In Angola, the location of one of the biggest gambits in Beijing effort to enhance energy security, the relationship's upside remains limited by

Chinese practices and traditional Angolan sensitivity to anything that smacks of colonialism or neocolonialism. While Angola was happy to accept Chinese loans and technical assistance, the inflow of large numbers of Chinese to actually work the projects added a degree of tension. According to the Angolan government, in 2010 there were 70,000 Chinese at work in Angola, ranging from crane and bulldozer operators to more-skilled railway technicians.[25] This practice of importing large numbers of Chinese workers has not gone over well with the Angolans and reflects a lack of sensitivity on the part of the Chinese. Lucy Corlin, a research associate at the Africa-Asia Centre of the University of London's School of Oriental and African studies, observes that the problem in Angola (as in the rest of Africa) is that "Chinese companies and politicians collectively have leaned heavily on high-level political relations rather than informed analysis and research"[26] Add to this that the Chinese live in their own enclaves, do not learn the local language, go to Chinese schools, and stand apart from the native population.[27]

But there is another side of the equation. Chinese workers have been attacked in Angola, and there are occasional kidnappings. Many Chinese companies have confronted hostility from government agencies, an imperfect legal system, corruption, high customs fees, and ill faith in business operations with local firms who resent their presence.[28] There are two other more political factors: the Chinese are an easier-to-attack proxy for the Angolan government (and the Angolan government does have its opponents) and China's involvement in the Cabinda Enclave has left its nationals open to attack from separatists. The Cabinda Enclave, separated from the rest of Angola by the Congo River, is a major oil-producing area, and its inhabitants have long resisted being part of the country. In 2010 separatists targeted Chinese working for the Angolan government.

The cooling of the Sino-Angolan relationship reflected the double-edged nature of national interests and how they factor into the rise of Asia, for China in particular. The initial Sino-Angolan surge in relations during the first decade of the twenty-first century was one of mutual benefit. For its part Angola benefited from Chinese loans and expertise and was able to lever China vis-à-vis the Europeans and, to a lesser degree, the United States. For China a close relationship with one of Africa's largest oil producers was an important step in securing future energy supplies. The extension of cheap credit to Angola also staved off competition, in particular France's Total, which was hoping to play a more active role in Angola's oil bonanza.

China's checkbook diplomacy in Angola also sparked criticism with the international community, in particular on the impact of China's "noninterference" in other country's political and economic affairs. Such a policy allowed China the option to venture into areas where the West has raised questions in terms of human rights, corruption, and opaque financial transactions. Angola's lack of transparency is well known. This lack was evident in 2000 when "Anglogate" hit France, complete with the revelation that oil company Elf-Aquitaine maintained a multimillion dollar slush fund derived from oil proceeds to pay African leaders, including top Angolan leaders. Subsequent efforts were made to "clean up" financial transaction with Angola. The IMF fought for greater clarity in the African country's finances in 2002 when another scandal emerged over the use of oil-guaranteed loans employed in the structuring of Angola's bilateral debt to Russia. According to an IMF report in March 2002, Angolan authorities refused to provide the IMF with details of the oil-guaranteed loans "because it would infringe on their national sovereignty."[29] With a patron like China, ready and willing to write large checks without any questions asked, who needs the IMF, World Bank, or nosy Western governments that have to account to the public? At the same time, the lack of accountability also backfires on the Chinese as money for projects has gone missing, delaying completion dates or resulting in mission reassessments.

By 2009 the Sino-Angolan relationship had cooled. This cooling was mirrored by a 33 percent drop in bilateral trade (down to $17 billion in 2009) and the decline of Angola as one of the top buyers of Chinese contracts, once among the top three and now fallen behind Iran and Venezuela.[30] Angola also blocked the $1.3 billion sale of a 20-percent stake held by Marathon Oil to China's CNOOC and Sinopec. Adding insult to injury, Angola then signed a deal to raise its existing cooperation with India. For Angola China's embrace has been a little too much, touching upon colonial sensitivities, especially as Beijing's colony of workers reached large and identifiable numbers. That embrace also became a point of public discontent; something that the government decided was not to its advantage. Last but hardly least, the Chinese deal brought pressure from the West, namely the United States, a critical trade and investment partner. In 2009 U.S. Secretary of State Hilary Clinton visited Angola, indicating that her country would increase investment in the oil industry and in agriculture. By 2011 it was evident that China had gained influence, but in doing so, it became much like former colonial powers in its behavior— a factor that ultimately came to limit China's clout.

Sudan represents an even more complicated problem for China. While China faces tough Western, Indian, and Brazilian competition in Angola, Sudan has a substantially reduced Western presence. Simply stated, the odious nature of the Sudanese government in Khartoum, in particular its active role in the genocide in Darfur over the last decade, has forced many Western oil companies to leave due to the pressure from human rights groups and government measures. The West has generally opted out of Sudan, including many non-oil sectors of the economy. The result has been a significant Chinese penetration into one of Africa's largest oil exporters. China's role has been critical for Khartoum: the Asian country is the major Sudanese trade partner, the key oil market, and the main supplier of weapons. Beijing has also played a major role in protecting Sudan from sanctions against Khartoum vis-à-vis the United Nations over Darfur human rights violations.

China came to Sudan in the late 1990s, a time when the African country's economy was in free fall. The second round of civil war with the south was destructive to agricultural production and internal trade. Although Western oil company explorations indicated that Sudan was sitting on what many thought to be one of the continent's largest oil reserves, Sudan had a huge negative public relations problem. It had earlier given refuge to Osama bin Laden, its leadership consorted with well-known Islamic radicals, and its human rights record (even before Darfur) was bad. Pressure on Western companies such as Chevron and Total was intense, and eventually they left. Consequently, China found Sudan bereft of Western companies and in need of an ally. And China needed the oil. In 1996 China National Petroleum Corp. bought into fields being operated by Western companies. It joined the Sudan's Energy Ministry in building the country's largest refinery and steadily increased its presence over the next decade. This presence was observed in Chinese companies building a 900-mile pipeline from the southern part of Sudan (where much of the country's oil is located), port facilities, and other support infrastructure. It has been alleged that this infrastructure buildup was done with Chinese companies working hand in glove with Sudanese military forces that launched a campaign to eliminate southern villages to make room for the pipeline.[31] There were also multiple reports of China having 4,000 soldiers (in civilian clothes) protecting Chinese workers as well as $3 billion being spent on infrastructure projects since 1999, including a refinery, port, Friendship Hall and Friendship Hospital in Khartoum, a bridge over the River Nile, a rice farm, and a textile mill.[32]

China's Sudan venture is ruffling Western feathers and certainly the linkages to Darfur's genocide upset human rights activists, but Beijing's national interests of securing energy supplies trumps those factors. Simply stated, it is sad that bad things are happening in Darfur and for that matter in South Sudan (up to the ceasefire in 2005), but it is necessary to keep China's economy growing, its population in a state of improving lifestyle, and the Communist Party in power. What complicates this situation is that China's love fest with the north does not hold it in good standing in South Sudan, which overwhelmingly voted in January 2011 to separate from Khartoum and to form a new nation. Between South Sudan and Abyei (a sliver of land between North and South Sudan) most of Sudan's oil reserves are located largely outside of Chinese-friendly hands. China will have to prove itself again in the south and probably once again wield its checkbook, a potentially expensive proposal.

The changing geopolitical scene was evident in early 2011 following the vote for South Sudan's separation. The government in Juba, South Sudan's capital, is keenly aware that the oil pipeline and port facilities necessary to get their oil to international markets must go through the north. Considering China's strong identification with the north, it was no surprise that it was announced in late January 2011 that the Juba government was negotiating with Japan's Toyota East Africa to construct a new oil pipeline to Kenya's Lamu port.[33]

Asia's rise is clearly having an impact around the world. Old relationships are being shaken up and new ones are being created. For the supporting cast (and we use this term loosely), China, India and the other Asian dynamos have much to offer, including badly needed funds for infrastructure and education, markets, and in some cases supportive diplomatic patterns. At the same time, the sword of national interests cuts two ways, with many African countries finding that when the Chinese come, they bring large numbers of their countrymen and do not necessarily hire local workers. Additionally, local businesses from Brazil to Zambia have deep concerns over competition from Chinese goods that could put them out of business. From the Asian perspective, pushing into emerging markets like Africa represents new challenges, including business environments that can be arbitrary, weak legal systems, and at times a lack of political stability. China's checkbook diplomacy has also meant that in some cases money has been lost to local power brokers instead of being spent on roads, schools, and other infrastructure projects. The same challenge confronts other Asian companies, but many of these, as in South Korea and India, are beholden to shareholders (be they families or market participants) and are profit driven unlike the state-owned Chinese companies. Nonetheless, the higher profile of Asia around the world in many of the supporting-cast countries is more appreciated than not as it has allowed African, Latin American, and Middle Eastern governments to use leverage to find common ground in the changing global system.

CONCLUSION

The economic turmoil of the 2007–11 years is leaving a different world in its wake. The stumbling of the Anglo-American economies and a painful rethinking of that model of freewheeling capitalism has left the field open to those economies still standing. Considering that continental Europe's more safety-prone and less entrepreneurial approach has also been hurt by the global downturn, more eyes and investor money have turned to emerging markets, first to the BRICs but also to a number of other economies (like Turkey, Indonesia, and South Africa) that have a track record of strong economic growth and prudent management and that are pursuing market-oriented policies. Last, but hardly least, these countries have embraced globalization, finding an increasingly complementary niche with both BRICs and OECD countries. All of this bodes well for Asia's rise as it provides an alternative to the troubled Western economies and Japan, where demographics are in decline and public finances are functioning as dampers to growth, processes that mean limited upside in the purchase of goods from Asian economies. At the same time, there are limits as to how far the rest of the emerging markets want to be a supporting cast for the rise of Asia and especially China.

Chapter 6

THE MAJOR ECONOMIC CHALLENGES

Asia's rise as a powerful economic zone is breathtaking in many ways, but substantial headwinds remain. It is the purpose of this chapter to focus on those challenges. One such challenge is the need to redefine development strategies in the wake of changes in the global economy, a process that entails defining the role of the state, trade, and currency issues. Other challenges are how to handle security concerns vis-à-vis the long-distance sourcing of raw materials and what to do with the vast sea of foreign exchange reserves on the investment front as well as how to deal with infrastructure needs, socioeconomic inequities including poverty, and environmental pollution. Equally important are regional differences, such as those that have developed between North and South Korea and Singapore and Indonesia. Central to dealing with Asia's economic challenges is China, the region's largest economy. China's success has been spectacular, but there have been costs. Asia's largest economy is in need of adjustment with more of a domestic emphasis, something China's leadership acknowledges but finds difficult to implement due to the structure of its political economy. At the same time, Asia's second largest economy, Japan, has its own set of economic challenges that could create considerable turbulence in the region's economic trajectory.

Asia's economic challenges are significant, and a failure to address them would bring into question Asia's rise, in both a business and political sense. The highly successful nature of Asia's economic development has pushed the region to a new level, but the challenges in climbing further upward are that much more daunting. The challenges also point to the fact that China's rise in the twenty-first century is not guaranteed and may become problematic. This is a sobering thought for many economic policymakers and business leaders.

THE POLICY DEBATE IN THE EARLY
TWENTY-FIRST CENTURY

The most challenging economic issue facing Asia in the early twentieth century is what comes next in terms of economic strategy. Asia's development story from the 1950s to the early twenty-first century is one of improvements in the standard of living for a substantial portion of humanity, a regaining of global market share, and the ascendancy of a handful of economies into the top rungs of the international system through pursuit of manufacturing and exports. Although some of the region's stories are less successful than others, there are more stories of success than failure. Asia looms ahead of Africa and Latin America, parts of the Middle East, and North Africa and is closing the distance in many economic and social indicators (per capita income, lifespan, and education) of many European and North American countries. Singapore and Hong Kong now rate higher in a number of socioeconomic indicators such as per capita income, life expectancy, and literacy than many European countries. Certainly in terms of economic productivity the Korean, Taiwanese, and Japanese workers overshadow many of their counterparts in the West. While France in 2010 was hard hit by strikes protesting the upward shift in the national retirement age from 60 to 62, China spent the same year becoming the world's second-largest economy on the planet. Yet the economic picture is hardly complete, and it could be argued that Asia now faces an even harder challenge ahead—how to manage success and convert it into a more balanced achievement both within national economies (especially in the cases of China and India) and within the region, with an eye to maintaining a constructive role in a global economy that is under considerable stress.

The key player in the "what next?" challenge is China. This country has the central role as it is the world's second-largest economy; is a major trade partner of the United States, Europe, and Latin America; and has an increasingly dominant role in Asia's economic development. A recognition of China's importance is by no means to ignore the significance of Japan, the world's third-largest economy, and India, Asia's other rapidly expanding economy. However, there is no denying the centrality of China to Asia's economic landscape and its expanding significance in the global system. This importance is evident in the major role that China has come to play in the G-20 group of major economies and in the long reach of its companies throughout the far-flung corners of the Earth (as presented in chapter 4). China's significance is also evident in how in the post-2008 world, global markets have come to follow the daily volatility of the Chinese economy.

Today's China is radically different from the China of 1949 (when the People's Republic of China or PRC was founded), of 1989 (Tiananmen Square), and, for that matter of 1997 (the Asian financial crisis). Indeed, China has lifted approximately 400 million people out of poverty in recent years as it creates an increasingly affluent nation. But its economic spoils are divided unevenly. There are substantial gaps between the coastal and interior regions, its infrastructure needs are massive, and the financial system is underdeveloped for the needs of such a large economy. These challenges can be observed in the growing need to reform the country's economic strategy. What worked so well in the past—an export machine guided by state banks and other investment instrumentalities—runs the risk in the decades ahead of slowing dramatically. The problem is twofold. First, the U.S. consumer, long the buyer of a massive cornucopia of products, was forced to retrench in the post-2008 economy. Second, economic opportunities in China have been steadily eroded by an aggressive expansion of state-owned companies. Both tracks of this problem filter through the issues of China's currency management, the investment of foreign exchange reserves (including the management of SWFs), and Beijing's interaction with the rest of the G-20 countries. Above all else, China has become very inter-dependent on its trading relationships with the United States, Japan, and Europe. With the problems facing the West, this relationship puts greater pressure on China to change its approach to the economy.

China faces deeply embedded structural constraints. Unless these constraints are addressed successfully, they could impede China from reaching its full potential. Since 1978 market-Leninism and its accompanying set of relationships have generally worked, despite periodic hiccups such as Tiananmen Square in 1989 and the increasing outbreak of public discontent over official corruption, predatory developers, and a growing gap between rich and poor. What is increasingly problematic is the entangled interests of China's political leadership and the country's largest businesses. This development is creating a problem in that powerful interest groups have considerable political influence, which is felt in economic policy. In turn, this role of the powerful risks shutting out innovation and reducing opportunities for average people.

Urbanization is an enormous economic issue in China and much of Asia as well. China's cities are expected to grow by at least 300 million by 2020. Correspondingly, the population of rural China is likely to be 145 million less than at present.[1] Rapid urbanization has implications for housing and environmental protection, of course, but also for education, food procurement, health care, traffic congestion, crime control, and ethnic diversity. In China this points back to the management of the economy and the importance of the ruling party to deliver the package of goods that keeps its citizens happy.

There are other economic challenges as well. For example, in China there is the issue of how should public versus private enterprise be managed? In 2002 the Chinese government initiated a Go-Out policy to create 30 to 50 national champions from the most promising and strategic SOEs. In 2006 Chinese leadership announced that a handful of sectors were to become "pillar" industries, which would be dominated by companies under government control. These industries were auto manufacturing, telecommunications, mining, energy production (including clean technology), and steel manufacturing. China is working along similar lines to earlier experiments conducted by the French, Japanese, and Singaporeans in state capitalism. But the creation of national champions is not without complications and potential downsides. For example, at present the message is that private enterprise is acceptable as long as it does not intrude on a government-favored sector. This restriction deters private enterprise from getting too large or too successful. It can, however, detract from creating truly competitive companies.

One example of the public sector versus the private sector was Zhejiang Gonow Auto Co. Regarded as one of China's more successful private-sector success stories, Gonow was founded in 2003 and produced popular minivans and trucks. The company also developed a considerable export business, sending its products throughout the newly developing markets, from Egypt to Peru. In 2009 Gonow started a line of sport utility vehicles and opened a third assembly line. The high-flying performance of Gonow, however, put it in the spotlight for an aggressively expanding and consolidating auto sector. In April 2010 it was announced that Gonow had agreed to merge with Guangzhou Automobile Group, a state-owned auto maker run by Zhang Fangyou, a communist operative since 1975 who was selected for the job by government officials. As Zeng Yehui, head of brand management at Gonow, observed, "the policy didn't push us to cooperate, but it did encourage us and guide us. The cooperation between Guangzhou Auto and Gonow is in accordance with the country's policy direction."[2]

The global crisis of 2008–9 appeared to reinforce the role of state companies. The government's stimulus package of close to $600-billion launched in 2009 to stave off an internal economic slowdown and to help stabilize the global economy appeared to favor government-owned or government-connected companies and fed an asset bubble in property and investment sectors. At the same time, SOEs were given cheap loans from the country's state-owned banks and were able to commence strategic restructurings with an eye to industry consolidation.

While there are issues about the role of state companies over private domestic companies, the question of company ownership also complicates China's relationship with its trade partners. This is especially the case when Chinese companies are involved in foreign purchases, something that is increasingly occurring with the Asian country's growing wealth. The amount of money being invested outside the country is considerable and is not limited to sovereign wealth funds. China's outward investment from 2005 to 2009 included $72.2 billion in energy and power, $33.4 billion in finance and real estate, $62.5 billion in metals, $3.2 billion in transport, and close to $3.0 billion in other sectors.[3] This substantial flow of Chinese investment tripped national sensitivities when CNOOC sought to purchase U.S. oil company Unocal for $18.5 billion in 2005. CNOOC's ownership by the Chinese government became a lightning rod for U.S. opposition, which claimed that the purchase represented a potential breach of national security. Critics of the deal repeatedly asked of U.S. politicians and pundits do you want to have one of our leading energy companies in the hands of a potentially hostile power? Within 40 days of the initial Chinese bid, it was withdrawn, leaving a bad taste in the mouth of many Asians.

Although the Unocal case reflected protectionist sentiment in the United States, the issue of the ownership of Chinese companies and national security emerged in India as well. In April 2010 India officially imposed a ban on the importation of Chinese purchasing equipment made in China unless it was totally satisfied with a supply-chain audit. The Indian government also made inquiries about the ownership of China's Huawei Technologies and ZTE Corp., indicating that New Delhi was worried over having spying technology embedded into their products.[4] The situation for Chinese companies was not helped when in January 2011 three of Huawei's employees were arrested for taking photos of vital paramilitary installations along the Indo-Nepali border. The Chinese insisted the three were tourists on holiday in the remote Nepal-India border region and had mistakenly entered India, Indian authorities had a very different view of the matter.

Other nations have also expressed reservations about the involvement of large state-owned Chinese companies in their economies. The issue emerged in Australia in 2009 when Aluminum Corp. of China (Chinalco) sought to invest $19.5 billion in Rio Tinto's iron ore, copper, and aluminum assets. While this offer was not an outright takeover of the Australian-based mining company, Chinalco wanted two of the company's seventeen board seats. Australian concerns were that Chinalco, that is, China (the company's major buyer), would have too much control over future production of iron ore and other Australian commodities. Rio Tinto rejected the offer, but this decision took into consideration that the Australian government's Federal Investment Review Board (FIRB) was examining the bid with a view to Australian national interests. The result of the lost Chinaclo bid was best captured by an academic study from the University of Nottingham: "Chinalco may have lost one, albeit, important battle. In the years to come, however, the world will see similar moves by other Chinese firms. The Long March of China's national champions toward the world's top firms has only just begun."[5] True to this statement, many of the same issues surfaced when SinoChem sought to be part of a consortium to purchase Canada's Potash Corporation of Saskatchewan in 2010. The bids of SinoChem and others were rejected by the Canadian government for political reasons.

While there have been complications over China's outward investment, foreign investment into China has been complicated by competition with state-owned companies. China's weapons industry was a flashpoint in this regard when state-owned company China North Industries Group and U.S. buyout firm the Carlyle Group competed to purchase a third company, Xuzhou Construction Machinery Group (XCMG). XCMG was one of China's largest producers of commercial vehicles and trucks as well as military vehicles. The Carlyle Group in 2005 offered $375 million to acquire 85 percent of the company. The offer was rebuffed, and Chinese government approval was not forthcoming. The Carlyle Group made subsequent bids for smaller portions of XCMG, but each offer was turned down. However, in 2010 when China North Industries made a bid for the company, it was accepted and state approved.

The Chinese regard the arms industry as an issue of national security, and having China North Industries emerge as a more broadly diversified company can be argued as being positive for China's national interests. One can imagine the American public reaction if a Chinese company sought to purchase either Lockheed Martin or Raytheon, two major U.S. defense businesses. At the same time, China has consistently maintained that it has the welcome mat out for foreign companies to set up shop in China—as long as these companies come with technology transfers and do not compete with local state-favored sectors.

The complexity of the foreign investment issue is not going away, but it is worth a little more discussion. Anytime a purchase by one company of another takes place, a number of considerations emerge. Among these considerations are does the acquisition or merger make sense, who benefits, and does the transaction trigger monopoly laws? Critically important is who owns the company. Governments are obviously interested and usually involved in a regulatory role. In many regards mergers and acquisitions are a normal part of business. It is when national security interests become involved that acquisitions become a point of concern. What is initially meant to be a business decision transforms into international politics, shifting from corporate chiefs and their lawyers to foreign policy decision makers and politicians. As demonstrated above with the United States, Canada, Australia, and India, there are trip wires on this issue; the same can be said about foreign companies entering China. Yet, the obviousness of the Chinese government's ownership raises issues of who controls a company's goals and raises questions about transparency and disclosure. The vast majority of Western companies do not fit this profile as they are privately owned and generally have to meet higher levels of disclosure. State ownership provides advantages, but it can also be a handicap in international markets in which players demand a more level playing field.

The CCP is now intertwined with China's largest companies, which are generally state-owned and often run directly by the party. This raises the issue of whose interest does the CCP represent—that of the Chinese peoples or that of the major companies? This question may oversimplify the argument, but if this perception becomes more evident to the public eye, it could badly erode the CCP's legitimacy. In particular, it puts a spotlight on the key contract between the people and the party—the economic right to pursue wealth. And over the last decade, there has been greater state involvement in the economy, with state-owned or connected enterprises pushing out the private sector. Indeed, new data from the World Bank show that the proportion of industrial production by companies controlled by the state increased in 2009, halting a long downward slide in the production of these companies. Perhaps more significantly, investment by state-controlled enterprises spiked last year, reflecting the government's stimulus program. But a growing worry is the crowding out of China's still fledgling private sector by state companies that are well connected to members of the ruling party.

Another dimension of the interlocking nature of state-owned companies and the CCP is the difficulty that such a set of arrangements makes in changing policy direction. In a sense, China has made massive strides away from the old command economy, but a considerable amount of heavy lifting remains in the banks and corporations. The banking system has issues with legal accountability, and the corporate sector lacks best practices on the level of the topnotch multinationals. Regulatory agencies have been created, staffed, and given some degree of authority, but political factors still play a significant role. According to economist Barry

Naughton, "the need to develop a legal and regulatory system is increasingly urgent, and the demand for legal rights and regulatory fairness is increasingly widespread in the population. But thus far, progress in developing a regulatory apparatus has been limited by the fact that transparency, accountability, and oversight run into limits when they touch on the ultimate structure of political power."[6]

China clearly needs a change in policy direction, considering the structural transformations occurring in the United States. But the tightly entwined nature of the political economy makes big changes potentially system threatening. If certain props to the market-Leninist system are removed, will the CCP edifice collapse? In the past China has witnessed spectacular regime collapses, sometimes replaced by periods of acute societal and political fragmentation. China's leadership as well as most Chinese citizens would like to avoid traveling down that road, but pressures are mounting for change. These pressures are particularly evident with regard to trade policy. At times China seems to be playing a disruptive role with respect to the global system. In recent years its current account surpluses are the largest in the world by far. As noted, its foreign currency reserves are massive, and this despite the low incomes of much of its population. This situation is unprecedented for a major trading country and places great pressures on the global economy. Further, these surpluses are generated, in large part by China's massive intervention in the foreign exchange markets in order to prevent the appreciation of its currency. It calls this intervention a matter of national sovereignty. But the practice promotes trade frictions with its Western trading partners. It also represents an implicit tax on Chinese consumers and a subsidy to its producers. China is alone among the major world economies in rejecting a flexible exchange rate policy, which would promote adjustment of its balance-of-payments position and help to avoid a buildup of large imbalances. As noted by C. Fred Bergsten, Charles Freeman, Nicholas R. Lardy, and Derek Mitchell, "China makes no effort to hide its preference for low-quality, politically motivated bilateral and regional arrangements over more economically meaningful (and demanding) multilateral liberalization through the World Trade Organization or . . . individual trading partners."[7]

How does China encourage its exports? It employs at least three strategies. First, it suppresses labor rights and wages. Second, it subsidizes export production in key industries. Finally, China maintains strict nontariff barriers to imports. It could also be argued that China's lax copyright laws and demands for technology transfers further give unfair advantages to Chinese companies. Most large trading countries are unable to engage in such activities over a sustained period of time. Since China is the world's largest surplus country and second-largest exporter, and thus has enormous impact on world trading patterns and policies, its actions pose severe challenges to the existing global trading regime.

Related to the issue of export-driven economics is that of inflation related to wages. In the post-2008 world, the slower-tracked recovery in the advanced economies and the stronger recovery in Asia and other emerging markets led to a divergence in terms of growth and inflationary pressures. Asian economies faced in 2009, 2010, and early 2011 rising commodity prices, including food. In December 2010 India had riots related to higher onion prices. As higher food prices put pressure on consumers, workers are more inclined to put pressure on companies to raise wages. As workers struggle to catch up with their wages in the face of higher prices, companies will feel inclined to increase prices to protect their profit margins. Add to this process a slowly shrinking surplus labor pool in Asia as demographics shift to slower population growth. As the Asian Development Bank in its 2011 report noted, "the decline in surplus labor, along with strong demand due to high economic growth, has increased the pressure for higher wages. Indeed, trends in 2000–2008 indicate fast-rising nominal wages in PRC, averaging about 15% a year."[8] The implications of this prediction are that inflation looms as a major risk in the early 2010s, something that is beyond usual monetary policy and requires a move away from the structural constraints of the export-driven growth model. And this is not an issue for only China but for many of the countries in the region that are part of the Chinese-export-manufacturing supply chain.

THE FINANCIAL SECTOR CHALLENGE

Much of the emphasis on Asia's economic development has been on the creation of a highly competitive export-driven manufacturing-industrial sector. The export of manufactured goods generally helped Asian countries overcome the limitation of underdeveloped domestic economies and allowed them to accumulate wealth. That wealth, however, was often funneled into national savings at banks. The option of investing in local stock markets was limited as the money was tapped for development needs. The knock-on effects of this practice have been better educational systems and upgraded infrastructure. Nonetheless, the development of the financial sector beyond banks functioning as a place for deposits and loans (usually to well-connected companies) has until recent years lagged behind Western stock and debt markets.

A fully functioning financial system is expected to be a central point in the efficient allocation of capital, to mobilize and pool savings, and to ease the exchange of goods and services. It is also important to clarify that the financial system is not limited to banks but extends into those instrumentalities that deepen and widen what the financial system can do to improve national development. Under this last-mentioned flag would be SWFs, capital markets for both equity and bonds, and other companies such as private equity funds.

Changes through the first decade of the twenty-first century have left Asia wealthier. This wealth manifests in four forms: foreign exchange reserves, public pension funds, SWFs, and SOEs. While the emergence of sovereign wealth funds is an old story in Singapore (which gave birth to the Government of Singapore Investment Corporation and Temasek Holdings), China's entry into this field was more recent with the formation of the China Investment Corporation (CIC) in 2007.

The challenge is that once Asia has the wealth, what does it do with it? Where should China's massive foreign exchange reserves be put? CIC invested in both Morgan Stanley and Blackstone Group in late 2007 and then watched their investments plummet in one of the world's worst financial meltdowns since the 1930s. Most Asian SWFs have invested in U.S. Treasuries and become hostage to the fortunes of the U.S. economy. This was a painful issue during the 2010–11 period as the U.S. government decided to pump up the economy rather than deal with a large fiscal deficit.

While economies such as Japan, South Korea, Singapore, and Hong Kong have relatively sophisticated financial systems, those of China and India fit into what can be called emerging financial systems. This is not to infer that the Chinese and Indian financial systems are inferior. They survived the 2008 financial turmoil in far better shape than most Western systems, helped along by their still relatively isolated financial systems and passing on subprime securities. While the lower level of financial sophistication limited damage to most Asian banks, the shallow nature of capital markets limits the ability of local institutions to finance such large-cost items as infrastructure. Journalists Mukesk Jagota and Anant Vijay Kala write, "India is increasingly relying on overseas investments for long-term funds as a shallow local debt market and highly-regulated pension and insurance funds limit the supply of such cash."[9] Looking ahead, Asia's financial challenge is how to invest its formidable foreign exchange earnings. A related challenge is how Asia is to deepen its local stock and debt markets. Certainly the investment issue is a difficult one and will remain so.

THE EDUCATION CHALLENGE

Directly related to the challenges of economic restructuring, poverty reduction, and deepening financial systems is education. In many ways education is one of the keys to unlocking the long-term sustainability of Asia's rise in the twenty-first century. In the past education has played a central role in providing a functioning leadership elite in government and the private sector as well as skilled workers. For example, in developing Asia the proportion of young people with no schooling declined by almost 20 percentage points from 1970 to 2010, with enrollment rates increasing at all levels.[10] However, the pace of improvements vary across the region. The Asian Development Bank observed in 2010 that "the secondary completion rate in the PRC; the Republic of Korea; and Hong Kong, China was 85% and above; India's was lower than 2%."[11] It should be added that while India scored low with the secondary education completion rate (a statistic weighed down by a less dynamic representation in rural India), its institutions of higher education maintained a strong reputation for excellence, necessary for the advancement of its high tech sector.

The education challenge is not just a social issue but a question about the ability of Asian economies to overcome what is sometimes called "the middle income trap" in which economies stumble in developing high value-added activities to replace low-skilled, labor-intensive businesses. Along these lines, it is critical to comprehend that income growth is not correlated with the growth of human capital.[12] Malaysian Prime Minister Najib Razak, keenly aware of his country's slowing pace of economic growth, states, "We need to take the high-skill, high-income route quickly to become and remain competitive. Failure is not an option."[13]

For all of the challenges facing Malaysia's educational system, these challenges are more severe in Asia's poorer counties. That group encompasses Afghanistan, Cambodia, Laos, Nepal, and Bangladesh. Even in Pakistan the literacy rate is a low 54 percent. This education challenge represents a substantial hurdle to the further modernization of local economies, that is, the further introduction of technology and the boosting of the value-added production process. Consequently, the challenge is likely to be improvement of the penetration of education throughout the region, with a view to maintaining regional momentum on educational reforms.

THE LONG LINES TO THE COMMODITY TREASURE HOUSES

Natural resource security looms large as a key concern for many Asian countries. This is much more so for East Asia. Economies such as Taiwan, China, Korea, and Japan are dependent to varying degrees on obtaining oil, natural gas, and a substantial number of other commodities, ranging from wheat and meat to iron ore and coal. As demonstrated in the chapter 5, these trade lines are highly significant to Asia's future, especially as these resources are critical to fueling future growth. At the same time, there are a number of challenges that come with the long line of communications to points around the world. These challenges include security of shipping, personnel, and plants; an intensifying rivalry with a number of countries (within Asia and elsewhere) over key resources; and increasing scrutiny over the role of Asian countries in local economies and politics.

It should also be emphasized that food is part of the issue over the long lines to the commodity storehouses. As Asia becomes increasingly more affluent and the push grows for an emulation of the Western lifestyles, Asian diets are changing. There is a greater demand for protein (i.e., meat) in the diet, and this demand means more resources go to animal husbandry. All of these factors place more pressure on Asia's fertile land and water resources. It also raises a number of other questions, captured by the Asian Development Bank in 2011: "Can Asian cities deliver water to their residents? Can the region feed itself and, if not, will the rest of the world provide enough food?"[14] The ability of Asia to make certain it has food security points back to its ability to buy the imports it needs, and that means security at sea.

The risk facing many of Asia's trading nations is increasingly related to the return of piracy in the Indian Ocean, in particular in the area around the failed state of Somalia. What is represented as Somalia on the map is a war zone of competing clans and factions as well as Islamic radical groups. With an almost complete breakdown of central authority, some Somalis took to raiding the sea lanes around them. International shipping of any type became a target as pirates would seize ships and hold them and their crews for ransom. Throughout the first decade of the twenty-first century, this problem intensified, finally forcing major powers to station naval ships in the region. South Korean ships were vulnerable to such attacks, but the South Korean navy recaptured one of their nation's ships as well as capturing Somali pirates in early 2011.

The pirate issue is not limited to the waters around Somalia but includes the waters around Indonesia. Pirate attacks have long occurred around the Straits of Malacca, a critical chokepoint for East Asian shipping heading to and from the Middle East, Africa, and Europe. Considering the massive sprawl of islands that make up Indonesia, patrolling the waters has been difficult. While there have been calls for greater international cooperation in dealing with this problem, overlapping border disputes have made this cooperation difficult.

The security issue also extends into national security. While pirates are one concern, they are dwarfed by concerns for the effects on shipping of war. For China, Korea, and Japan, this is a major strategic issue as trade has become a key element in the development of their economies. Moreover, much of East Asia's manufacturing machine is fueled by imported energy in the form of natural gas and oil. From Beijing's standpoint, a war with the United States could result in being cut off from its Sudanese and Angolan oil supplies by the U.S. Navy operating out of Singapore or in alliance with India. Japan certainly feels the same chill generated by the stronger and more aggressive presence of the Chinese navy in Asian waters. Taiwan obviously feels an even deeper chill along these lines.

The issue of commodity security is not limited to China. Asia's largest country in itself represents its own set of risks for countries that make extensive use of what are referred to as rare earth metals. These metals— lithium, scandium, and yttrium—have become critical components for manufacturing cell phones, computers, screens, hybrid cars, and disk drives produced in such countries as Japan, the United States, and South Korea. While rare earth metals are found around the world, with the former Soviet bloc of countries and the United States being large-scale holders and with other amounts sprinkled about South Africa, Australia, Brazil, and India, China is estimated to hold about 37 percent of the world's resources of these elements, some 36 million tons. What is most important is that as of 2010 China controls more than 97 percent of the production of these rare earth metals because much of what is in other countries is not easily accessible. This monopoly makes China the major player in the rare earth metals trade.

In the early twenty-first century, demand from around the world for rare earth metals escalated. At the same time, China's own needs for rare earth metals grew, raising the question of whether at some point Asia's largest country would shift from exporter to importer. By 2011 that issue became more salient. Adding to the pressure on the rare earth metals trade was its emergence as a political issue when China and Japan diplomatically bumped heads over a territorial dispute over uninhabited islands in the East China Sea. During the dispute it was reported that China stopped exports of the metals, something denied by Beijing but asserted by Tokyo. If nothing else, the threat of cutting Japanese industry off from its major source of rare earth metals raised the pressure on Tokyo to acceding to Beijing's will.

One view about China's economic policy vis-à-vis rare earth metals is that its slowdown in exports is geared to boasting the development of its domestic manufacturing industry by trading resources for technology. China's raw materials supply helped stimulate foreign companies to buy and to depend on China while also helping to push the creation of local companies geared to using these metals. Wishing to further develop what is a growth industry (with its linkage to high tech goods), China established an export quota system, driving up the cost to foreign companies and promoting local enterprises, which also included foreign companies that set up operations. On top of the export quotas, there are a number of tax breaks, including an export duty of 25 percent and a 17 percent VAT rebate.

China's Ministry of Industry and Information Technology has championed a policy of restructuring the rare earth metals sector to make it more Chinese with an eye to moving up the value-added ladder. According to Damie Ma of consultants Eurasia Group, "instead of exporting purely unprocessed rare earths, the intention is to consolidate production and create more value-added applied materials that contain rare earths by keeping a crucial link of the supply chain in the country."[15]

The result of the 2010 island dispute between China and Japan was to sharpen the debate about how much trust to extend China. From the Japanese perspective, China appeared to have little compunction in withholding a key export in order to force Japan to capitulate, something that many other Asian countries watched with uneasiness. Although China denied that it halted rare earth metal exports, many Asian governments wondered if Beijing would not hesitate to use economic leverage in the same fashion when their national interests were at odds with the region's largest economy. For many Asian governments, the words of Japan's foreign minister in October 2010 held a degree of truth: "it's certainly not good for our own resource security to rely on a single country." He added, "We're in the process of diversifying our supply sources."[16]

THE ENVIRONMENT

We have noted that much of Asia has been growing at a blistering pace for more than 10 years. But with this growth and the energy requirements accompanying this growth has come serious environmental problems. Asian growth has belched out greenhouse gases. In the 10 years leading up to 2008, for example, Asia's energy use grew by 70 percent. The future is coal based: half of Asia's primary energy consumption, and 70 percent of China's, is coal. However, development is laying waste to much of the region's natural richness. The Chinese miracle is built on a bulldozed landscape. In Malaysia, Thailand, and the Philippines, once-vast stands of virgin forest are gone. Asia's sushi fad bodes ill for the bluefin tuna even on the far side of the world.

One changing dimension in Indonesia related to globalization, however, is a growing awareness of the environment. Perhaps a better way of stating this is that most Indonesians are becoming more concerned about the corporate abuse of their land, water, and air. In a sense, they have little choice, considering how corporate mistakes are affecting daily life. During Asia's financial crisis of 1997–98, Indonesian farmers slashed and burned forests, creating a memorable blackish haze (now annual) over the entire region that has spread well beyond the county's borders. At the same time, Indonesia has been hit by a number of mining disasters and other industrial accidents, which have left waterways horribly polluted and the land scarred.

One of the most egregious industrial accidents occurred in May 2006. Villages in Sidoorjo (near Surabaya), East Java, were hit by a huge mudflow, which was caused by a natural gas exploration well. By October 2006, the accident had evolved into a major environmental disaster, drawing international attention. The scope of the problem was such that the mudflow displaced 15,000 people, eight villages were inundated by mud, and major rail and road arteries were severed. Efforts to divert the mudslide into a river failed.

The mud problem epitomized the difficult nature of tackling environmental problems in Indonesia. The government response was lamentably slow, and the idea of corporate responsibility was sadly lacking. The company involved in the environmental disaster was part of the well-connected Bakrie Group. How well connected? The group's leader, Aburizel Bakrie, was at the time serving as coordinating minister for People's Welfare, part of the government team monitoring the disaster. In most countries this would be a conflict of interest. Costs for the cleanup were estimated to be around $1 billion, which the company worked hard to avoid, obviously preferring that the government pick up the bill.

Indonesia has substantial natural resources, which are important to the country's well-being. The country must be able to extract these resources, process them, and get them to markets, both domestic and foreign. At the same time, there has to be a balance vis-à-vis the environment. Indonesia's forestry industry is a good example of globalization gone bad. Demand for Indonesian timber began in the 1970s but accelerated during the 1980s and 1990s. This industry is heavily concentrated on the islands of Kalimanton, Sumatra, Sulawesi, and West Papua (Irian Jaya). While illegal logging and overlogging were problems under the Suharto regime, the breakdown came in 1997–98. Forest cover loss rates, already high and rising in the mid-1990s, were worsened by devastating forest fires in Kalimanton and Sumatra. As the World Bank notes, "the deforestation rate was higher than expected: 1.7 million hectares a year from 1985–97, compared to previous estimates of 0.6 to 1.3 million hectares a year. For the Outer Islands as a whole, well over 20 million hectares of forest were lost; this is one-fourth of the forest cover that existed in 1985, equal in area to the U.S. State of Florida."[17] The environmental degradation caused by such large-scale devastation has an impact well beyond national borders. The entwined issues of environmental pollution and corporate responsibility have another side: the idea on the part of the local officials to use legal proceedings to exact changes from multinational companies. This is not to argue that multinationals are without blame for cutting quotas.

Industries such as mining and oil are rough-and-tumble businesses, and management teams are used to dealing with difficult legal environments. Certainly Freeport-McMoran Copper & Gold found themselves in the legal crosshairs more than once in Indonesia. Newmont Mining has also been in court over alleged pollution of Buyant Bay in northern Sulawesi, despite a study commissioned by the World Health Organization that found the bay was not polluted and that local villagers did not display toxic levels of mercury in their systems—a similar conclusion to the Indonesian Environment Ministry.[18] Indonesia since the fall of Suharto has developed a reputation of being a more difficult business environment, and one result is that mining companies have not opened up a new mine in the country since 1998.

Another entwined environmental and globalization issue concerns disease. Like a number of other Asian nations, Indonesia has had problems with bird (avian) flu. By early 2007 bird flu was responsible for close to 70 human deaths, the highest number in Asia. This has been a difficult issue, and international cooperation has been complicated by bureaucratic slowness—and a desire by Jakarta to have equal access to drugs and technologies as richer countries.[19] Indeed, Indonesia intentionally delayed the process in April 2007 to make certain that it did not just "surrender" the information pertaining to the spread of the disease but got something back in terms of medical assistance.

THE POVERTY CHALLENGE

While a different approach to economic management is needed, security is required for key commodity inputs, and the environment must be improved, another significant issue overshadows these concerns—poverty reduction. Asia has done much to transform and improve its economic position. According to a joint OECD, the World Bank, WTO, and ILO (International Labor Organization) report, in 1975 six out of ten Asians lived in absolute poverty (defined as less than $1 of income a day), a plight that afflicts less than two out of ten Asians in 2010.[20] The same report notes that in China, with its 1.3 billion people, the authorities managed to reduce people living in poverty from 53 percent in 1981 to 8 percent in 2001; this change suggests that over 400 million people have risen out of abject poverty in that country since it began to open to the outside world.

The widespread and sustained movement of people out of poverty in China is significant. This decrease in poverty has helped the country close what was once a massive gap in terms of GDP size, sophistication, and influence. Yet, for all of those advanced, the standard of living remains below many other industrialized economies. The Asian Development Bank reported in 2010 that "despite growth-concomitant massive reduction in poverty, it remains widespread in the region: Two-thirds of the world's poor still call the region home; more than 1.8 billion Asians subsist on less than $1.25 a day. Equally important, this portion of the population is the most vulnerable to food-price inflation, something that became more pronounced from 2008 on."[21]

Which parts of Asia have the largest number of poor? While Japan, South Korea, Hong Kong, Taiwan, and much of coastal China are affluent and have standards of living comparable with the West, the same cannot be said of much of South Asia, parts of Indonesia, Laos, and Cambodia. The latter countries are largely poor. Even in China extreme poverty is still evident, especially in the north and west of the vast country. More poor people live in eight states of India than in the 26 poorest African countries combined. Consequently, it is critical for economic growth to continue, which returns policymakers back to the post-2008 crisis issue of what to do next in terms of economic strategy. In turn, this raises the challenge of how to further improve on poverty reduction.

THE JAPANESE PROBLEM

As the most advanced of Asian economies, Japan's problems are different from the rest of the region. Poverty, education, and the environment are not the same grave challenges as they are in the Philippines, China, or Indonesia. Japan represents a different mix of problems, combining a massive and still growing public sector debt and daunting demographics as well as painful questions over immigration, procreation, and child care. While Japan's problems commenced in the late 1980s, and despite some headway having been made in the early of the 2000s, the Asia Pacific country confronts a very uncertain future.

In January 2011 the rating agency Standard & Poor's downgraded Japan's sovereign rating from AA to AA-, and in February Moody's changed its outlook on AA2-rated Japan to negative. These ratings were a considerable distance from the once-coveted AAA rating the country once held. For a country that is one of the world's top three economies, the lowered ratings were a blow, especially as they placed the Asia Pacific nation on the same level as China (which has seen its ratings moving up). Few analysts missed the symbolism of that development. The Standard & Poor's ratings downgrade signaled that the severe challenges facing Japan in the early twenty-first century are getting worse and that the nation's leadership is sadly not up to the task. Japan is drifting—and not a little. Japan's problems have tremendous ramifications for the rest of Asia, considering the importance of Japanese trade and foreign investment. Equally important, if Japan eventually moves down the road to a full-blown debt crisis, the event would have massive ramifications because Japan's economy is too big to bail out and a Japanese debt crisis could be highly disruptive to the international financial system.

Japan has a major debt problem.[22] According to the OECD, Japan's debt-to-GDP has been on a steady upward trajectory since the 1990s. In 2010 debt-to-GDP was 194 percent, and it is expected to reach 210 percent by the end of 2012. Equally worrisome is that the debt level cannot stabilize and decline in a meaningful fashion unless the government monetizes the asset side of its balance sheet. Standard & Poor's in January 2011 stated that "the downgrade reflects our appraisal that Japan's government debt ratios—already among the highest for rated sovereigns—will continue to rise further than we envisaged before the global economic recession hit the country and will peak only in the mid-2020s."[23]

The Japanese government's response has often been that the debt ratio is really not that bad because over 90 percent of the debt is held by domestic buyers, with only 6.4 percent held by more fickle foreigners. While this may have held up as a sound argument in the past (and Japanese domestic buyers have been constant for Japanese Government Bonds or JGBs), the negative demographics afflicting Japan are going to reduce national savings as older people use their money for medical and living expenses. Along these lines, one IMF Working Paper (2010) observed that "Japan is undergoing rapid population aging, which is likely to limit the market's absorptive capacity of public debt."[24] There will be fewer people of working age to pay for the rest and buy up the new JGBs on offer. Simply stated, population shrinkage will reduce economic output and add to labor costs, both reversing the tax base and number of potential debt buyers.

Thus, any cure for Japan's debt is complicated by the country's dismal demographics. Depending on a number of studies, Japan's population, which started shrinking in 2006, is expected to fall from the 126 million in 2010 to anywhere between 100 to 80 million by 2050. What this population decrease means is that Japan has to give considerable thought to how to manage its debt on a long-term basis. This need is especially urgent as spending is likely to increase at a faster rate because an aging population leads to rising outlays in the form or rising payments for pensions, health care, and other government entitlements. Considering the strong Japanese antipathy against immigration (which is occurring at a trickle), the replacement population is not likely to emerge from external sources.

An additional complication to Japan's ability to climb out of its growing debt hole is the March 11, 2011, earthquake in the Tohoku region. Registering 9.0 on the Richter scale, the quake was followed by a devastating tsunami and the meltdown of a major nuclear power plant, Japan's economy struggled in the aftermath. While the Tohoku region accounted for around six percent of Japan's GDP, seven percent of its population, and seven percent of its capital stock, the critical issue was the disruption in power supply related to the problems at the nuclear plant. Such disasters are expensive: for example, the 1995 Kobe disaster cost around 2 percent of GDP. This time around estimates range from $150 billion to $350 billion or 3 to 4 percent of GDP.[25] Considering the fiscal restraints and high debt level already facing Japan, the cost of reconstruction only adds to the strain.

Japan's debt management, therefore, is tied into a complex matrix of socioeconomic problems that include dealing with sensitive issues of procreation, child care, the role of women, and immigration—things that are a minefield for any society. The Democratic Party of Japan governments have sought to provide greater incentives for children. Nonetheless, the negative social factors do have an impact on Japan's debt problem, and worry is going to increasingly penetrate into domestic financial circles and possibly lead to an internal bond buyer's revolt, at least at the margin. What would happen if domestic buyers refused to show up at a JGB auction?

What makes the debt problem so difficult is that Japan's political life is highly problematic. Naoto Kan, the current leader of the Democratic Party of Japan (DPJ), is the country's fifteenth leader in the past 25 years. He is the second DPJ prime minister, following the abrupt resignation of Prime Minister Yukio Hatoyama in June 2010. There has been a feeling that the DPJ, both under Hatoyama and Kan, have failed to lead on economic issues, instead colliding with the country's bureaucracy in an effort to wrest control over economic policies. According to a S&P comment, "the Democratic Party of Japan-led government lacks a coherent strategy."[26] Another international rating agency, Fitch, observed that Japanese policymakers show little inclination to wean their country from its debt habit.

In 2010 and 2011, the DPJ presided over a weak coalition and was dependent on other political parties to pass legislation, a situation that is complicated by the very vocal and constant calls for the government to resign by the other major party, the Liberal Democratic Party (LDP). The LDP, which presided over much of the debt buildup, has vowed to fight over every vote with the DPJ in order to make the latter's government fall. Sadly, this political landscape does not provide fertile soil for the type of reforms needed to deal with the debt issue.

Where do these problems leave Japan? While we do not see any indication that Japan is about to default or have any problems in repaying its debt over the short term, the country will continue to be afflicted by an ongoing erosion of its economic and political standing in the international system. Moreover, the moment when the Japanese domestic buyers wake up and see that the Emperor is wearing no cloths is moving closer. All of these realities imply that a crisis looms on the country's horizon. In 2011 the Economist Intelligence Unit observed that "unless policymakers grasp the nettle of tax reform the country is setting itself up for a future sovereign crisis. The timing of such a crisis is highly uncertain and could be far in the future, but the worry is that Japan may already have passed— or close to passing—the point of no return in terms of its ability to repair its fiscal position."[27]

As the third-largest economy in the world (after the United States and China), Japan is too big to bail out. When it comes to debt management crises, even Japan must eventually feel the pull of fiscal gravity. Japan's future promises an elevated degree of political uncertainty, higher debt, a weak effort to contain the fiscal red ink, and perhaps further changes of government. Even with a change of government, it is doubtful that any political party or dynamic individual will emerge to make the tough decisions needed to turn Japan around.

CONCLUSION

Asia's economic success has been of historic significance; the path forward will reflect the ability of the region to continue to demonstrate a high degree of flexibility, innovation, and discipline. What made the region successful before—an embrace of education, a hard work ethic, sacrifice, and a strong desire for the advancement of all—will be tested as new challenges arise. The most critical of these new goals is how to move to the next stage of economic development, which requires the ability to shift strategies from export-driven and capital-guided growth to a greater emphasis on domestic demand and interregional trade and investment. While these goals are significant in China's case, they are also factors throughout much of the region. The so-called middle-income trap looms large as does such issues as the rule of law, education, poverty alleviation, and the need to deepen and strengthen the financial sector. Related to all of this is the need for Asia to play a greater role in guiding the global economy and to deal with such matters as regulation, economic policy, and governance, all important elements in the post-Great Recession landscape, especially considering the challenges of pollution, water supply, energy use, and food security. Asia has gained considerable power, but with that power comes the greater responsibility to make the global economic system work. Leadership and vision become all the more important as the size and scope of economic challenges guarantee that the path will be bumpy.

Chapter 7

POLITICAL CHALLENGES IN ASIA

Asia's political challenges are substantial. They include how to manage growing wealth disparities, official corruption, insurgencies, ethnic-religious tensions, nuclear proliferation, border disputes (land-based and maritime), and traditional geopolitical rivalries. Looming over all of these issues is the grand debate about the applicability of political systems, for Asia—a division between autocracies (also called authoritarian regimes of the hard and soft kinds) and democracies. Although the political systems debate usually pits autocratic China against democratic India, it cuts across any discussion about political development in Asia from the neodynastic regimes in Central Asia and North Korea to the rough-and-tumble pluralistic systems in Taiwan and South Korea. The debate also raises some serious questions about how far Asia as a whole can travel down the road to becoming a more unified economic bloc. For Europe and North America, regional economic trade regimes were achieved with a greater ease because all the actors involved were democracies, something not at work in Asia. At the same time, the widespread nature of autocratic regimes builds in an inherent risk factor for the region in terms of such issues as political succession, socioeconomic stresses, and nationalism.

It is the purpose of this chapter to concentrate on Asia's political challenges, with a focus on "domestic" issues. Earlier chapters have touched upon economic relations between Asian countries, BRICs, and to some degree, other emerging markets. Consequently, this chapter begins with the debate over political systems, followed by the interrelated topics of insurgencies, ethnic-religious tensions, nuclear proliferation, border disputes, and transnational crime. The last three issues broaden beyond the domestic focus but are nonetheless significant political challenges, and all three have significant domestic ramifications. While economic development is important, political development is equally important.

Weak institutions and civil societies ultimately undermine or derail economic achievement—or at the very least, limit the upside.

THE GRAND DEBATE

The grand debate over Asia's political future is whether it will be democratic or autocratic, with India presented as the democratic champion and China the autocratic leader. India is frequently referred to as the world's largest democracy, while China is sometimes depicted as an authoritarian political machine bent on either regional or global domination. It is usually forgotten that only in the twentieth century did an independent India find its way to democracy. China, of course, maintained its traditional autocratic tradition. Coming out of dynastic bedrock, the grand debate also has a cultural element. It has been argued that Asians, especially those imbued with Confucian values of hierarchy, are more prone to authoritarian political systems. The respect for authority and stability lends itself to a long history of dynastic rule in China, Korea, Japan, and even Vietnam and Mongolia. Even in the nineteenth and twentieth centuries the liberal democratic tradition was at best anemic. It operated under control by European powers in the form of colonies (that did not support elective government by the local populations), China's political fragmentation during the Republican-Warlord era following the end of the Xing dynasty (1911), and Japan's elite-dominated parliamentary system; Asia's political tradition did not reflect a Western, liberal system. Even Japan's parliamentary system—such as it was—gave way to a military-dominated government in the 1930s that brooked little dissent, adopted certain Fascist overtones, and led the country into wars of conquest.

The China versus India argument misses some important aspects of Asia's political future. A more nuanced landscape exists. One of the key points lost in the grand debate is that China and India do not represent all of Asia. Other countries have a part in the political development drama. These other countries also wrestle with important issues as to how to define their civil societies in terms of good governance and poverty-reducing growth. The Asian political picture changed in the aftermath of World War II. Japan was forced to adopt a more representative and "democratic" system. Though the desire for political order soon asserted itself in the form of the Liberal Democratic Party, which soon came to dominate national politics, Japan embarked upon a more recognizably parliamentary form of government. An opposition, including Socialists and Communists, existed and competed for seats in the Diet, but the LDP was able to co-opt or recruit some of the most able politicians, develop a close working relationship with the national bureaucracy, and build strong linkages to the Japanese business elite. While these accomplishments made the LDP unbeatable in national elections into the early 1990s, it also resulted in Japan's economic miracle during the 1950s and 1960s.

For many other Asian countries, Japan's apparent success by the 1970s made an impression. At the same time, the United States (concerned about the spread of communism) was supportive of a wide range of nondemocratic regimes from South Korea to Taiwan as well as into Southeast Asia with Indonesia (strongly anti-Communist after 1965) and into South Asia with Pakistan's military regimes. The other side of the political coin, the Asian left, had little to offer in the form of democratic experimentation in the light of the totalitarian leanings of Mao's China; communist Vietnam, North Korea, and Mongolia; and the dystopian Maoist experiment in Cambodia by the Khmer Rouge. In the last example, the Khmer Rouge's policies systematically set out to return Cambodia to being a rural country by depopulating the cities and liquidating the upper and middle classes. Cambodia still struggles with the effect of the short (1974–78), yet nearly terminal Khmer Rouge experience.

Asia's great economic leap forward became the springboard for a renewed debate about the region's political development. By the 1980s Asia was no longer an economic backwater. Japan was the world's second-largest economy, and South Korea, Taiwan, Hong Kong, and Singapore were regarded as cutting-edge economies with Indonesia, Malaysia, and Thailand not far behind. Even China was making considerable strides. But in the 1980s most of Asia was hardly democratic, with authoritarian regimes of one stripe or another dominating, the exceptions being India and the Philippines—hardly economic success stories. Then the democratic landscape in Asia appeared to improve. In the 1990s Indonesia underwent a democratic wave with the end of the Suharto regime, East Timor emerged as a new state, and Cambodia held a series of elections during the decade. Despite the stumble of the 1997–98 Asian economic contagion, the region's emergence was hardly done. The next decade was to witness significant progress by Asia on the economic development path, and this progress helped to elevate the debate over politics once again, especially as the emerging powers were China and India. The economic crisis of 2008–10 in which the West (as the self-proclaimed champions of democracy) weakened itself sharpened Asia's grand debate over competing political systems. When the West is removed from the equation about political development, then models for many boil down to something along the lines of India v. China.

CHINA'S PATH

China's political system, as touched upon in the previous chapter, has a strong correlation to the country's economic development. Under the Beijing Consensus, China's leadership offers economic opportunities for its citizens in exchange for the citizens putting their trust in the ruling Communist Party, which is to provide personnel security and social stability.[1] The last includes adequate food supplies and affordable housing. In a sense, China's small elite in the CCP manages all aspects of society by using the bureaucracy, the military, and the media. For all the goals to be achieved, the ruling party is market-Leninist, willing to pursue a market-based economy (of some type with a large and competitive state sector) and ruling as a single party with no opposition parties allowed. The CCP, therefore, is the sole legitimate political actor, and no other political actors are allowed, hence the visceral reaction to the Falun Gong movement in the 1990s. Regarded as a spiritual movement by its adherents, Chinese authorities were deeply concerned by its growing following and labeled it a "heretical organization" or a cult and banned it.[2]

In the early twenty-first century, the Chinese political system came under considerable pressure from the outside world and from within as its population became more affluent and worldly. China's push into the global economy was one of its major successes, but it was also the source of apprehension as more Chinese were exposed to external forces. This exposure has created a major challenge for China's leadership as a greater opening to the outside, the West in particular, opens up an unpredictable and possibly dangerous path. The real challenge for Chinese leadership is how to keep a firm grip on political power while permitting relatively free areas of economic enterprise.

Since Deng Xiao-ping's first reforms thirty years ago, China has been cautiously inching toward market forces while retaining a solid political grip. The state-owned sector has shrunk correspondingly (from 77.6 percent in 1978 to 29.5 percent in 2007). However, significant government controls on the economy remain, such as price controls on grain and gasoline. But the twelfth Five-Year Plan of March 2011 relies more on market forces in some areas (adjusting factor prices to more accurately reflect costs, liberalizing interest rates, and cutting the number of SOEs). Still, Beijing plans to regulate overproduction through project approvals and loan credits in such traditional industries as steel and cement as well as in new industries, including solar and wind power.

So how does China plan to release its grip on the economy while retaining a tight political hold? One fallback for Chinese leadership is nationalism. Michael A. Ledeen, a former commissioner on the U.S.-China Economic and Security Review Commission from 2001–03, observes, "Unlike traditional communist dictators—Mao, for example—who extirpated traditional culture and replaced it with a sterile Marxism-Leninism, the Chinese now enthusiastically, even compulsively embrace the glories of China's long history. Their passionate reassertion of the greatness of past dynasties has both entranced and baffled Western observers, because it does not fit the model of an 'evolving communist system.' "[3]

The use of the nationalist card to bolster the state reveals that the ideological pillars upon which the regime stands have eroded. But reliance on nationalism leaves the government's ideological reference points at a position that can be exceedingly volatile. While China's use of grievance-based nationalism vis-à-vis Japan stirs the citizenry and reinforces the sense of being Chinese, it puts a factor into the political mix that is difficult to control, especially if public attention turns to complaints over corruption, rising food costs and rents, and the encroachment of the state on the private sector. One of the major challenges for China's leadership, who have a considerable vested interest in the nation's political economy, is how to maintain the loyalty of their people as the level of knowledge about the outside world increases. The Chinese authorities thus work very hard to dominate the flow of information, something that Google, forced to cooperate with the censors in order to work in China, has had to wrestle with. The Richard Waters and Joseph Menn of the *Financial Times* write that "Beijing's strenuous efforts to filter the tide of online content washing ashore into the world's largest Internet market set a standard for other regimes."[4]

Internet control is a critical factor. Related to the control of the Internet is the survival of the CCP's regime. The structure of controls distracts from any governance failures and maintains the party's favored status. One observer (a foreign media entrepreneur based in China) astutely noted of the interplay between the CCP, Internet, and branding that "residents agree to support the 'brand values' defined for China by the CCP. They are rewarded for doing so, penalized for abstaining from the general effort and punished severely for taking a contrary stance."[5] China probably has one of the most developed cyberwarfare forces in the world. Attacks on the United States and other countries have been traced back to China and indicate the probability of government encouragement or involvement. One of the nightmare scenarios facing China's leadership has to be the fear that a younger generation of computer literate Chinese slip the leash of state control and turn their disdain and anger on the authorities. This could be a spontaneous action, much as what occurred in Tunisia and Egypt in 2011. Chinese authorities were active in censoring all news of the Middle East's political turmoil in order to make certain that its people did not get similar ideas of using the global social network.

Of course, there is another side to this issue as well. If the Internet was thought to sound the death knell for authoritarian regimes by undermining their attempts at control, in fact the opposite is also taking place. The Internet is used by authoritarian regimes to eavesdrop, hunt down dissidents, and further control the flow of information. For example, every computer has a unique IP address, and every posting to a website can be traced to the originating computer. This ability to trace computer usage means that getting households wired to the Internet will give authoritarian regimes the ultimate surveillance tool—a spying device in every household and office. So Chinese authorities can accumulate evidence against potential activists, charge, and jail them, all before the wider public even hears their names. China is not unique. Burma's military junta (which is close to China), for example, has made use of a firewall developed by U.S. software maker Fortinet.[6]

One possible scenario for China's political development is that the regime heads into a period of nationalistic buildup, censorship, and tighter control over the country's sociopolitical affairs. In this future China's Beijing Consensus-market-Leninism could end up with a regime based on nationalism, the glories of the past, tight censorship, and a military buildup. In many ways this trajectory is similar to what was evident in European fascism during the 1930s, complete with government policies seeking and promoting food self-sufficiency. The danger, according to some analysts, is that such a regime ultimately becomes confrontational. As Ledeen notes, "the short history of classical fascism suggests that it is only a matter of time before China will pursue confrontation with the West. That is built into the DNA of all such regimes. Sooner or later, Chinese leaders will feel compelled to demonstrate the superiority of their system, and even the most impressive per capita GDP will not do. Superiority means others have to bend their knees, and cater to the wishes of the dominant nation."[7]

Considering the worries over China's potential trip down the road to fascist militarism (which are probably overstated), is there any possibility of a democratic or quasi-democratic political development path? Nobel Peace Prize winner Liu Xiaobo (imprisoned for his views) poses a question: "Our countrymen are still like infants who depend entirely on adult care and who know only how to wait for a wise ruler to appear. Can it be that Chinese people will never really grow up, that their character is forever deformed and weak, and that they are only fit, as if predestined by the stars, to pray for and accept imperial mercy on their knees?"[8] In answer to his own question, Liu indicates that China's population will at some point stop depending on reform from above: "for the emergence of a free China, placing hope in 'new policies' of those in power is far worse than placing hope in the continuous expansion of the 'new power' among the people."[9]

What does the new power among the people entail? A combination of social mobility, Internet interconnectiveness, and a questioning of authority is needed. The Beijing Consensus, market-Leninism, and for that matter, Asian values do not necessarily translate into the endless rule of the CCP. Things can and most likely will change. The argument that the Chinese are not suited to nor capable of a more open political system is not supported empirically. The CCP is far less doctrinaire and more representative than it used to be. At the lower party ranks, there is some degree of electoral competition. One also must wonder about the validity of the argument in light of India's ability to maintain a system of parliamentary government and the gradual evolution to open, more pluralistic political systems in Taiwan, South Korea, Indonesia, and Japan. The Indian democratic experience puts cold water on the argument that such a large country as China cannot be democratically governed (an argument arising from the view that China seems always one step away from chaos). Taiwan, South Korea, and Japan also show that societies, like that of China, strongly influenced by Confucian cultures can adopt democratic systems.

But there is another point as well. Authoritarian political regimes are not without their advantages. The Chinese political system is able to make large and complex decisions quickly because an authoritarian regime faces few political checks on it power. This advantage is most obvious with regard to infrastructure building. China has built airports, dams, high-speed rail, and water and electricity systems to feed its growing industrial base. China can and did move a million people out of the Three Gorges Dam flood plain, these people having virtually no recourse to protest. By contrast, in democratic India every new investment is subject to checks by competing political parties, trade unions, peasant associations, and the courts. Chinese political leaders are adept at catering to the interests of Chinese elites and the emerging middle class. They build on their fears of populism, which have been problematic throughout Chinese history. That is why there appears to be little middle class support in China for a Western-style multiparty democracy—at least in significant numbers. Chinese political leaders may not tolerate any political challenge to the Communist Party, but they are attuned to the urban middle class and powerful business interests that generate employment. They try to stay on top of popular discontents, and they can shift policy in response.

Where does this leave the grand debate over Asian political development vis-à-vis China? In much of the region there is a strong predilection toward autocracy with a view toward maintaining political order, conducive to economic development. A stable political environment has been a major factor in China's great market-driven leap forward in the late twentieth and early twenty-first century, and this political stability is evident in other countries, such as Singapore and Vietnam. It also factors into the high incidence of military rulers in Pakistan. China's size and economic significance, however, does put it under particular scrutiny. China faces pressures on the old system. Challenges, however, do not mean the old system is incapable of transforming itself, but it creates a high degree of uncertainty over the political development of Asia's largest country. And it does not rule out a gradual transition to a more pluralistic system.

THE INDIAN EQUATION

What about the other side of the grand debate? India's experience is important on a number of fronts. Unlike Pakistan and Bangladesh, India has maintained a long line of civilian governments and has survived religious-ethnic tensions, insurgencies, and an extended state of emergency. To a significant degree, India's development has been the opposite of China's: its political development morphed to democracy, and its economic development shifted from a closed economy to an open one. The journalist Niranjan Rajadhyaksha observes that "independent India has been a curious combination of an open society and a closed economy, and embedded in this arrangement was the implicit assumption that ordinary people were intelligent enough to choose their rulers but not intelligent enough to choose what to buy and produce."[10]

India's political development offers much to admire. Elections occur on a regular basis, the rule of law is largely respected, and opposition voices are heard, all of which creates a fractious political system. That fractious political system has, at times, led to a difficulty in implementing economic policies, with some blaming it for India's falling behind China in economic development. Sumit Ganguly, professor of political science and director of American and Global Security at Indiana University, notes, "To a considerable degree, the economic hurdles that confront India result directly from the country's fractious and increasingly coarse politics. . . . The width of the political spectrum and the virtual absence of one-party dominance in India's parliament for over two decades have meant that the forging of a political consensus on many issues of national significance can easily be held hostage to either parochial political or rigidly ideological concerns."[11] Fractious internal politics erode governance and weaken the political center's ability to contend with insurgencies and Islamic extremism as well as India's relations with Pakistan, from the latter's support to terrorists and from the threat of its conventional armed forces (the two countries have fought four wars).

The long life of India's insurgencies represents one failure of the country's democratic model. Two major insurgencies have been running for several decades: a discontented Muslim majority in the disputed Kashmir and Jammu region and the Naxalite movement in the State of West Bengal. While Kashmir and Jammu encompass security issues with Pakistan, the Naxalites are a homegrown Maoist group that emerged in the late 1960s because of unhappiness with the structure of land ownership. Although Indian security forces appeared to have crushed the Naxalites by the early 1970s, the movement staged a comeback in the first decade of the twenty-first century. The insurgency has spread over 16 states, operating in a swath of land roughly the size of Portugal.

India's other insurgencies are largely located in Northeast India, a region connected to the rest of the country by a narrow bridge of territory called the Siliguri Corridor. The region consists of seven states, Assam, Meghalaya, Tripura, Arunachal Pradesh, Mizoram, Manipur, and Nagaland. Far from New Delhi and surrounded by Burma and China, this region is the home of local separatist groups (Assamese, Naga, and Mizo guerilla groups); the situation is complicated by the coexistence of tribal groups and migrants from other parts of India. The borders are also relatively porous, allowing a sizeable contraband trade of everything from diamonds and guns to heroin.

Why the insurgencies, especially when India's economy is on the rise? One possibility is that India's growing embrace of market-driven economic development is aggravating long-standing socioeconomic inequalities. Kunal P. Kirpalani, writing for the *South Asia Masala* blog in 2010 observed that "what seems to be a common grass-root cause in South Asian insurgencies is socioeconomic and political developmental deprivation. India's Northeast is no exception. It is a region that lags behind most of India developmentally. While the southern and western states reap the benefits of India's booming economy, the economic situation in the Northwest has deteriorated."[12] Ganguly is not as certain that socioeconomic inequality is the reason for the revival of insurgencies. He contends that "this argument, though seemingly persuasive, is not entirely satisfactory because substantial economic inequity has been a constant of the Indian socioeconomic landscape since independence."[13] Another dimension of the insurgency issue is the globalization of communications and the adoption of technology, both of which function to drive up awareness of social inequities and corruption. Additionally, local and central governments have failed in these regions to contend with long-standing problems such as land reform.

The issue of Islamic radicalism also represents a challenge, something that India shares to some degree with China. That comparison, however, has limits as China's Muslim minority is largely located in the northwest and is ethnically Uighur. India's Muslim population is around the same size as Pakistan's population, and members of that community have served as presidents, diplomats, and generals. A concerted and extended effort has been made to maintain a secular India, despite the existence of religiously based parties such as the Hindu nationalist BJP (Bharatiya Janata Party). Even the BJP when in office was forced to modify its approach and put a little distance between itself and some of the more radical Hindu nationalist groups. All the same, India has periodically been subject to radical Islamic terrorist attacks, the most notable being the 2008 Mumbai attacks, which killed 164 people.

India thus offers up a democratic model to Asia and developing countries in general. It is, however, a model that has its own set of problems, much as does China's autocratic model. What makes this model of interest to the rest of the region is that China is advertising its undemocratic system. Joshua Kurlantzick, a *Current History* contributing editor, writes of China and Russia that "indeed, they are advertising their undemocratic systems—according to which they have moderately liberalized their economies while avoiding concurrent political reform—as development models that Asian countries should emulate. China and Russia also emphasize a doctrine of noninterference, arguing that countries should not intervene in other nations' internal affairs—interference that could include sanctioning human rights violators or supporting prodemocracy movements."[14] In this regard, prodemocratic forces often point to India as a viable counterexample.

CIVIL SOCIETY AND PEOPLE POWER

While the rest of Asia pays close attention to China and, increasingly, to India, it is questionable to what extent other countries regard either as a political development model. The grand debate is heard and digested, but each country has its own set of issues that determine the strength of its civil society and capacity to accommodate political change. A caveat to this would be the strategically located countries where political developments could ripple into larger neighbors. These countries includes North Korea, Taiwan, and Burma that border China or are close to major economies such as South Korea and Japan. It is certainly a factor for Hong Kong, which is a Special Administrative Region (SAR) and has a relatively higher degree of political freedoms than does mainland China.

One thing that is evident in examining political development in Asia is the different perceptions of civil society. In a Western, liberal sense, civil society usually refers to groups and organizations, many of them voluntary, that support modern secular democracy and capitalism. It can also function as a counterforce to the state and function as a "public sphere," "where citizens argue with one-another about the great questions of the day and negotiate a constantly-evolving sense of the 'common' or 'public' interest."[15] A less liberal view of civil society is that such society is meant to be supportive of economic growth and poverty reduction and in many circumstances supportive of state goals to achieve those ends. While one might claim that China is the latter and India the former, the civil society issue is not limited to those two countries. Critics of civil society, of course, will point out that the uncontrolled development of a multitude of nonstate actors will only lead to chaos, especially if nonstate groups have radically different views. In Asia this debate has implications for the issue of "people power" movements, which have become significant factors in political change in the Philippines, Indonesia, and Thailand.

People power gained importance as a major political force in the Philippines in 1986. The country was then ruled by the Marcos dictatorship, which was known for its corruption and crony capitalism as well as the extravagance of Marcos's wife, Imelda, and her 2,000 pairs of shoes.[16] When the leading democratic dissident Benigno "Ninoy" Aquino, Jr., returned to the Philippines in 1983, he was assassinated at the airport. This blatant act of repression by the Marcos regime galvanized nationwide opposition. Massive demonstrations followed, bringing the country to a standstill and eventually forced Ferdinand Marcos to leave the country. People power thus played a major role in overthrowing a dictatorship and restoring democracy to the Philippines.

The Philippines' people power movement, sometimes referred to as the Yellow Revolution for the yellow banners used by the prodemocracy forces, resulted in a mixed legacy. It has been cited as a forerunner to and inspiration for the soon-to-come political earthquake that hit Eastern Europe and the Soviet Union and showed how spontaneous mass action can topple repressive regimes. On the other hand, the Philippines political system struggled through the rest of the twentieth century and into the next with major problems: corruption, attempted military coups, and the constitutional ouster of one president, Joseph Estrada.

Estrada's ouster also involved people power. The president was publicly accused by a governor and former close friend of giving the nation's leader a payoff. Although the governor was tainted by his own corruption investigation, his allegations caused the Philippine House of Representatives to file an impeachment case against Estrada. The impeachment suit moved quickly through the House to the Senate, where an impeachment court was formed. Estrada pleaded not guilty, and in an 11–10 vote, senators refused to open an envelope that contained evidence. The prosecution panel walked out in protest, and soon the streets were filled with anti-Estrada demonstrators. Estrada was defiant about public opposition, but his position deteriorated when on January 19, 2001, the armed forces chief of staff Angelo Reyes withdrew his support for the president. Reyes's primary consideration in giving his support to Vice President Gloria Macapagal-Arroyo was the widespread opposition of the people to President Estrada. The ousted leader was later arrested for plunder, which act set off his supporters who also used people power to mobilize protests. The military, however, crushed this round of popular turmoil.

People power as a political force in Asia did not end with the Philippines. Perhaps one country worth a little more discussion is Indonesia, Southeast Asia's largest country. The value of its experience is that it is non-Confucian and is predominately Muslim but has some overlays from earlier exposure to Hinduism, Buddhism, and Christianity. In the late twentieth century, Indonesia moved into the democratic fold, and it appears the debate over whether to follow either an Indian or Chinese model was not a factor.

Indonesia demonstrates the ability of a large country to make the transition from a soft authoritarian system into a democracy. Soft authoritarianism in this case was defined by a political system that was decidedly hierarchical with President Suharto and his court (family and close retainers) at the apex of the power pyramid, followed by layers of businessmen and high-ranking bureaucrats and military officers, all presiding over a growing middle class and large working and peasant classes. The New Order government, which dominated Indonesia from the mid-1960s to 1997, also had the trappings of a democratic government—a constitution, regular elections, opposition parties (allowed but controlled), and a limited freedom of the press. The reality was that Suharto dominated the political system, being reelected each time, that opposition parties quickly ran up against the limits of what they were allowed, and press freedom was tolerated only to a point.

When the Asian economic crisis revealed the rot in Indonesia's ruling structure, President Suharto was ousted by a people power movement. It can be argued that the systemic collapse of the economy and its rescue by the IMF demonstrated the high level of corruption that had come to stifle entrepreneurship and middle class aspirations of upper social mobility. In Suharto's place, Vice President Bacharuddin Jusuf Habibie constitutionally replaced the outgoing president and then put the country on the path to a more democratic political system of truly competitive elective politics. Although Habibie's tenure was relatively short (1998–99), he presided over an open election that led to three peaceful constitutional changes in government. Despite challenges, such as Islamic radical terrorism, corruption, and occasional issues over freedom of the press, the Freedom House, which is based in New York and which is a prodemocracy advocacy organization, regards Indonesia as the only fully "free" country in Southeast Asia and puts it in the same group as India, South Korea, Japan, Taiwan, and Mongolia.

But questions remain about the extent of people power and civil society. In Indonesia people power sprang from an increasingly frustrated civil society. Beginning in a spontaneous fashion, Indonesia's people power movement quickly found form and outlet in a largely unused constitution and in underused opposition political parties. Students at the universities in Jakarta also played a major role in stimulating the opposition. Despite considerable upheaval, Indonesia's political system was able to return to stability and to move along a democratic path. The other result was the birth of East Timor, a former Portuguese colony, taken over by Indonesia in the 1970s.

The path for people power in Thailand was not as straightforward as Indonesia. From 1991 to 2006, Thailand evolved along a more democratic path. Economic growth, despite a downturn in 1997–98, was strong and globalization also expanded the country's linkages to the outside world. Thai civil society, however, became polarized during the tenure of Prime Minister Thaksin Shinawatra, who was known for his strong personality, populist leanings, charges of corruption, and willingness to stir things up. Thaksin managed to alienate the country's urban elite, the military, and the monarchy, actions that resulted in his ouster following large-scale demonstrations against him in 2006.

While people power helped oust Thaksin, people power was used to protest his ouster. What emerged in Thailand was an awareness that there were deep political cleavages, representing two civil societies, one grounded in the rural parts of the country, the other in the urban areas and centering on Bangkok. Researchers Robert B. Albritton and Thawilwadee Bureekul make the following observations: "People living in rural areas live a significantly more precarious existence. Their livelihood is constantly threatened by nature and they are exposed to lack of personal security in a significantly more anarchic society. This leads to a greater dependence upon social networks for 'getting by' in life and, as in almost any society. Rural dwellers are significantly more communal, as well as being interested in the welfare of their neighbors (which can be either positive or negative, from some perspectives.)."[17] They also point out that communalism also causes a higher trust level in government.

Albritton and Thawilwadee's study also focused on the civil society in Thailand's urban sector, noting that city dwellers were more inclined to be "modernistic," being individualistic and less beholden to others, including the state. As the academics note, "for these urbanites, individual independence from society and government leads to a greater interest in protections from government interference that scholars often associate with what are generally described as 'civil liberties.' "[18] Ultimately these two sides, each with its own civil society outlook, which encompassed democracy, clashed, leaving 2007–11 a very unstable period in Thai political life. In a very real sense, competing civil societies—people power movements—sought to cancel out each other's view of what democracy means. Moreover, people power provided a nonconstitutional, non-ballot box option in seeking a political outcome. The result was to leave deep-set cleavages in Thai society, tarnishing Thailand's attraction as a place for investment and undermining growth.

The grand debate remains an open-ended argument, best left to a broader comparison of autocratic versus democratic political systems rather than lining up India vis-à-vis China. China and India, however, will continue to gather attention in this debate because of their emergence as new powers and because of the relationships they are developing. For the record, India is willing to seek influence in Burma, one of the most repressive regimes on the planet; while China has close relations with South Korea, one of Asia's most boisterous democracies. The main challenge for most of Asia is how to deepen their civil societies in order to withstand multiple challenges from both political and economic changes. Be they autocratic or democratic, how do Asian countries balance maintaining political order with change within their societies? As the examples of Indonesia's democratic development and of Vietnam's and China's authoritarianism show, there is no single or easy answer.

TRANSNATIONAL CRIME

Transnational crime represents a pernicious political challenge throughout Asia. It encompasses many different kinds of criminal activity. It includes organized crime's broad range of enterprises, such as the trafficking of narcotics, guns, women, body parts, artifacts, and rare animals as well as organized crime's ability to subvert formal political systems. Another transnational crime is high seas piracy. Criminal organizations operate transnational networks from key drug producing countries, namely Pakistan, Afghanistan, and Burma. Afghanistan is at the heart of heroin production, with trade routes that extend through Central Asia, the Middle East, and China to Europe and the United States. In 2007 this South Asian country was estimated to cultivate 93 percent of the world's opium poppy. It is involved in the full narcotics production cycle, from cultivation to finished heroin.[19] Burma, at the center of the Golden Triangle, is a distant second behind Afghanistan on the heroin-opium front. However, Burma has emerged as one of the leading producers of methamphetamine, tapping old trade networks through Laos, Cambodia, Thailand, and China.

Afghanistan's drug cultivation and export cast a long shadow over the political development of neighboring countries. Central Asia, in particular, has been ao open frontier for the international drug trade as the governmental institutions in most states are weak, law enforcement poorly equipped, and corruption widespread. In a study of the state-crime nexus in Central Asia, conducted by the Central Asia-Caucasus Institute & Silk Road Studies Program, Erica Marat observes that "for each Central Asian state today, there is a greater chance of destabilization caused by rivalries among competing fractions of political, business or military elites, rather than confrontation with terrorist organizations. Instability arises from the mobilization of criminal non-state actors, illicit businesses, and chaotic inter-state migration. Corruption and personal interests in economic enrichment among political actors also play an important role."[20]

Methamphetamine was once a relatively harmless pick-me-up, but advances in chemical science have made this a far more potent drug, producing temporary hyperactivity and euphoria. It can be sold as powder, as tablets, or in crystal form, all forms of which make smuggling easy. The downside to the drug are tremors, violent behavior, drowsiness, and depression. The world's main production area is the Golden Triangle, sometimes now referred to as the Ice Triangle after one of the names used for methamphetamine.

Burma is an ideal place for methamphetamine production. The government is one of Asia's most repressive and corrupt and lacks control over sizeable parts of the country. Long an opium-heroin producer, climactic conditions forced a reassessment of the business model for many cartels. Methamphetamine offered a substitute and required zones beyond any government's control. Burma's criminal groups, many of them ethnic Chinese with networks across the region, were ready and able to step in. Two other key factors in this mix are Asia's overall rising affluence, which means more money to spend by more people on drugs, and China's reforms, which have vastly improved its road, rail, and air infrastructure, all conducive to smuggling drugs out of Burma. Sadly, China's growing closeness to Burma has meant an upward swing in drug use and addiction.

BORDER DISPUTES

Asia has a significant number of border disputes that remain potential causes for international tensions. On several occasions, border claims have led to conflict. Border disputes include clashes between the Soviet Union and China in the 1960s and 1970s, overlapping claims in the South China Sea that resulted in an outbreak of fighting between China and Vietnam (in 1974 and 1988), and the long-simmering problems of Kashmir and Jammu that pits India and Pakistan against each other (with the last undeclared war being fought in 1999). The list goes on. It includes competing Russian and Japanese claims over the Kurile Islands, which Soviet forces occupied at the close of the World War II, an act that Japan refuses to accept and the reason why Tokyo will not sign a formal peace treaty with Moscow. Further disputes arise from Japan and South Korea's competing claims over the Liancourt Rocks and from Thailand and Cambodia's ongoing border quarrel, which resulted in combat as recently as early 2011.

Asia's economic success has been based on international trade and commerce, factors that are dependent on international cooperation and cross border stability. Considering the push toward greater regional economic cooperation, it might be expected some of the historical sting of border disputes, some dating back to colonial rule, would have faded. In the early twenty-first century, this does not appear to be the case as economic success has emboldened nations and given them a greater stake in border disputes that could have significant value in terms of access to natural resources such as oil and natural gas. At the same time, public opinion has gained a stronger voice in diplomatic policies, sometimes pushed along by nationalistic politicians. As Tim Johnston of the *Financial Times* wrote of the 2011 Thai-Cambodian border dispute, "Thailand and Cambodia, both-members of the Association of Southeast Asian nations have an uneasy relationship that has been made more turbulent by the lack of clarity surrounding their shared border, an issue which has long provided a ready source of fuel for nationalist chauvinism on both sides"[21]

While the Thai-Cambodia conflict is important, the major border disputes that represent major potential political challenges involve China, Pakistan, Japan, and both Koreas. To clarify, China's claim to much of the South China Sea touches on border issues with Indonesia, Malaysia, Vietnam, and the Philippines; China and India still have ongoing differences over their mutual border, especially when adding Tibet into the mix; India and Pakistan have a long-standing (since 1949) feud over Kashmir and Jammu; and Japan, South Korea, and China have ongoing disputes over their maritime borders (complicated by the possibility of substantial undersea oil and gas reserves). All of these disputes touch upon strong veins of nationalism that are not far from the surface. They could also threaten to draw in other non-Asian actors such as the United States.

India and Pakistan's borders represent an ongoing invitation to a larger crisis, possibly another war. War is the danger arising from border disputes and nationalism. Although in most cases war is not a serious possibility since cool heads usually prevail, still border disputes contribute to what is becoming an arms race in Asia. Additionally, economic prosperity is allowing Asian countries to upgrade their weapons systems. Ashwani Kumar, member of Parliament from India's Congress Party says, "It goes without saying that India must be seriously concerned with the rise of China's strategic power, including its military and economic power. India has consistently opposed an arms race—but India will not be found waiting in taking all measures necessary for the effective safeguarding of its territorial integrity and national interests."[22]

China has been building its military prowess to an unprecedented degree in recent years. Three programs stand out. First, China has created an active land-based ballistic and cruise missile program that is among the most ambitious in the world. Second, it has transformed and enlarged its submarine fleet. Finally, China has concentrated on what it calls "informatisation," which describes how the People's Liberation Army needs to function as one force, using sensors, communications, and electronic and cyberwarfare. Thanks to a combination of satellites, radar, reconnaissance drones, and underwater-sensor arrays, China now has a good idea of what is going on far into the Pacific. In short, China is developing a meaningful deterrent to threats. India and other neighbors have reason to be concerned.

India is not alone in looking at China's growing military might as a reason to upgrade its military. While the United States and most European military budgets are set to decline (related to economic considerations), Australia, Singapore, Malaysia, and Vietnam are adding submarines, planes, helicopters, and tanks. Ross Babbage states that "the most fundamental changes to the security environment are being caused by the nature, scale and speed of China's military expansion. . . . China is starting to contest the Western Allies operational sanctuary in pace, the security of their naval vessels at sea,the security of Western Pacific airspace and the security of allies surveillance, situational awareness, logistic and other information networks."[23]

Without taking anything away from the concerns over China's military buildup, the escalation in weapons buying throughout the region raises the military ante—even when China is not involved. Additionally, there are a number of border disputes that do not involve China. Thailand and Cambodia are one example, but Cambodia and Vietnam have also had their differences in the past, some leading to combat. The danger, of course, is that something begins small and escalates. Siemon Wezeman, a senior fellow at the Stockholm International Peace Research Institute who specializes in tracking defense spending, observes that "little incidents could easily escalate into bigger incidents, and then little nasty wars."[24]

NUCLEAR PROLIFERATION

For policy makers from Washington to Tokyo, nuclear proliferation is a major concern. In Asia it is the penultimate part of the arms race. China, Russia, India, and Pakistan have nuclear arsenals, and North Korea is probably in the nuclear club. Japan and South Korea have the technology within reach that would allow them to join the club. With the exception of North Korea, the nuclear club has not threatened to unleash its weapons of mass destruction on its neighbors. Yet, the risk remains that one of those little incidents will transform into one of those nasty little wars. In this scenario, India and Pakistan usually come to mind, considering the record of conflict between the two countries.

Another major risk factor is nuclear weapons in the hands of an unstable regime or rogue state. While this scenario is often put forward about Pakistan if a Taliban-like takeover were to occur, North Korea represents the sum of all fears: an opaque state, headed by a dictatorial leader with a past littered with assassinations, border provocations, and a sizeable military establishment. In 2009 North Korea claimed to have successfully tested a nuclear weapon as powerful as the atomic bomb that leveled Hiroshima.

North Korea has thus made steady progress in developing nuclear power, but the regime is not regarded as stable. The country has gone through a famine that began in 1996 (with an estimated million deaths), has seen numerous purges, and has occasionally lashed out at South Korea (as with the sinking of a South Korean naval ship in 2010 and the shelling of a small island town also in 2010). The six-party talks (with Russia, the United States, Japan, South Korea, China, and North Korea) have sought to keep tensions under control and maintain some type of dialogue. Yet, North Korea remains a closed regime, highly opaque and increasingly dependent on China for its economic survival. At the same time, the aging dictator Kim Jong-il is seeking to implement a lengthy handover of power to one of his sons, Kim Jong-un. Adding to the concerns over North Korea was the speculation that the regime was responsible for passing nuclear technology to Syria. North Korea is for many policy makers the sum of all fears—a rouge state that is headed by a nontransparent elite in the process of political succession and armed with long-range missiles, probably with a nuclear capacity. North Korea is perhaps the worst example of the nuclear danger in Asia, but nuclear proliferation looms as a key issue in Asia, casting a long shadow over economic achievements and the region's rise.

CONCLUSION

Asian economic achievements are substantial, but the political landscape carries many challenges, some of which can halt the rise of the region's power. To some degree, Asia's globalization came largely in an economic form, with a second, more political wave rolling into the region over the last decade. The political wave encompasses the challenges of identity and social mobility as well as the need to deal with hurdles that can hinder further advances. Technology, in particular the advancement of communications, has introduced into the process of political development one more element of complexity, shrinking time and reducing geographical barriers. While Asia's political challenges should not be overstated, neither should they simply be swept aside, as these challenges represent major issues especially for the region's autocratic states.

Chapter 8

THE WEST AND THE RISE OF ASIA

While economic and political challenges are substantial within Asia, there is a related set of economic and political challenges in how the West reacts to the changing geopolitical landscape in the Eurasian landmass and Asia Pacific regions. This reaction includes everything from the Western belief that liberal democracy is the end result of history to the increasingly fierce competition over markets and natural resources in the Middle East and Africa, Central Asia, and Latin America. It also touches upon the challenges of foreign investment, both Western investment in Asia and Asian investment in the West. Despite the considerable push toward globalization in the late twentieth and early twenty-first century, nationalism remains very much a factor in Western-Asian relations, a powerful force that has been largely allowed expression but generally contained on the policy side. History has demonstrated where unleashed nationalism can take Europe and Asia. Nonetheless, against the backdrop of impressive trade statistics, capital inflows and outflows, major corporation market penetration, and glossy airline commercials emphasizing the joys of global intermingling, there is an undercurrent of tensions driven by concerns over job losses, declining standards of living, and overall competitiveness. There is a lot at stake requiring that Asia and the West manage the relationship, reduce tensions, and maintain forums to deal with such things as trade strains, international terrorism, rogue nations, and the environment. Failure to manage these issues leaves the door open to a deeper set of problems and a return to more blatant power politics that defined the early twentieth century and led to World War II.

EAST AND WEST AND A CHANGING WORLD ORDER

At the close of the Cold War, the United States enjoyed what was known as the unipolar moment, a brief passing period in which Washington was the sole remaining superpower. That situation was to rapidly change. U.S. power was quickly eroded by an attack on its own soil in 2001, two related and costly wars in Afghanistan and Iraq, and a major financial-economic crisis in 2008–9. The Bush years ended in 2008 with U.S. power considerably weakened and the prestige of the West in decline. This sense of decline was reinforced by the European Union's sovereign debt crises that became pronounced in April and May 2010, forcing Greece and then Ireland into EU-IMF bailouts.

At the beginning of the second decade of the twenty-first century, the West, broadly defined as the United States, Canada, Australia, and Europe, found its power–both economically and politically—weakened. The once relatively cohesive U.S.-European alliance that sustained the West during the Cold War gradually diverged over issues ranging from strategic objectives vis-à-vis Russia and China to the environment and Middle East security. The United States was long the leader of the West and perceived itself, in the words of former secretary of state Madeleine Albright, as "the indispensable nation."[1] The changed circumstances from the 1990s and most of the first decade of the twenty-first century to post-Great Recession era has been a traumatic passage. Along these lines, the rise of Asia reflects the "rise of the rest," a process by which new powers accumulate the wherewithal to project influence beyond their borders and increasingly compete with the United States and the rest of the West.

The challenge now facing world leaders is to establish working guidelines for a global, political, and economic system. In the early twenty-first century, these guidelines translate into how will incumbent great powers respond to emerging challengers who seek to penetrate or move up the great power ranks?[2] Related to that is how might these responses be conditioned by considerations of economic interdependence? In a sense, the balance between big power aspirations and economic interdependence provide the broadest parameters for the emerging multipolar world order that must deal with the rise of Asia and in particular China and India.

This need is reflected in the transition from a U.S.-led G-7 group in the 1990s to a G-8 (Russia added) to a G-20 in 2008. While this group, including the likes of China, India, Brazil, Saudi Arabia, and South Africa, held up relatively well in its first two years of operation, the cohesiveness in policy making soon gave way as the clear and present danger of economic collapse receded. Complicating matters, the economic recovery for the advanced economies was painfully slow, hindered by the need to deleverage from high levels of debt. In Europe this deleveraging process led to a sovereign debt crisis in Greece, Ireland, and Portugal and harsh austerity in the United Kingdom in 2010–11. Adding to this uneven global recovery, the 2011 Japanese earthquake and tsunami even further underscored the nature of a set of advanced economies struggling against strong headwinds. This is a global system lacking a dominant superpower, and that lack opens the door to uncertainty. As Ian Bremmer, president of the Eurasia Group, and Nouriel Roubini, professor of economics at New York University, observe, "the result will be intensified conflict on the international stage over vitally important issues, such as international macroeconomic coordination, financial regulatory reform, trade policy, and climate change. This new order has far-reaching implications for the global economy, as companies around the world sit on enormous stockpiles of cash, waiting for the current era of political and economic uncertainty to pass."[3] As the Libyan crisis demonstrated, reaching consensus, let alone coordinated policy actions, is going to be difficult in the years ahead.

The more challenging nature of global politics was evident in 2011 with the crisis over Libya. In February and March 2011, Libya's government was rocked by widespread political demonstrations against the Gaddafi regime. Although the uprising was nearly successful, Colonel Muammar Gaddafi was able to hold on, rally loyalist forces, and threatened to crush the rebellion, darkly suggesting a bloodbath. A lively debate ensued at the United Nations, with France and the United Kingdom, backed by the United States, pushing for the creation of a no-fly zone, an area in which Libyan government aircraft would not be allowed to fly, especially if they were conducting combat operations against their own civilian population. On March 17 the United Nations passed a resolution establishing a no-fly zone, a measure backed by France, the United Kingdom, and the United States. In contrast, China Russia, India, and Brazil abstained, allowing the vote to pass but not supporting it.

In the aftermath of the U.N. Security Council vote, the United States, France, the United Kingdom, Spain, Canada, and Italy actively engaged military targets in Libya. While the allied effort halted Gaddafi forces seeking to take the rebel stronghold of Benghazi, the global community's response was hardly unified. The West, with the support of a handful of other countries such as Qatar and the United Arab Emirates, found itself very much at odds with China and Russia, which were verbose in their criticism. Russian Prime Minister Vladimir Putin likened the allied attacks to a "medieval call for a crusade."[4]

China was also critical of the U.S. involvement in Libya stating in the *People's Daily* that "the military attacks on Libya are, following on from the Afghan and Iraq wars, the third time that some countries have launched armed action against sovereign countries. In today's world where some people with Cold War mentality are still keen on the use of force, people have reason to express concerns about the effects of the military action."[5] Another Chinese publication, *Global Times* (owned by the *People's Daily*) provided another round of Chinese thought on global affairs: "The West will not give up their jurisdiction over justice and injustice. They truly believe that they are the world's custodian and the embodiment of justice. The Jasmine Revolution actually deepens their sense of purpose, and the West cannot bear the prospect that their will might be negated by Gaddafi."[6]

For its part, the United States portrayed the Libyan crises as being supportive of a multilateral approach and approved by the United Nations. It also was clear that this operation was not a U.S.-run one but that NATO was the legitimate authority, especially with leadership from France and the United Kingdom. This policy reflected a different approach on the part of the United States from the Clinton administrations and reflected deep-seated concerns over the limits of U.S. power against a backdrop of a debt-straddled economy. The Obama administration was keenly aware of the U.S. electorate's concerns over how much such an intervention would cost and for how long it would last. President Obama also clarified in March 2011 that the United States should not be asked to act alone but that it should stand ready to offer its unique capabilities in leading multilateral interventions with feasible narrow objectives.[7] Philip Stevens of the *Financial Times*, writes, "The U.S. remains the world's indispensable power, but it is becoming a more reticent one."[8]

Libya thus provides an example of a consensus that things are bad. However, there are very sharp philosophical differences as to what should be done and why. Even Western views, in particular European (Germany, for example, decided to sit this one out), differed and were influenced by concerns over oil and natural gas supplies (Italy, France, Spain, and Portugal are big oil and gas importers from Libya) and over the possibility of refugees waves hitting the European Union. In December 2010 Gaddafi warned EU leaders that their region may "become black because millions want to come to Europe."[9] With the Libyan government lacking control and with political unrest forcing people to seek shelter in Europe, the EU faced some difficult questions.

While the West clearly favors a democratic outcome in North Africa, China's commentary clearly gives the impression in the West that China favors the survival of the Gaddafi regime, even if it remains in power by conducting a bloodbath of repression. In contrast to China, Japan supported the no-fly zone. The reasons for the Japanese having a different view from Beijing boil down to Chinese concerns that the West may continue to support regime change in those cases in which it hopes to replace an autocracy with a democracy. China worked hard to filter the news about the Jasmine Revolution sweeping the Arab world in which the targets were autocratic regimes and in which protesters' demands favor free elections and more transparent governments. To the CCP such calls remain dangerous. Moreover, if Western governments are willing to help push along regime change, what would hold them back if a prodemocracy movement threatened to topple the communist government in China? By playing through the United Nations and casting doubt on the validity of the Libyan intervention, Beijing also sought to question the validity of any such action vis-à-vis the communist government in China. Also in a realpolitik sense, if Colonel Gaddafi managed to survive and reclaim control over Libya, China would be in position to argue that it was not hostile to his regime and hence have a better chance at buying Libya's oil and gas.

The path into the future, therefore, is conditioned by an increasingly less defined and more unstable global order. Relations between Asia and the West must be observed through this lens. In a sense, everyone understands that there is a geopolitical chessboard, but the problem is that the players are scrambling to understand the rules, which appear to have changed and are most likely to change still further. That said, the implications of an economic convergence between a rising Asia and an economically struggling West take on a profound nature.

THE WEST, ASIA, AND CONVERGENCE

As Asia closes the economic gap with the West, the issue of convergence and the responsibilities that come with that level of achievement assume greater significance. Along these lines, China and some of the more successful newly industrialized countries such as South Korea, Singapore, and Thailand can no longer plead poverty. In trade talks with the West, Chinese as well as a number of other Asian countries is using the mantra that it "is a developing country." This claim is meant to provide cover for a multitude of complaints by others such as causing cross border pollution, letting currencies float freely (India as well as China), and handling difficult international political issues (ignoring genocide, engaging with odious regimes, and dealing with the global trade in blood diamonds, prostitutes, and rare animal parts). Pleading poverty is an important part of China's justification for its behavior. In one form or another, making this argument has allowed the country to avoid responsibility over blatant human rights atrocities in Africa, to excuse its slowness in dealing with pollution issues (such as its heavy reliance on coal, which is also mined under often horrid conditions), and in its prolonged reluctance to appreciate the renminbi, which has created ongoing trade tensions with the United States and Europe.

While the developing-country mantra continues to be used, it is becoming less and less effective as China emerges as a major economic competitor; not to mention its becoming the world's second-largest economy in 2010. Of course, poverty still exists in China—around 150 million people out of 1.3 billion still live on less than $2 a day. Yet, as Gideon Rachman of the *Financial Times* observed in 2010, "China's insistence that it is a poor, developing nation is beginning to wear a little thin. This, after all, is a country that is sitting on more than $2,500 billion worth of foreign reserves."[10] (As of April 2011, the number is now $3 trillion and growing rapidly.) Rachman went on to argue that China's "insistence that it is still a 'developing country' has become a shield to protect itself against vital political and economic changes that matter profoundly to the rest of the world."

Directly related to this issue of China's status as a "developed" or "developing" country is how the West perceives Asia's major power, as is seen in the literature, much of it American, that either portrays China as a looming disaster (i.e., communist rule is increasingly dysfunctional and will eventually end like most Chinese dynasties before it) or as a resilient power, increasingly building its capabilities to dominate the global system. Gordon Chang, a lawyer who has worked in China, argues that the country's deep-seated corruption and political inflexibility is setting the stage for a titanic collapse. Writing in 2001, Chang stated that "on paper, China looks powerful and dynamic even today, less than twenty-five years after Deng Xiao-ping began to open his country to the outside world. In reality, however, the Middle Kingdom, as it once called itself, is a paper dragon. Peer beneath the surface, and there is a weak China, one that is in long-term decline and even on the verge of collapse. The symptoms of decay are to be seen everywhere."[11]

Chang's worrisome tone over China's fragility has been picked up in other works, including those of Minxin Pei at the Carnegie Endowment for International Peace and Susan Shirk, a deputy assistant secretary of state responsible for Sino-American relations during the Clinton administration and currently a professor at the University of California at San Diego. The latter has referred to China as a "fragile superpower" due to its volatile internal politics.[12]

At the other end of the spectrum are those who see China as a threat, a powerful country on the way to global dominance, secure in what

Andrew Nathan of Columbia University has called "resilient authoritarianism."[13] Add to this resilient authoritarianism (also called autocracy) a strong dose of nationalism fueled by a sense of historic grievances and thwarted grandeur, and the West has on its hands a powerful country geared for vindication at the very best and revenge at the very worst. As Richard Bernstein and Ross H. Munro wrote of China's rulers in their book *The Coming Conflict With China*, "they believe that an appeal to patriotism, and the existence of a Great Enemy in the world that perpetuates the former imperialist insult to China standing and pride, are a sure way of ensuring loyalty in a population that is otherwise subject to many domestic discontents. Anti-Americanism has become a matter of national dignity."[14]

Echoes of Bernstein and Munro can be heard in Martin Jacques's *When China Rules the World: The End of the Western World and the Rebirth of a New Global Order*. The argument here is more one of historical trends. The West long dominated the global system, and now its time is slipping away. In its place is a more Asia-centric world, with China at the core. While the rise of Asia's other tiger economies—South Korea, Singapore, Taiwan, Thailand, Indonesia, and Malaysia—are significant, China's is substantially more important. Unlike South Korea and Taiwan (and for that matter Japan), China was never a vassal state. Add the elements of size (no one is larger in Asia), historical awareness, and increasing assertiveness, China's rise is much more weighty and has far greater implications. According to Jacques, the West is deceiving itself by thinking that China's path to economic modernity will be accompanied by a gradual democratization. Indeed, China places a much greater emphasis on civilization than does the West, which has over the past several generations been wrestling with multiculturalism and political correctness, both with spillage into foreign policy and economic policy making. All of this has left China on a very different track from other Asian powers such as Japan and India, which are more at ease with the dominant Western international system. How China handles itself—being a citizen of a Western-flavored global system or of recreating a tributary system inherent in dynastic China—will determine the tone of relations with the West. Yet, Jacques's assertion is something that the West should bear in mind: "the underlying argument of the book is that China's impact on the world will be as great as that of the United States over the last century, probably far greater."[15]

Many of the same themes are picked up by Charles Glaser, professor of political science and international affairs and director of the Institute for Security and Conflict Studies at the Elliott School of International Affairs at George Washington University. In a 2011 piece in *Foreign Affairs*, he correctly summarizes the big questions: "Will China's ascent increase the probability of the great-power war? Will an era of U.S. – Chinese tension be as dangerous as the Cold War? Will it be even worse, because China, unlike the Soviet Union, will prove a serious economic competitor as well as a geopolitical one?"[16] The last question really draws in the issues of Asia's convergence with the West and the potential for an evolution of competing alliance systems, something that would not be conducive to international trade and investment. It could also make Taiwan a pivotal point of conflict. Yet, China's internal changes cannot be seen in isolation within the framework of Asian-Western relations.

Even if China is on a different track from the West than are Japan and India, it too is changing. Chinese politics have become slightly more pluralistic and liberal in recent years. The Chinese Communist Party has instituted a number of domestic political reforms, and the system has become more transparent and efficient. The party still remains firmly in control of national affairs, but there is more participation, particularly at local levels of government, than in the past.

The West needs to consider means to deal with China. Professor David Shambaugh of George Washington University suggests a number of ways that the United States might respond to an assertive China.[17] These include discarding its "long-standing paternalistic attitude and missionary illusions" about China. He argues that the United States has been far too condescending for far too long and that this attitude is inappropriate now that China is a major world power. Shambaugh also advocates reducing the U.S. national debt because it gives China too much leverage over U.S. policy making. He calls for increasing the study of the Chinese language in U.S. schools. Finally, he proposes strategies for engaging China in fruitful dialogue on the myriad of issues that now affect both countries.[18]

China's economic relationship with the West, and the United States in particular, is evolving rapidly, and scholars and such practitioners as business people, bankers, and economic policymakers alike are struggling to examine likely future scenarios. One prominent view is that Asia's policy makers would be wise to emphasize consumer-driven growth rather than the traditional export-driven growth that had propelled so many Asian countries to rapid development in the past twenty-five years. Policy makers note that their Asian counterparts should plan for a global rebalancing of demand: faster Asian domestic demand growth and slower growth of exports to outside the region. The converse would be true of the West.[19]

China's interests are inextricably tied to those of the United States as well. Both countries have thrived because of the economic and financial ties that have bound many of their interests together. As noted earlier in this book, China is the holder of vast sums of U.S. Treasuries, and it is the world's largest creditor. This economic tie has increased the stakes for both countries and pushed their complementarily interests. Of course, the United States is in China's debt, but China is also reliant on the United States. It is in Chinese interest for the U.S. economy to succeed and for the dollar to remain strong. In turn, these outcomes would increase the value of China's vast U.S. dollar holdings. There is also a political cost when the value of the U.S. dollar declines. Chinese nationalist feeling runs high when government investments turn sour. Indeed, Chinese SWFs caused a public outcry when they invested too early in U.S. investment banks during the financial crisis.

China's emergence as a world-class power is, of course, having profound effects on economic, political, military, and diplomatic relations with the West. But it is also forcing the West, and the U.S. in particular, to come to terms with the fact that it is no longer quite as dominant as it once was. From 1995 to 2005, the United States could legitimately claim to be the worlds' sole superpower. It is still the world's most powerful nation, but it is less dominant then before. One consequence of this U.S. decline is that Western, and especially U.S. policy makers, need to recognize that there may be alternative strategies for economic development than purely Western-centered ones. China's emergence poses challenges, but it also offers opportunities. The U.S. and Chinese economies are becoming more complementary. But it is in the interest of both powers to promote harmonious political ties as well when appropriate.

There is another point worth stressing—most Asian countries, be they democratic or not, admire U.S. democracy. China's leadership has a very different political system, and it clearly does not believe that the U.S. political model is in any way appropriate for itself for the foreseeable future. But Chinese officials do acknowledge that the United States enjoys a highly advanced, smoothly functioning polity that connects the people to the government in a way that ensures stability. China may not want to emulate the American political system, but it admires it nonetheless for its obvious success. As noted by the scholar William H. Overholt, the United States is the "least distrusted" of the big powers.[20] This attitude leaves the door open to the possibility that more pragmatism exists as a guiding lights for foreign policy in Washington, London, Paris, Beijing, and Tokyo.

No matter which direction China heads, it will demand the attention of the West. A China that stumbles in an economic crisis, now turned political, would be massively disruptive to surrounding countries as well as to the world in general, from Germany and France to Venezuela, the

United States, and Brazil. An aggressively assertive China embarked upon the recreation of a dynastic-like tributary system in Asia would be equally disruptive, especially if various trip wires were hit in Taiwan, Korea, or the Himalayas (vis-à-vis India). This leaves the West with a dilemma of how to accommodate the rising power.

CHINA IS NOT A MONOLITH

Part of the exercise for the West is to understand that China is not a mono-lithic structure. Although there is a "Chinese" foreign policy, the country thus far lacks a grand strategy. It is difficult in the early twenty-first cen-tury to clearly state what China stands for. During the Maoist era, it was a revolutionary state, seeking to spread its version of communism to Asia, Africa, and Latin America. In the Maoist world view, there were three worlds, with the Soviet Union and the United States being Beijing's major external dangers. With the passing of the Soviet Union, China's internal market-oriented economic reforms, and the development of a fulsome trade and investment embrace with the West, words such as "revisionist," "class enemies," and "running dogs of capitalism" have left the official vocabulary. That said, China lacks a well-articulated grand strategy, and there is more than one view of how to deal with the West in the nation.

For its part, China's foreign policy debate takes into consideration both domestic concerns and external threats, much as outlined by the U.S. debate. One school of Chinese thinking posits the United States as the major threat. Wang Fisi, dean of the School of International Studies at Peking University (in Beijing), observes:

> This notion is based on the long-held conviction that the United States, along with other Western powers and Japan, is hostile to China's political values and wants to contain its rise by supporting Taiwan's separation from the mainland. Its proponents also point to U.S. politicians' sympathy for the Dalai Lama and Uighur separatists, continued U.S. arms sales to Taiwan, U.S. military alliances and arrangements supposedly designed to encircle the Chinese mainland, the currency and trade wars waged by U.S. busi-nesses and the U.S. congress, and the West's argument that China should slow down its economic growth in order to help stem climate change.[21]

Those who hold these views believe that China should act in several ways. China should be aggressively creating an alliance with those countries— Iran, North Korea, Russia, Venezuela, and Zimbabwe—that are often at cross-purposes or outwardly hostile to the United States and the West.

Additionally, China's holdings of U.S. Treasuries should be used as leverage against Washington. Finally, China's military should be modernized more rapidly, with a more aggressive stance taken by the navy and air force as well as toward cyber warfare and space development.

Another line of thinking is to follow Deng Xiao-ping's Tao *gang yang hue* (low profile). In many ways this stance was China's approach when it enacted the earlier economic reforms. A welcoming China made an ideal place for foreign investment, something initially needed in terms of both capital and technology transfer. China's profile was relatively low in the 1980s and 1990s, though as the country's economic reforms proved successful rising nationalism made this approach less appealing. Still, China's position was not seen as a major threat, leaving the neighborhood less likely to seek deeper security arrangements with the United States and other Western countries.

When China shifted direction in the late 2010s and adopted a more nationalistic tone in its foreign policy, alarms went off in many other Asian capitals. A number of Asian governments opted to revitalize relations with the Unites States as a hedge to a more aggressive China.

What scenarios then loom for Asian-Western relations? One option is to acquiesce to the creation of a Finlandized Asia, with China at the core. The other option is to create a system of realism-based politics in which various political actors are not wed to ideology and are pragmatic or opportunistic in their policy decisions. The risk in both scenarios is that they can lead to conflict.

A gradual Finlandization of Asia would create a set of relationships that imitate the dominance of the militarily and economically more powerful Soviet Union in the affairs of a smaller and weaker Finland during the Cold War. In return for giving the Soviet Union a large say in Finland's foreign and economic affairs (the Nordic country was not allowed to join the European Union at an earlier stage or NATO), the Finns were generally left alone to govern themselves. Furthermore, the Finns were not forced to be members of the Warsaw Pact like other formal parts of the Soviet Empire. In Asia such a setup would translate into a region more closely aligned to China's national (or civilizational) interests, though still involved in global trade. Part of such a scenario would be the willingness of the West, namely the United States, to retreat from Asian affairs in the hope of appeasing China. In this scenario Taiwan would probably have to be sacrificed, and the U.S. military presence radically scaled back in the region, including in Korea and Japan. This approach would also be based on the view that the cost of standing up to an aggressive China by the West and regional allies is a lost cause.

At this juncture the Finlandization issue is not something that holds wide appeal, neither with the West nor other Asian countries. It may be an overstatement, but still reflects the Asian sentiment that the rise of Asia is seen as exciting, a vindication of vision, hard work, and solid morals that value political order and stability. At the same time, there is unease among other Asian countries with this development if Asia's rise results in it becoming part of a Chinese tributary system. Japan has been on the receiving end of anti-Japanese demonstrations and riots in China several times, and the 2010 island incident with its corresponding rare earth metals embargo did not create goodwill in Tokyo. China's active hand in Burma, the Maldives, and Pakistan has not endeared it to India. China's strong arm reach into the South China Sea has done little to put to rest concerns over Beijing's imperial reach in the Philippines, Indonesia, Vietnam, and Singapore.

The most likely outcome of Asia's rise in global affairs is a greater accommodation of the region's interests in how the global economy is steered through such mechanisms as the G-20 and the United Nations, a challenging prospect considering the often divergent interests and the slowness of such mechanisms to reach policy outcomes. At the same time, the geopolitical game between China and the United States is likely to sharpen, with a corresponding level of alliance building between Washington and key Asian capitals such as Tokyo and New Delhi. Another level of alliance making is also likely to develop between Asian's powers with an eye to limiting Chinese dominance.

The alliance-building dimension of Sino-Western relations was evident in November 2010 when President Barrack Obama visited Asia's democracies—India, Indonesia, South Korea, and Japan. China was conspicuous by its absence on the U.S. president's itinerary. *New York Times* journalist Mark Landler, Jim Yardley, and Michael Wines wrote that "those countries and other neighbors have taken steps, though with varying degrees of candor, to blunt China's assertiveness in the region."[22]

The motivation to keep the United States engaged in Asia comes from different national interest. India is in many ways China's major continental rival. It has already fought one war with China in the 1960s (in which it performed poorly), has ongoing border disputes over parts of the Himalayas, and has differing views over Tibet. India also resents Beijing's growing influence in Pakistan (based on trade, weapons, and the improvement of transportations links), its entrenched position in Burma, and its efforts to extend its reach into the Indian Ocean (regarded as New Delhi's backyard). While China is also an important trade partner for India, it is clearly a geostrategic rival. This rivalry is only enhanced by the stark differences between India's parliamentary political system and China's authoritarianism. The policy offshoot of all of these differences is that India is China's economic and political rival, who is willing to maintain constructive relations but will not be bullied. And in this case size (plus nuclear weapons and a large military) does matter. India has critical depth and is increasingly willing to use it to carve out its own sphere of influence and create its own alliances.

For the United States, India's significance as both an ally and trade partner was reflected by its growing importance during the presidencies of Bill Clinton and George W. Bush. President Obama furthered the relationship with his 2010 visit. The U.S.-Indian summit revolved around security issues, business opportunities, and the agreement to create a $10-billion infrastructure debt fund.

THE OTHER ASIAN-WESTERN CONUNDRUM

While China's economic and military rise represents a major challenge to the West, Pakistan and Afghanistan represent another type of challenge, one that is constructed around international terrorism, political instability, and nuclear weapons. In this regard, Asia's rise carries with it considerable historical baggage in the form of ethnic and religious tensions, border disputes, and dysfunctional political development. The long conflict in Afghanistan, which commenced in 1979 with the Soviet invasion, led to massive war damage in Pakistan's northern neighbor, a sizeable refugee population, and deep ties between various Afghan groups and Pakistan's military intelligence, the Inter-Services Intelligence (ISI). The Russians left Afghanistan in 1989, but the ensuing civil wars eventually led to the rise of the Taliban, who established a brutally repressive regime based on a very narrow definition of radical Islam.

Under the Taliban strict Sharia law was enforced, with men made to grow beards, with music and dancing prohibited, and with religious minorities persecuted. Additionally, women's schools were closed, education for girls ended, and women were not allowed outside of the house unless in the company of a male family member and dressed in a head-to-toe berka. The Taliban's radical interpretation of Islam made it few friends, with the only three governments recognizing it, those being Pakistan, Saudi Arabia, and the United Arab Emirates. In time the Taliban provided bases for al-Qaeda, which in 2001 launched the 9/11 attacks against the United States. The U.S. response was relatively rapid, resulting in the toppling of the Taliban and the hunting down of al-Qaeda in Afghanistan. It also put U.S.-Pakistan relations under considerable pressure as Washington forced the regime of General Perez Musharaff to either align with the West or the Taliban and al-Qaeda. Musharaff aligned his country with the United States.

The U.S.-led invasion of Afghanistan and the subsequent NATO occupation did not end the South Asian country's troubles. Afghanistan represents one of the most significant foreign policy challenges in Asia in the early twenty-first century. Pakistani journalist Zahid Hussain writes, "What was started as a fight to overthrow the Taliban and hunt down al-Qaeda forces has escalated into a wider regional conflict with Afghanistan now the center of a new Great Game and Pakistan, India, and Iran vying for influence."[23] Why has this situation evolved? First, Afghanistan's borders are porous, and the peoples who inhabit the landlocked country have sizeable communities in Pakistan and to a lesser extent in Tajikistan, Uzbekistan, and Turkmenistan. But it is the overlapping nature of the Pashtun communities along both sides of the Afghanistan-Pakistan border that complicates matters. There are 13 million Pashtuns living in Pakistan and roughly the same in Afghanistan. A long-standing tradition of a low federal profile in the Pakistani border area, namely the Federally Administered Tribal Area (FATA), has made it very easy for Pakistan to serve as a safe haven for Afghan Taliban and al-Qaeda forces that were earlier forced from Afghanistan.

Second, some elements of the Pakistani government have demonstrated a degree of tolerance for its own homegrown radical Islamic groups and indeed a number of analysts point to ISI involvement in supporting them. Additionally, many of the ISI's officers have ethnic and cultural ties to Afghan insurgents and sympathize with them. Added to these factors is a reluctance on part of the Pakistani military to stir up the tribal forces due to the rugged nature of the very mountainous terrain and a long history of violence in the FATA; the result is a security situation that has slipped inside Pakistan. This slippage is revealed by the development of an aggressive local Taliban, capable and willing to conduct high-level terrorist attacks against the military. The Pakistani military has engaged in a number of campaigns against Islamic militants, suffered casualties in those actions, and been the victim of a large number of deadly terrorist attacks.

Third, Afghanistan retains a high level of geopolitical significance. For Pakistan a pro-Islamabad Afghan government (as it had with the Taliban) provides security in the north, allowing it to focus more fully on its main rival, India. It is thought by some analysts that the ISI continues to support the Taliban as it believes that group's leadership are a strategic asset, a reliable backup force in case things go bad in Afghanistan.[24]

Four, Afghanistan looms large because of the U.S. policy of using drones to conduct aerial attacks on Taliban and al-Qaeda forces across the border that has stirred deep anti-U.S. sentiment in Pakistan. While the drones have killed a number of Taliban and al-Qaeda leaders, they have also inadvertently claimed the lives of women and children. These latter deaths have caused a backlash against Pakistan's government and military. As a consequence, U.S.-Pakistani relations have run hot and cold over the period following 9/11, greatly complicating security policies vis-à-vis Afghanistan and al-Qaeda. The tone of U.S.-Pakistan-Afghan relations is not helped by occasional reports that Osama bin Laden and top leaders of the Afghan Taliban (like Mullah Omar) are alive and well in the FATA.

The engagement of the United States and the West in Afghanistan is not producing the desired result of creating a stable, economically viable state. Instead, Afghanistan remains a country torn by personal, ethnic-religious, and regional rivalries, which are overlaid by transnational criminal influences and the ongoing role of intelligence agencies of Pakistan, India, and Iran. The U.S.-NATO occupation force, part of whose role is to reconstruct the country, faces considerable challenges.

The war in Afghanistan has lapped over into the India-China-Pakistan triangle. India has its own set strategic considerations that undermine any sustained warming of relations with China. Having an ally in Afghanistan helps India's strategic goals of denying Pakistan a strategic advantage and, India hopes, stretching its rival's resources to the point that it cannot sustain greater involvement in backing militants in Kashmir or in supporting terrorist attacks on India soil. At the same time, India's Afghan policy gives it an ally in a neighborhood feeling the pressure of Chinese power. Brahma Chellaney, an Indian foreign policy expert, notes that "for India, the potential emergence of a superpower on its northern border, the built up Pakistan as a military counterweight with transfers of nuclear-weapons and missile technologies and continues to hold captured Indian territories (including almost one-fifth of the original state of Jammu and Kashmir), is hardly a comforting thought."[25] China also continues to claim more Indian territories, something that weighs heavily in New Delhi. This leave's Asia's two largest countries without a fully defined border. The situation forces India to keep a substantial number of troops along the border, reducing its strategic reserve for Pakistan. All of these concerns contributes to India's greater interest in developing closer links to the United States and Japan, something that in turn worries a China anxious about containment.

The issues front and center over Pakistan and Afghanistan are key to the security of Central Asia, South Asia, and the Middle East. While

Afghanistan has been of ongoing concern, Pakistan represents a far more radical situation. What happens if radical Islamic forces take control? What would such forces do with control of a nuclear weapon? Does Pakistan fragment into a number of smaller states, based more on ethnic or tribal allegiances?

ASIA AS A CHANGING GEOPOLITICAL CHESSBOARD

Asia in the early twenty-first century represents a major political and economic challenge to the West. The challenges include how to accommodate a rising China (as well as a rising region), with the related issues of Taiwan, Chinese economic clout, and Chinese expansion of naval power into the Indian Ocean; what to do about North Korea, with its nuclear threat and the issue of reunification of the Korean peninsula; and how to deal with the strategic triangle of Pakistan, Afghanistan, and India. Beyond that are a plethora of other challenges: high seas piracy, the drug trade, human trafficking, and environmental damage. All of these present a menu of items that the West must consider in dealing with a region that is more self-assured because of economic success.

Certainly the changing nature of power in Asia is of deep concern in Berlin, Washington, and London. Like it or not, the West and Asia have become highly interdependent. Trade and commerce have bound them together, clearly evident in the dynamic of Sino-American and Japanese-European relations. The challenge ahead is to manage a changing geostrategic chessboard that reflects a more multipolar world, where the United States may still be the indispensible nation, although not as indispensible as it once was. Any time such changes are made, the path is filled with uncertainties and potential flashpoints. The road ahead will be one of changing national interests and alliances, especially as the West is likely to be less unified in approaching security issues. Germany's decision to be aloof from the Libyan intervention led by the United States, the United Kingdom, and France in 2011 is a case in point. Dealing with Iran and North Korea or reacting to a new India-Pakistani War might lead to other cases of policy divisions among the Western powers. What would Germany do if China invaded Taiwan and U.S. and Japanese forces entered the battle?

The potential scenarios that loom for the West and Asia are substantial and the potential flashpoints numerous. The challenge is to maintain an ongoing dialogue in a number of forums, often easier said than done. Related to this problem is the high level of interdependence between the two regions, especially in the extensive land mass that is Eurasia. All of these challenges point to the need to lessen tensions over key issues, including the West's pressing need to clean up its fiscal messes:. Europe's problematic peripheral economies (Greece, Portugal, Ireland, and Spain) and the United States (with its large fiscal deficits) Considering the difficult nature of deleveraging in the West, the strong reserve positions of Asia and the region's ability to maintain strong economic growth and divergence in economic policies are factors that will dominate dialogue in the years ahead. Other factors, such as the fate of Afghanistan and Pakistan and how to accommodate a rising China and India, make the future of Western-Asian relations challenging.

CONCLUSION

Conditions in Afghanistan and Pakistan will continue to be of major concern to both local players as well as to the West. Heavily engaged in Afghanistan, the West is also deeply involved in Pakistan as the Afghan conflict easily laps over borders. When NATO scales back, which is being signaled by the Obama administration, political insecurity in Afghanistan is likely, and the return of the Taliban cannot be ruled out. Pakistan, already in the throes of a civil war between secular and radical Islamic forces, runs the risk of further instability and of the Pakistani Taliban making greater inroads. The West could well face a nuclear-armed, Taliban-controlled Pakistan.

The West has a considerable amount at stake in how it manages growing Asian power in the twenty-first century. The range of issues touches upon trade and investment practices, security concerns, and intercultural relations. It touches upon the rise of China as Asia's most significant power; how other Asian countries, in particular, Japan and India, handle the rise of China; and how to balance the needs of the global economy with China's national interests. The rise of Asian power also mirrors the relative decline of the West and the diminishing ability of the United States to dominate outcomes. The days of unilateralism—short lived though they were—are gone. A new multipolar world is forming that does not so easily take its cue from the West. Multipolar systems are inherently more difficult to control, and political stability is not necessary the most likely outcome. At the same time, Western power is not eclipsed, only diminished, something that Asia's rising powers must take into consideration. The world is left with the likelihood of an extended period of major power jostling as new alliances are formed and relationships are tested against more openly expressed national interests, which in some cases will be less supportive of globalization, open markets, and private enterprise.

Chapter 9

CONCLUSION

> If anything, the emergent Asia is showing that economic strength cannot by
> itself be the new international currency of power.
> —Brahma Chellaney, *Asian Juggernaut*

The reintegration of China and India into the global economy, the continued dynamism of Southeast Asian economies, South Korea's ability to maintain a strong economy despite the danger posed by North Korea, and the massive accumulation of foreign exchange reserves by China, Japan, Hong Kong, and Taiwan represent a changing international political economy that clearly indicates that Asia matters now more than it has in several centuries. The ascendancy of China and India, in particular, have ramifications for the structure of international relations, especially as they represent contrasting (some would argue competitive) development models beyond what the West has to offer. For more established powers—the United States, Japan, Europe, and Russia—China and India have growing significance on the geopolitical chessboard, and this significance is forcing a recalculation of friends and foes and national interests. At the same time, globalization in both the political and economic sense is having a profound impact on Asian societies, ranging from Pakistan and India to North Korea and Burma. Thus, Asia may be changing the world, but the world is also changing Asia.

But these changes are not without consequences. As Samuel P. Huntington noted in 1968 in his *Political Order in Changing Societies*, the process of modernization is disruptive. While the term modernization is infrequently used as it implies Western cultural superiority (in equating modernization to Westernization), the word globalization could be substituted. Although globalization also has a tendency to be associated with Americanization (considering that country's sometimes overwhelming mass-oriented, consumer-driven culture), Asia's transformation into a very significant part of the international economic system means globalization is less and less a strictly Western and U.S. trend. As Chinese and Indian multinationals become major players in key commodity markets, industrial sectors, and high tech, their actions create ripples in local societies; in the past, Western transnational corporations dominated these sectors. And it is important to underscore that they are joining the ranks of earlier Asian trailblazers from South Korea, Hong Kong, Singapore, Taiwan, and Japan.

LESSONS LEARNED

What lessons have been learned through the course of this book? First, Asia is on the rise, but there are serious problems that can constrain the trajectory and slow the process of economic convergence with the West. Some of these problems are political in nature, and some economic as with environmental impact of industry and the role of the state in the economy. There remains a vast disparity between countries such as Japan, Singapore, and South Korea on one side and Pakistan, Nepal, and Laos on the other. Serious border disputes linger as well, making prospects for greater economic integration more challenging, especially in relation to the other two major blocs that have achieved a more cohesive dimension: the European Union and the North American Free Trade Area.

Second, the primary problems facing Asia are increasingly political in nature. In some ways the economic challenges are the easy part; the hardest challenge is how to create long-term affluent societies that are able to enjoy the fruits of their labors. Related to this problem is how to create civil societies capable of dealing with public frustrations over often slow government policies pertaining to corruption, the environment, disease control, nuclear safety, and basic law and order.

Third, Asia's rise did not occur in a vacuum; the gains made by countries such as China and India were complementary to the development of other emerging market countries, in particular the BRICs and Turkey, Indonesia, Colombia, and South Africa. The more pronounced linkages between Asian countries and countries in Latin America and Africa reflect a major change in the global economy and new power alignments, some of which de-emphasize the role of the West.

Four, China has emerged as Asia's next powerful state, a status reflected by its massive foreign exchange reserves, the size and scope of its economy (the world's second largest in 2011), and increasingly its more sophisticated military. Despite China's status, its dominance as a regional and world player is not assured. The country faces multiple challenges, some of which could set the country back severely if not properly managed. Moreover, China's sometimes aggressive stance and success has made other countries more wary and led some to cautiously develop alliance in order to contain Beijing's rising power.

Five, although the West did itself serious damage in 2008–10, with first a homegrown financial crisis, followed by a sovereign debt crisis, it is not finished. Despite substantial economic problems, the West is still more affluent than Asia. U.S. demographics are in better shape than much of Asia's, especially when compared to China, South Korea, and Japan. Moreover, it was the West that moved to do something in Libya in 2011, while China and India carefully abstained from the United Nations vote to establish a no-fly zone and therefore prevent a massacre of the population in opposition zones. Furthermore, the West still has a large role to play in Asia—from the NATO operation in Afghanistan to strategic relationships with Japan, India, and South Korea (where the United States still has troops).

Six, Asia will remain central to any major business in the United States and the West. Despite different views on issues, both Asia and the West have much more to gain from trade and investment than from war. This mutual profit holds promise for the future course of relations between the two regions and their people.

And finally, ignorance of the outside world is not bliss for anyone growing up in the twenty-first century. With the high degree of globalization evident in daily life, touching upon everything from the cars people drive to employment prospects at an Indian-owned company for a citizen of the United States, knowledge of developments elsewhere is critical to life choices.

COOPERATION, CO-OPTATION, AND CONFRONTATION

In light of the points above, large questions loom as to the future. Although predicting the future is always difficult, there are three potential scenarios. Cooperation is the most likely and would be the most beneficial for the further development of trade and investment. Co-optation is a poor second option, while confrontation would not benefit anyone over the long run.

Asia's push to economic convergence with the West will gain further momentum. At the same time, the pressures stemming from economic development are only going to increase and put governmental and social institutions under greater stress. That stress will come from ongoing urbanization, heavy demand for such resources as potable water, and environmental pollution. Global warming (or climate change) is also going to result in the flooding of coastal areas (a severe problem for a country like Bangladesh), desertification (serious for Inner Mongolia), and drought (of concern to China and India). One potential future is an Asia reeling under all of these problems, weak central governments unable to cope with rising crime amid warlordism, and large parts of countries such as China and India becoming terra incognita, places where no one wishes to travel and only does so at great personal risk. Parts of Pakistan and Afghanistan already are dangerous zones even for those who are born there. This grim scenario would also include large migrations of people from their homelands and active terrorist campaigns launched for a host of reasons. The great dynamic burst of industrial might in the second half of the twentieth and early twenty-first centuries would be a distant memory as machinery rusts in looted factories and the former great harbors once clogged with ships are largely empty except for a few fishing boats. In this scenario a new dark ages has descended because problems that needed to be solved were left to fester so that finally they overcame governments and social institutions. The rule of the land has become war, disease, and lawlessness.

Cooperation

However, the future does not have to be a grim place. In terms of cooperation, Asian countries can decide to work more closely to resolve the problems facing the region. Cooperation means a greater use of regional institutions such as ASEAN, free trade agreements, and the Asian Development Bank. It would also translate into a closer working relationship between Japan and China as well as between these two countries and India. One variation of this is ASEAN Plus Three (APT), the three being China, Japan, and South Korea (but not India). Economic cooperation could be extended into joint development of areas of the waterways between countries that are subject to overlapping claims.

Central to cooperation would be an accepted balance of power among the key countries including the United States and its allies, Japan, and increasingly India, vis-à-vis China. This would be a more multipolar world, more akin to the system of alliances and counteralliances that marked Bismarck's Europe in the late nineteenth century.

Along these lines, the United States would have to give more credence to China as a world power and rely more on diplomacy to achieve national interests. At the same time, China would have to be less strident in developing cozy relationships with U.S. enemies, and it would also have to practice more diplomatic prudence about dealing with unsavory regimes in possession of badly desired resources as in Africa. There could also be a more productive relationship between the two countries in terms of securing food supply, something that China is sensitive about after the rice shortages that hit Asia in 2008.

Cooperation would also provide a smoother support system for China when its population dynamic shifts. In many respects, China is in a rush to achieve a higher standard of living before its population becomes old. According to a report by the multinational bank, HSBC, Americans have a fertility rate of 2.1, high enough to shield them from the sort of demographic collapse looming in parts of Asia, including China. Beijing and Shanghai are 1.0, South Korea is 1.1, and Singapore 1.2.[1] China's work force, essential to the current economic sprint to convergence with the West, is expected to reach a tipping point in the mid-2020s. This date provides time to make key decisions (such as fully scrapping the one-child policy), and a benign international environment and a working system of economic cooperation between Asia and the West would benefit all in this matter. Such cooperation would offer the opportunity to learn from other countries, especially from European nations that are also facing substantial problems with graying populations.

Co-optation

The second scenario involves co-optation and envisions an Asia that has surrendered to the dominance of China. In this scenario the Middle Kingdom has returned, and the rest of the world sits at its feet—or at least an Asia that has agreed to become Beijing's vassal (much in the manner described as Finlandization in chapter 8). This world would be marked by the end of the U.S.-South Korean military alliance, some form of Korean reunification (with China having considerable influence over the combined state), the withdrawal of U.S. troops from everywhere except Japan, and a marked increase in China's political and military reach, including into the Indian Ocean and the Persian Gulf. This projection of Chinese power would be augmented by formal alliances with Iran and long-time ally Pakistan. China would either cooperate with most Asian countries that fell into its sphere of influence, or it would be hostile to those that did not, most probably to Japan and India, especially if U.S. power continues to erode.

Co-optation would lead to a new Cold War, encompassing the bulk of the world's population. It would present an almost Orwellian landscape of the world divided into three superstates: Oceania (the Americas,

Australia, South Africa, and the United Kingdom), Eurasia (the Soviet Union and Europe), and Eastasia (China, Japan, and part of India). The remaining parts of the world would be a battle zone for the competing superstates.

Although this Orwellian scenario is extreme, a somewhat looser form of large coalitions could form (and reform), much like the European power system did throughout much of the nineteenth century. Some of these European coalitions eventually collided, setting the stage for long and deadly conflicts. Such conflicts would also spell an end to economic globalization as the tendency would be to curtail trade and investment and instead promote national agendas of protectionism, fierce competition over global resources (as in Africa and Latin America), and greater regional self-sufficiency.

Confrontation

The last scenario is outright confrontation between China on one side and the United States and Japan on the other, possibly over an attempt by Beijing to take control of Taiwan. Confrontation could also come between India and Pakistan and result in the use of nuclear weapons. And the radical Islamic factor would certainly find fruitful territory to spread, possibly opening the door to the creation of new hard-line theocracies. These hard-line Islamic regimes would complicate efforts for trade cooperation and open borders. Moreover, nuclear weapons have proliferated, adding one more factor to potential destruction. With confrontation both political and economic globalization would be over, or, at the very least, considerably reduced in size and scope.

The confrontation scenario ultimately is what would happen if the Cold War under the co-optation scenario turned hot. While confrontation seems farfetched, both U.S. and Chinese war gaming includes conflict between the two countries. Taiwan, in particular, remains a point of contention, and U.S. and Chinese interests are often at odds in parts of Africa, Latin America, and the Middle East.

Confrontation could also occur if Pakistan and India came to blows over such items as Islamabad's support of terrorist attacks in India, over the disputed Kashmir area, or over maintaining influence in Afghanistan in the aftermath of a U.S. withdrawal. Pakistan has a very heavy strategic focus on what happens in its northern neighbor. If a pro-Pakistan government comes to power in Afghanistan, Pakistan grains strategically in its rivalry with India. However, if the Afghan government continues to be pro-Indian, as is the current Karzai administration, which leans heavily toward a New Delhi active in development projects, Islamabad will have to protect its north because it feels squeezed by Indian and pro-Indian forces. Since both Pakistan and India have nuclear weapons, any threat of a major war immediately draws in other countries, including the United States and China. A new India-Pakistan war could be very deadly with no winners.

In January 2007 historian Niall Ferguson warned that it took only one act of terrorism in 1914 to cripple the world's financial markets. He noted that the world at that time was flush with liquidity due in large part to global integration and financial innovation (very much like the early 2000s). Inflation was tamed, and emerging markets were booming. A highly globalized world was poised to have another good year. On June 28 the assassination of Archduke Franz Ferdinand shattered the old world and quickly took Europe into a major conflict. As for the financial side, "the financial crisis happened even faster. Within days of the Austrian ultimatum, the delicate web of international credit was torn to pieces."[2]

Ferguson's point is that this scenario could play out again. Imagine if a visiting U.S. vice president travels to Baghdad and is assassinated. An angry United States believes the act was carried out by Iran. An ultimatum is sent to Tehran, which looks to Russia and China for support. The clock is running, and the countdown to a major war has begun. Along the same lines, how do China, India, and Japan respond to a nuclear conflict started by Iran? Or how would the West and India respond to the rise of a Taliban-like regime in Pakistan, armed with nuclear weapons? How would the powers respond to the implosion of the North Korean government or the launching of a nuclear attack by North Korea on South Korea or Japan? Taiwan also figures large under these scenarios as it draws the United States into conflict with China. All of these possibilities represent potential flashpoints for war.

Considering the wide-ranging nature of change involved in globalization and the related rise of Asia, a major reassessment of how the West, in particular the United States, responds is critical. The nature of Asia's growing power and assertiveness requires that the United States reconsider some of its weaker policy choices that have fostered an overwhelming dependence on the consumer and on spending. The culture of the shopping mall needs to be replaced by policies that promote education, savings, and better management of infrastructure. As younger generations become captives to computer screens and a manufactured Hollywood culture, essential infrastructure is falling into disrepair, savings levels are running negative, and the number of math and science students has fallen. Looking into the future, the United States and other Western powers have to give serious thought as to what kind of world they want to live in. Failure of the United States to address these issues in the wake of a converging Asia sets the stage for a U.S. decline that will be traumatic for North Americans as well as the rest of the world.

One of the essential messages of the rise of Asia, therefore, is that to remain competitive, the United States needs to change. As Robyn Meredith of *Forbes* states, "Let the rise of India and China be a catalyst to reestablish America's competitiveness. Let it be this generation's space race. If inward-facing India and communist China can transform themselves and face the world, so can the United States of America."[3] The adjustments that are required are going to be painful and protracted, and demand a much different way of looking at how to compete. They also entail a scaling down of aspirations—no more living beyond one's means and putting time horizons beyond the end of the next business quarter.

CONCLUSION

Asia's rise comes at a time when the international order will remain volatile, buffeted by the crosscurrents of further globalization of the financial, labor, production, and consumer markets on one side and by a profound and sometimes violent quest to maintain cultural identity on the other as well as in some cases a need to fight the loss of jobs or to bridge growing income disparities. This push-pull aspect of economic development clearly has disruptive elements as Asian countries seek to establish some type of working regional order for the long-term. Critical to this search is finding a more sound equilibrium between economic and political development. Along these lines, Asia's rise, largely pushed along by economic advances, runs the risk of being sidetracked by political challenges created by internal and external forces. Asia's rise will continue to have a limited upside if some of these political issues, such as how to create a stable and prosperous Pakistan or how to further open Chinese society in an orderly fashion in order to address long-standing grievances, are not addressed. Greater economic wealth in Asia will not convert into a stable future if the heavy lifting of political development is avoided.

Asia will increasingly have greater influence in the still-nascent and fluid post-Cold War world. This influence becomes all the more critical as whatever forces are guiding the global economy will be in more hands, including a growing contingent from Asia, be it from Beijing, Tokyo, or New Delhi. A stronger guiding influence will also come the emergence of civil societies throughout Asia, be they under the roof of authoritarian capitalism or democratic capitalism. At the end of the day, issues such as the environment, a better life for one's children, and comfort in old age face everyone, providing a commonality of concerns no matter the political system. The major challenge is how to manage these needs as they cross over borders and affect one's neighbors in a shrinking world system. Asia is carving out a larger role in that process, mirroring its growing power. The early twenty-first century is proving to be a major testing ground for this newfound power, with such diverse issues as Europe's sovereign debt crisis, the Middle East and North Africa's political spring (2010–11), and Japan's earthquake, tsunami, and nuclear disaster (2011) representing only the tip of geopolitical and economic iceberg. The process is not going to be easy, and the Asian commitment to fining order and stability in the twenty-first century will be strongly tested.

NOTES

PREFACE

1. Kishore Mahbubani, "America's Place in the Asian Century," *Current History*, May 2008, 195.

CHAPTER 1: INTRODUCTION

1. *Annual Report 2007* (Paris: World Trade Organization, 2007), 38.

2. Morton Abramowitz and Stephen Bosworth, "America Confronts the Asian Century," *Current History*, April 2006, 147. The authors observe of the rise of Asia that its "companies are serious, often dominant players in virtually every industry. East Asian brands are now global brands. Commodity markets are shaking from the repercussions of East Asia's growth and its escalating demand for energy, steel, aluminum, lumber, and countless other resources."

3. Martin Walker, "Globalization 3.0," *Wilson Quarterly*, Autumn 2007, 19.

4. Dominique Strauss-Kahn, "2010—A Year of Transformation for the World and for Asia," paper, International Monetary Fund, Asian Financial Forum, Hong Kong, January 20, 2010, 1.

5. Stewart Gordon, *When Asia Was the World: Traveling Merchants, Scholars, Warriors and Monks Who Created the "Riches of the East"* (Philadelphia: Da Capo Press, 2008), 188.

6. Angus Maddison, *The World Economy: A Millennial Perspective* (London: Palgrave Macmillan, 2001), 85.

7. Kenneth Pomeranz, *The Great Divergence: China, Europe and the Making of the Modern World Economy* (Princeton: Princeton University Press, 2000), 4.

8. Robert W. Fogel, "Capitalism and Democracy in 2040: Forecasts and Speculations," National Bureau of Economic Research, NBER Working Paper, no. 13184, June 2007, i.

9. Michiyo Nakamoto, "Displacement Activity," *Financial Times*, August 23, 2010.

10. Richard Portes, "Sovereign Wealth Funds," *Vox*, October 17, 2007. http://www.voxeu.org/index.php?q=node/636.

11. "A Chinese Wind-Power IPO, Puffed Up," *Economist*, December 5, 2009.

12. Naill Fergusson, *The War of the World* (New York: Penguin 2006), xli. Some of the same ideas were earlier articulated by political scientist Samuel P. Huntington in his seminal *Political Order in Changing Societies* (1969). Although there is far less emphasis on the war dimension, Huntington's thesis is that the process of development (i.e., the introduction of change into society) is not necessarily stabilizing, but rather it often causes political instability. Huntington argues that the brunt of change hits a country's political and social institutions. New demands are made on these institutions, which often struggle to accommodate. However, some institutions are unable to change and are afflicted by political decay. Consequently, a gap occurs between institutional ability to respond and accommodate to change and public aspirations. When this gap occurs in an acute fashion, political instability in the form of coups, civil unrest, and civil conflict become manifest.

13. Azar Gat, "The Return of Authoritarian Great Powers," *Foreign Affairs*, July/August 2007, 60. There is an extensive literature pertaining to authoritarianism. See the classic works of Philippe Schmitter and Guillermo O'Donnell, *Transitions from Authoritarian Rule: Tentative Conclusions about Uncertain Democracy* (Baltimore: Johns Hopkins University Press, 1986); Guillermo O'Donnell, *Modernization and Bureaucratic-Authoritarianism: Studies in South American Politics* (Berkeley: University of California Press, 1973); and Juan Linz and Alfred Stepan, eds., *Breakdown of Democratic Regimes: Latin America* (Baltimore: Johns Hopkins University Press, 1978). Also see Marsha Pripstein Posusney and Michele Penner Angrist, eds., *Authoritarianism in the Middle East: Regimes and Resistance* (Boulder: Lynne Reinner, 2005); Hisham Sharabi, *Neopatriarchy* (Oxford: Oxford University Press, 1988); Daniel Pipes, *In the Path of God: Islam and Political Power* (New York: Basic Books, 1983); and Stephen J. King, "Sustaining Authoritarianism in the Middle East and North Africa," *Political Science Quarterly* 122, no. 3 (Fall, 2007): 433–59.

14. Fareed Zakaria, "The Rise of Illiberal Democracy," *Foreign Affairs*, November/December 1997, 34.

15. Those alternative political arrangements encompass elements of what have been referred to as "corporatism" and "technocracy." Corporatism represents a particular pattern of relationships between the state and civil society that is the product of a long-standing traditional view that the state should play the central role in mediating among competing groups and interests in society. For a historical account of the corporate tradition, see Howard J. Wiarda, "Corporatism and

Development in the Iberic-Latin World: Persistent Strains and New Variations," *Review of Politics* 36 (January 1974): 12–24. The rest of society, and in some cases the economy, is guided by the bureaucratic center. Added to this is the element of technocracy that incorporates the recognition of the need to cope with the larger questions of development, conflict, and change from a technical and/or scientific perspective. Elements of this are evident in China, Singapore, and Thailand. For more on this subject, see Jorge I. Tapia-Videla, "Understanding Organizations and Environments: A Comparative Perspective," *Public Administrations Review* 36, no. 6 (1976): 63.

16. Alan S. Blinder, "Fear of Offshoring," Working Papers 83, Center for Economic Policy Studies, Department of Economics, Princeton University, 2005, http://ideas.repec.org/e/pbl41.html.

17. Ibid.

18. "Jasmine Stirrings in China: No Awakening, But Crush It Anyway," *Economist*, March 5, 2011.

19. See Danile Deudney and G. John Ikenberry, "The Myth of the Autocratic Revival," *Foreign Affairs*, January/February 2009, 78.

20. Roger C. Altman, "The Great Crash, 2008," *Foreign Policy*, January/February 2009, 2–3.

CHAPTER 2: THE GREAT DIVERGENCE

1. For a more comprehensive view of the sweep of Asian history, see John Fairbank, Edwin Reischauer, and Albert Craig, *East Asia: Tradition and Transformation*, rev. ed. (Florence, KY: Wadsworth Publishing, 1989), and Rhoads Murphey, *East Asia: A New History*, 5th ed (New York: Longman, 2009).

2. Kenneth Pomeranz, *The Great Divergence: China, Europe, and the Making of the Modern World Economy* (Princeton: Princeton University Press, 2000), 4. Also see Scott B. MacDonald and Albert L. Gastmann, *A History of Credit and Power in the Western World* (Rutgers, NJ: Transaction Press, 2000).

3. As historian K.N. Chaudhuri notes, "The recurrent rise and fall of political empires and dynasties in Asian history must be seen alongside the assimilative power of Islam, Hinduism, and Confucian ethnics to restructure the volatile forces present in the state system into conditions of steady state. Their failure in the late eighteenth century to assimilate European militarism and separate civilizational identity also marked the end of a life cycle." *Asia Before Europe: Economy and Civilization of the Indian Ocean from the Rise of Islam to 1750* (Cambridge: Cambridge University Press, 1990), 41.

4. For an excellent summary of the Portuguese and the pepper trade, see Anthony Disney, *Twilight of the Pepper Empire: Portuguese Trade in Southwest India in the Seventeenth Century* (Cambridge: Cambridge University Press, 1978).

5. Percival Spear, *A History of India*, volume 2, *From Sixteenth Century to the Twentieth Century* (New York: Penguin, 1990), 69.

6. John Micklethwaith and Adrian Wooldridge, *The Company: A Short History of a Revolutionary Idea* (New York: Modern Library, 2003). As Micklethwait and Wooldridge note in their history of the company, "The East India Company was more than just a modern company in embryo. 'The greatest society of merchants in the Universe' possessed an army, ruled a vast tract of the world, created one of the world's greatest civil services, built much of London's docklands, and even provided comfortable perches for the likes of James Mill and Thomas Love Peacock" (21).

7. Bamber Gascoigne, *A Brief History of The Great Moghuls* (London: Constable & Robinson, 2002), 243. Also see John F. Richards, *The Mughal Empire* (New York: Cambridge University Press, 1993), 281.

8. Plessey must also be seen in a broader context. It was one battle of many in the Seven Years War, which spanned the globe. That conflict was concluded at the Treaty of Paris in 1763 and marked an important turning point in the fortunes of Asia and Europe. At least in the minds of the Europeans, Asia was part of the global economy and increasingly was up for grabs. For many Indians, Chinese, and Indonesians, the Treaty of Paris really did not involve them, only the pesky Europeans who increasingly showed up in their waters and were beginning to interfere in local affairs.

9. Philip Richardson, *Economic Change in China, c1800–1950* (New York: Cambridge University Press, 1999), 16.

10. G. B. Sansom, *The Western World and Japan* (New York: Vintage Books, 1949), 7.

11. Immanuel C.Y. Hsu, *The Rise of Modern China* (New York: Oxford University Press, 1975), 243. According to Hsu, "this treaty was imposed upon the vanquished at gunpoint, with the careful deliberation usually accompanying international agreements in Europe and America. A most ironic point was that opium, the immediate cause of the war, was not even mentioned—the question of its future status cautiously avoided by both sides."

12. Jane Jacobs writes that "China's wrong turning, capricious though it was, carried the double blow of surrender of its technological lead and simultaneous retreat into a fortress mentality." *Dark Age Ahead* (Toronto: Vintage Canada, 2005), 18.

13. See Yoshiie Yoda, *The Foundations of Japan's Modernization: A Comparison with China's Path Towards Modernization* (Amsterdam: Brill, 1995).

14. W. J. Macpherson, *The Economic Development of Japan 1868–1941* (New York: Cambridge University Press, 1995), 17.

15. Ian Buruma, *Inventing Japan 1853–1964* (New York: Random House, 2003), 20.

16. R. L. Sims, *Japanese Political History since the Meiji Renovation 1868–2000* (London: Hurst & Company, 2001), 288.

17. Ranbir Vohra, *The Making of India: A Historical Survey* (Armonk, NY: Sharpe, 2001), 205.

18. As two World Bank economists wrote, "Nehru was a Kashmiri Brahmin and was also a Fabian socialist with Marxist sympathies who had suffered an

upper-class English education. All of these go with a distrust of business, and some of them at least with ignorance of the allocational role of the price mechanism, admiration for Russian planning, and genuine concern for the poor." Vijay Joshi and I.M.D. Little, *India: Macroeconomics and Political Economy 1964–1991* (Washington, D.C.: World Bank, 1994), 8.

19. Vohra, *The Making of India*, 203.

20. The Philippines was by far the most advanced of the first group, but it had gone through the trauma of the fall of the Marcos dictatorship and a period of democratic consolidation before the authorities could fully concentrate on economic reform. Of the last two waves, China was by far the most significant newcomer, considering its large billion plus population and geostrategic position. China went from being an inward-looking and heavily agriculturally oriented economy in the 1970s to the manufacturing workshop of the world by the early 1990s, with its share of world trade quadrupling from the prereform period. As Nicholas D. Kristof and Sheryl WuDunn stated in 1994: "If China can hold its course, it will produce the greatest economic miracle in recorded history. Never before has such a large proportion of humanity risen from poverty so rapidly. Studies that measure the size of an economy in terms of purchasing power indicate that China's economy is already the third largest in the world, after those of the United States and Japan. At present rates, the Chinese economy will surpass America's within a few decades to become the biggest in the world." Nicholas D. Kristof and Sheryl WuDunn, *China Awakes: The Struggle for the Soul of a Rising Power* (New York Vintage Books, 1994), 14–15.

CHAPTER 3: THE RISE OF CHINA

1. For more information on Deng Xiao-ping, see Harrison Salisbury, *The New Emperors: China in the Era of Mao and Deng* (New York: Harper Perennial, 1993); Richard Baum, *Burying Mao: Chinese Politics in the Age of Deng Xiaoping* (Princeton: Princeton University Press, 1996); Rodcrick MacFarquhar, ed., *The Politics of China: The Era of Mao and Deng* (New York: Cambridge University Press, 1997); Michael E. Marti, *China and the Legacy to Deng Xiaoping: From Communist Revolution to Capitalist Evolution* (Dulles, VA: Potomac Books, 2002); and Benjamin Yang, *Deng: A Political Biography* (Armonk, NY: East Gate Books, 1997).

2. William Overholt, "China and Globalization," testimony presented to the U.S.-China Economic and Security Review Commission, May 19, 2005, RAND Corporation, 3.

3. John Gittings, *The Changing Face of China: From Mao to Market* (New York: Oxford University Press, 2005) 99.

4. For a favorable but nonetheless interesting biography of Zhu Rongji, see Laurence J. Brahm, *Zhu Rongji and the Transformation of Modern China* (Singapore: Wiley, 2002).

5. For a focus on the gradualistic nature of China's reform process and dealing with globalization, see Doug Guthrie, *China and Globalization: The Social, Economic and Political Transformation of Chinese Society* (New York: Routledge, 2006).

6. For a focus on the gradualistic nature of China's reform process and its dealing with globalization, see Guthrie *China and Globalization*.

7. "Rising FDI in China: The Facts behind the Numbers," *UNCTD Investment Brief*, November 2, 2007.

8. Bruce J. Dickson, *Red Capitalists in China: The Party, Private Entrepreneurs, and Prospects for Political Change*, (New York: Cambridge University Press, 2003), 1.

9. Yong Deng and Thomas G. Moore, "China Views Globalization: Toward a New Great-Power Politics?" *Washington Quarterly*, Summer 2004, 118.

10. See Marcus W. Brauchli and David Wessel, "Asian Crisis Spawns New Look for Business," *Wall Street Journal*, June 2, 1998. Also see Keith Robin and Scott B. MacDonald, "Foreign Investment Transforming Asia's Economies," *BridgeNews Forum*, October 26, 1999.

11. Ifzal Ali and Juzhong Zhuang, "Inclusive Growth Toward Prosperous Asia: Policy Implications," Asian Development Bank, ERD Working Paper SeriesManila, July 2007, 2.

12. Ibid, 3.

13. Dali L. Yang, "Forced Harmony: China's Olympic Rollercoaster," *Current History*, September 2008, 244.

14. *Asian Development Outlook 2011: South-South Economic Links* (Manila: Asian Development Bank, 2011), 28.

15. Paul Maidment, "China's Aging Population," *Forbes.com*, July 24, 2009, http://www.forbes.com/2009/07/24/china-shanghai-demography-population-opinions-columnists-one-child-policy.html.

16. For a fuller discussion of many of these points, see Wang Feng "China's Population Destiny: The Looming Crisis," *Current History*, September 2010), 244–51.

17. For a fuller discussion of these points, see Linda Yueh, ed., *The Future of Asian Trade and Growth* (London: Routledge, 2010).

18. See http://world-exchanges.org/member-exchanges.

19. David M. Lampton, "What If China Fails? We'd Better Hope It Doesn't," *Wilson Quarterly*, Autumn 2010, 61.

20. Stephen Wilson, "India Can't Match High Bar Set by China's Olympics," Associated Press, October 4, 2010, http://www.usatoday.com/sports/olympics/2010-10-04-1674918158_x.htm?csp=34sports.

21. *World Economic Outlook*, October 2010 (Washington D.C.: International Monetary Fund, 2010), 62.

22. Shujie Yao and Dylan Sutherland, "Chinalco and Rio Tinto: The Long March for China's National Champions," University of Nottingham, China Policy Institute, Briefing Series, issue 51, July 2009, 12.

23. "No Dim Sum," Lex, *Financial Times*, March 16, 2009.

24. "Fortune 500," *Fortune, CNN Money*, SSB, *Large Corporations of China 2007* (Beijing: State Statistical Bureau, 2009).

25. "A Wary Respect," Special Report on China and America, *Economist*, October 24 2009.

CHAPTER 4: CONSTRUCTING THE NEW ASIAN ECONOMY

1. Anoop Singh, "Asia Leading the Way," *Finance and Development*, June 2010, http://www.imf.org/external/pubs/ft/fandd/2010/06/index.htm.

2. Tadahiro Asami, "Chiang Mai Initiative as the Foundation of Financial Stability in East Asia," Institute for International Monetary Affairs, Tokyo, March 1, 2005, 6.

3. "Min Zhu on Asia's Economy and More," *Finance and Development*, June 2010, http://www.imf.org/external/pubs/ft/fandd/2010/06/zhu.htm.

4. Ibid.

5. Arving Panagaviya, "Trading Choices of South Asia," *South Asia: Growth and Regional Integration* (Washington, D.C., World Bank, 2007), 175.

6. *Asian Development Outlook 2010 Update: The Future of Growth in Asia* (Manila: Asian Development Bank, 2010), 49.

7. Panagaviya, "Trading Choices of South Asia," 175.

8. Ibid.

9. Jay Cooper, "More Firms Look to India to Fill Research Needs," *Investment News* (New York), May 7, 2007, 48.

10. Rashmee Rashan Lall, "IITs Ranked Number Three in the World," *Times of India*, October 13, 2006, http://articles.timesofindia.indiatimes.com/2006-10-13/rest-of-world/27820510_1_technology-and-science-institutes-mit-and-california-university-stanford-and-cambridge.

11. "Arcelor-The Inside Story," *Telegraph*, (Calcutta), May 4, 2008. This book review examines Amit Ray's *Cold Steel: Lakshmi Mittal and the Multi-Billion Battle for a Global Empire*.

12. Niranjan Rajadhyaksha, The *Rise of India: Its Transformation from Poverty to Prosperity* (Singapore: Wiley [Asia], 2007), 21.

13. James Lamont, "Potholes in the Road," *Financial Times*, February 5, 2010.

14. Pramit Mitra, "Running on Empty: India's Water Crisis Could Threaten Prosperity," Center for Strategic and International Studies, *South Asian Monitor*, Washington, D.C., February 8, 2007, 1.

15. Somini Sengupta, "In Teeming India, Water Crisis Dries Pipes and Foul Sludge," *New York Times*. September 28, 2006, http://www.nytimes.com/2006/09/29/world/asia/29water.html?ei=5087%0A&en=bb650dc7840f1933&ex=1159761600&pagewanted=all.

16. Ibid.

17. Amy Kazrin, "Labour to Unlock," *Financial Times*, October 5, 2010.

18. Sumit Ganguly and Manjeet S. Pardesi, "India Rising: What is New Delhi to Do?" *World Policy Journal*, Spring 2007, 13.

19. Sadiq Ahmed and Ejaz Ghani, "South Asia's Growth and Regional Integration: An Overview," in *South Asia: Growth and Regional Integrations*, Sadiq Ahmed and Ejaz Ghani, eds. (Washington, D.C.: World Book, 2002), 4.

20. Dilip K. Das, "The South Asia Free Trade Agreement: Evolution and Challenges," *MIT International Review*, Spring 2008, http://web.mit.edu/mitir/2008/spring/south.html.

21. "Sino-Nepali Trade Still Lopsided," *Kathmandu Post*, October 1, 2010, http://www.ekantipur.com/the-kathmandu-post/2010/10/01/money/sino-nepal-trade-still-lopsided/213411/.

22. Syed Fazl-e-Haider, "Pakistan's Trade Bear-Hug with China," *Asia Times*, April 21, 2010, www.chinasecurity.us/index.php?option=com_content&view=article&id=469&Itemid=8.

23. Pete Engardio, ed., *Chindia: How China and India are Revolutionizing Global Business* (New York: McGraw Hill, 2007), xi. Also see Jairam Ramesh and Strobe Talbott, *Making Sense of Chindia: Reflections of China and India* (New Delhi: India Research Press, 2006).

24. *Asian Development Outlook 2010 Update*, 50.

25. Shalendra D. Sharma, "The Uncertain Fate of 'Chindia,' " *Current History*, September 2010, 253.

26. Anubhuti Vishnoi, "Beijing Sends Word: Can Help CBSE with Mandarin Course," *Indian Express*, December 12, 2010, . . . http://www.indianexpress.com/news/Beijing-sends-word-can-help-c. . ./723581/.

27. Sharma, "Uncertain Fate," 254.

28. Jeremy Page and Tom Wright, "China Tries to Shore Up India Ties," *Wall Street Journal*, December 14, 2010.

29. James Lamont, "Wen's Trip to India Revives Old Disputes," *Financial Times*, December 13, 2010.

30. Tim Johnston, "A Wider Radius," *Financial Times*, January 28, 2010.

31. Ibid.

32. "Asia's Regional Integration: Should the Region Be Looking to Europe as Exemplar?" *Standard & Poor's Global Credit Portal*, August 11, 2010.

33. Takahiko Hyuga, "Japan Says 'Ni Hao' as Brands Trump Diplomacy for China Deals," *Bloomberg*, December 16, 2010.

34. These scenarios are discussed in greater detail in Andrew Sheng, *From Asian to Global Financial Crisis* (New York: Cambridge University Press, 2009), chapter 12.

CHAPTER 5: THE SUPPORTING CAST: BRICs AND BEYOND

1. Interview conducted by Beth Kowitt, "For Mr. BRIC, Nations Meeting a Milestone," *Fortune*, June 17, 2009, http://money.cnn.com/2009/06/17/news/economy/goldman_sachs_jim_oneill_interview.fortune/index.htm.

2. Dominic Wilson and Roopa Purushothaman, "Dreaming With BRICs: The Path to 2050," Goldman Sachs Global Economics Paper, no. 99, October 1, 2003, 1.

3. Jorgen Elmeskov, quoted from Mark Deen and Simon Kennedy, "OECD Doubles 2010 Growth Forecast, Recovery to Widen," Bloomberg, November 19, 2009. http://www.bloomberg.com/apps/news?pid=newsarchive&sid=aRWN91h135.

4. David E. Hoffman, *The Oligarchs: Wealth and Power in the New Russia* (New York: Public Affairs, 2003), 6.

5. Dmitri Trenin, "Where US and Russian Interests Overlap," *Current History*, May 2008, 224.

6. Ibid, 222.

7. Werner Baer, The *Brazilian Economy: Growth and Development*, 6th ed. (Boulder: Lynne Rienner, 2008), 1.

8. Mac Margolis, "The One-Party Democracy," *Newsweek*, September 3, 2010, http://www.newsweek.com/2010/09/03/brazil-s-one-party-democracy.html.

9. Ibid.

10. Lindsay Whipp, "Japanese Money Falls under Brazilian Real's Spell," *Financial Times*, January 5, 2011.

11. Leslie Hook, "China's State Grid in Brazil Push," *Financial Times*, December 22, 2010.

12. Geoff Dyer, "The China Cycle," *Financial Times*, September 13, 2010, p. 9.

13. Quoted in Nicholas Watt, "Blue-Eyed Bankers to Blame for Crash, Lula Tells Brown," *Guardian*, March 26, 2009, http://www.guardian.co.uk/world/2009/mar/26/lula-attacks-white-bankers-crash.

14. Richard Lapper, "Brazil Accelerates Investment in Africa," *Financial Times*, February 9, 2010.

15. Quoted in "Analysis: Surge in Chinese Investment Reshapes Brazil Ties," Reuters, August 10, 2010, http://www.reuters.com/article/2010/08/10/us-brazil-china-idUSTRE67947R20100810.

16. Ibid.

17. John Lyons, "Brazil Is Posed to Pressure Beijing on Currency Policy," *Wall Street Journal*, January 4, 2011.

18. Quoted in Mike Woolridge, "Will Brics Strengthen South Africa's Economic Foundations?" BBC News, January 5, 2011, http://www.bbc.co.uk/news/world-africa-12113830.

19. Lapper, "Brazil Accelerates Investment in Africa."

20. John Ghazvinian, *Untapped: The Scramble for Africa's Oil* (New York: Harcourt, 2006), 277. Also see "Lesotho Meets China: The Chinese Are Everywhere," *Economist*, August 7, 2010.

21. See the work of political scientist Cecil Johnson, *Communist China and Latin America 1959–1967* (New York: Columbia University Press, 1970), 1.

22. Robert I. Rotberg, ed., *China into Africa: Trade, Aid and Influence* (Washington, D.C.: Brookings Institution Press, 2008), 4.

23. Martyn J. Davies, "Special Economic Zones: China's Developmental Model Comes to Africa," in *China into Africa: Trade, Aid and Influence*, Robert I. Rotberg, ed. (Washington, D.C.: Brookings Institution Press, 2008), 151.

24. Ghazvinian, *Untapped*, 278.

25. Benoit Faucan and Sherry Su, "Hostility Toward Workers Cools Angola-China Relationship," *Wall Street Journal*, August 10, 2010.

26. Quoted in Faucan and Su, "Hostility Toward Workers."

27. Henry Lee and Dan Shalman, "Searching for Oil: China's Oil Strategies in Africa," in *China into Africa*, Rotberg, ed., 122.

28. Faucan and Su, " Hostility Toward Workers,"

29. Tony Hodges, *Angola: Anatomy of an Oil State* (Lysaker, Norway: Fridtj of Nansen Institute, 2004), 167.

30. Ibid.

31. Ghazvinian, *Untapped*, 287.

32. Ibid.

33. Matt Richmond and Maram Mazen, "Sudan Vote May Shift Control of Oil Pumped by CNPC," *Bloomberg*, January 7, 2011.

CHAPTER 6: THE MAJOR ECONOMIC CHALLENGES

1. For a fuller discussion on urbanization in Asia, see Michael Backman *Asia Future Shock* (New York: Palgrave Macmillan, 2008). Mumbai India has a current population of about 19 million, but by 2020 it will exceed 28.5 million, becoming the world's largest city—larger than most nations.

2. Quoted in Michael Forsthe et al., "Chairman Mao Never Left Board as Communists Dominate China Inc.," *Bloomberg*, October 13, 2010.

3. From the Heritage Foundation dataset available upon request from the Heritage Foundation, Washington, D.C., as cited in Kevin D. Cramer, presentation to the University of Connecticut China Study Group on Chinese Outbound Investment, Stamford, CT, August 27, 2010.

4. Abhrajit Gangopadhyay and Jai Khrishna, "India Seeks Chinese Firm's Ownership Data," *Wall Street Journal*, May 16, 2010.

5. Shujie Yao and Dylan Sutherland, "Chinalco and Rio Tinto: The Long March for China's National Champions," Briefing Series, issue 51, China Policy Institute, University of Nottingham, July 2009.

6. Barry Naughton, *The Chinese Economy—Transitions and Growth* (Cambridge, MA: MIT Press, 2007), 108.

7. C. Fred Bergsten, Charles Freeman, Nicholas R. Lardy, and Derek Mitchell, *China's Rise: Challenges and Opportunities* (Washington D.C.: Peterson Institute for International Economics and the Center for Strategic and International Studies, 2009), 14.

8. *Asian Development Outlook 2011* (Manila: Asian Development Bank, 2011), 28.

9. Mukesh Jagoat and Anant Vijay Kala, "India, US Agree to Set Up $10 Bn Infrastructure Fund," *Wall Street Journal*, November 8, 2010.

10. *Asian Development Outlook 2010*, 62.

11. Ibid.

12. This point was brought out by J. Benhabib and M. Spiegel, "The Role of Human Capital in Economic Development: Evidence from Aggregate Cross-Country and Regional US Data," *Journal of Monetary Economics* 34, no. 1 (1994), 143–73.

13. Kevin Brown, "Malaysia on Hard Road to High-Skills Wealth," *Financial Times*, November 5, 2010.

14. *Asia 2050: Realizing the Asian Century* (Manila: Asian Development Bank, 2011), 34–35.

15. Quoted in Mure Dickie, Jonathan Soble, Leslie Hook, and Javier Blas, "Japan Cries Foul Over Rare Earths," *Financial Times*, October 25, 2010.

16. Quoted in Norman Pearlstine and Sachiko Sakamaki, "Maehara Says China Ties on Mend, Eyes Rare-Earth Deals," *Bloomberg*, October 25, 2010.

17. *Indonesia: Environmental and Natural Resource Management in a Time of Transition* (Washington, D.C.: World Bank, 2004), 24.

18. Tom Wright, "Jakarta's Newmont Suit Risks Investment Fallout," *Wall Street Journal*, March 30, 2007.

19. "RI Sends Bird Flu Samples Abroad Only after Agreement Signed: Minutes," *Jakarta Post*, March 26, 2007.

20. Organization for Economic Cooperation and Development, World Bank, International Labor Organization, and World Trade Organization, "Seizing the Benefits of Trade for Employment and Growth," prepared for submission to the G-20 summit meeting, Seoul, November 11–12, 2010, 32.

21. Asian Development Bank, Outlook 2010 Update (Manila, the Philippines: September 2010).

22. See "Crisis in Slow Motion," *Economist*, April 10, 2010. Also see Scott B. MacDonald and Jonathan Lemco, "Japan's Slow-Moving Avalanche," *Current History*, April 2002.

23. Quoted in William Sposato, "S&P Downgrades Japan, Says Government Lacks Debt Reduction Plan," *Bloomberg*, January 27, 2011.

24. Kiichi Tokuoka, "The Outlook for Financing Japan's Public Debt," IMF Working Paper, WP/10/19, International Monetary Fund, Washington, D.C., 19.

25. *Asian Development Outlook 2011*, 11.

26. Lindsay Whipp and Mure Dickie, "S&P Downgrades on Debt Worries," *Financial Times*, January 27, 2011, p. 15.

27. "Japan Economy Debt Downgrade," Economist Intelligence Unit, London, January 28, 2011.

CHAPTER 7: POLITICAL CHALLENGES IN ASIA

1. One of the most recent essays on China's political system is Richard McGregor's, *The Party: The Secret World of China's Communist Rules* (New York: HarperCollins, 2010).

2. For more information on the Fulun Gong, see Savid Ownby, *Falun Gong and the Future of China* (New York: Oxford University Press, 2008), and Maria Hsia Chang, *Fulan Gong: The End of Days* (New Haven: Yale University Press, 2004).

3. Michael A. Ledeen, "Beijing Embraces Classical Fascism," *Far Eastern Economic Review*, May 2008, 8–9.

4. Richard Waters and Joseph Menn, "Closing the Frontier," *Financial Times*, March 29, 2010.

5. X, "China's Holistic Censorship Regime," *Far Eastern Economic Review*, May 2008, 21. Mr. X is a foreign media entrepreneur based in China. His identity is concealed because of the certainty that publishing this essay under his name would lead to the loss of his livelihood.

6. S. Crispin "A Quantum Leap in Censorship," *Asia Times*, September 22, 2006. Fortinet's web-filtering products can be used to screen out the views of opposition parties and dissidents from web sites. For a fuller discussion of Fortinet and its capabilities, see www.Fortinet.com.

7. Ledeen, "Beijing Embraces Classical Fascism," 11.

8. Liu Xiaobo, "Can It Be That the Chinese People Deserve Only 'Party-Led Democracy?' " *Journal of Democracy*, January 2011, 154.

9. Ibid, 160.

10. Niranjan Rajadhyaksha, *The Rise of India: Its Transformation from Poverty to Prosperity* (Hoboken, NJ: Wiley, 2007), 169.

11. Sumit Ganguly, "India Held Back," *Current History*, November 2008, 370.

12. Kunal P. Kirpalani, "India's Northwest Insurgencies: A Somewhat Forgotten Story," *South Asia Masala*, June 10, 2010 http://asiapacific.anu.edu.au/blogs/southasiamasala/2010/06/10/India%E2%80%99s-northeast-insurgencies-a-somewhat-forgotten-story/.

13. Ganguly, "India Held Back," 372

14. Joshua Kurlantzick, "Asia's Democracy Backlash," *Current History*, November 2008, 377.

15. Michael Edwards. "Civil Society—Theory and Practice," *Encyclopedia of Informal Education*, http://www.infed.org/association/civil_society.htm. See also Robert Putnam, *Bowling Alone: The Collapse and Revival of American Community* (New York: Simon and Schuster, 2000).

16. For an interesting discussion of corruption in the Philippines, see David Kang. *Crony Capitalism: Corruption and Development in South Korea and the Philippines* (New York: Cambridge University Press, 2002).

17. Robert B. Albritton and Thawilwadee Bureekul, "Thailand Country Report: Public Opinion and Political Power in Thailand," Second Wave of Asian Barometer Survey, Asian Barometer Project Office, Working Paper Series,: no. 34, Taipei, 2007, 3.

18. Ibid, 4

19. *Afghanistan*, U.S. Department of State 2009 International Narcotics Control Strategy Report, Washington D.C., http://www.state.gov/p/inl/rls/nrcrpt/2009/vol1/116520.htm.

20. Erica Marat, "The State-Crime Nexus in Central Asia: State Weakness, Organized Crime, and Corruption in Kyrgyzstan and Tajikistan," Silk Road

Paper, Central Asia-Caucasus Institute & Silk Road Studies Program: A Joint Transatlantic Research and Policy Center, October 2006, 14.

21. Tim Johnston, "Cambodia-Thai Border Dispute Flares Up," *Financial Times*, February 4, 2011.

22. Quoted in Amol Sharma, Jeremy Page, James Hookway, and Rachel Pannett, "Asia's New Arms Race," *Wall Street Journal*, February 12–13, 2011.

23. Ross Babbage AM, "Australia's Strategic Edge in 2030," Kokoda Paper, Kokoda Foundation, Kingston, Australia, February 7, 2011, 1.

24. Quoted in Sharma, Page, Hookway, and Pannett, "Asia's New Arms Race."

CHAPTER 8: THE WEST AND THE RISE OF ASIA

1. Transcript of Madeleine Albright quoted on Jim Lehrer's Online Newshour, March 6, 1997. http://www.pbs.org/newshour/bb/fedagencies/march97/albright_3-6html.

2. These questions were asked in David P. Rankin and William R. Thompson, "Will Economic Interdependence Encourage China's and India's Peaceful Ascent?" in Ashley J. Tellis and Michael Wills, eds., *Strategic Asia 1006–07: Trade, Interdependence, and Security* (Seattle: National Bureau of Asian Research, 2006), 333.

3. Ian Bremmer and Nouriel Roubini, "A G-Zero World," *Foreign Affairs*, March/April 2011, 2.

4. Quoted in Tony Capaccio and Kitty Donaldson, "Allies Expanding No-Fly Zone as Strikes Lead to Delay in Attack," *Bloomberg*, March 21, 2011.

5. Quoted in Keith B. Richburg, "China, after Abstaining in U.N. Vote, Criticizes Airstrikes on Gaddafi Forces," *Washington Post*, March 21, 2011.

6. Ibid.

7. "Obama Deserves Support on Libya," *Financial Times*, March 30, 2011.

8. Phillip Stephens, "Obama to Europe: Ban Courage," *Financial Times*, March 25, 2011.

9. Quoted in Flavia Krause-Jackson, "Biblical Exodus from Africa Feeds Anti-Immigrant Rhetoric," *Bloomberg*, March 1, 2011.

10. Gideon Rachman, "China Can No Longer Plead Poverty," *Financial Times*, October 26, 2010.

11. Gordon Chang, *The Coming Collapse of China* (New York: Random House, 2001), xvi.

12. Susan J. Shirk, *China: Fragile Superpower* (New York: Oxford University Press, 2007).

13. Andrew J.Nathan and Bruce Gilley, *China's New Rulers: The Secret Files* (New York: NYREV, 2002).

14. Richard Bernstein and Ross H. Munro, *The Coming Conflict with China* (New York: Knopff, 1997), 4–5.

15. Martin Jacques, *When China Rules the World: The End of the Western World and the Birth of a New Global Order* (New York: Penguin Press, 2009) 15.

16. Charles Glaser, "Will China's Rise Lead to War? Why Realism Does Not Mean Pessimism," *Foreign Affairs*, March/April 2011, 80.

17. See David Shambaugh, "A New China Requires a New US Strategy," *Current History*, 109, no. 728 (September 2010), 219–226.

18. Ibid.

19. For example, see John Llewellyn and Lavinia Santovetti, eds., *The Ascent of Asia*, Nomura Global Research, Tokyo, February 2010.

20. William H. Overholt, *Asia, America and the Transformation of Geopolitics* (New York: Cambridge University Press, 2008), 225.

21. Wang Fisi, "China's Search for a Grand Strategy," *Foreign Affairs*, March/April 2011, 72.

22. Mark Landler, Jim Yardley, and Michael Wines, "As China Rises, Wary Neighbors Form Alliances," *New York Times*, October 31, 2010.

23. Zahid Hussain, *The Scorpion's Tail: The Relentless Rise of Islamic Militants in Pakistan—and How It Threatens America* (New York: Free Press, 2010), 209.

24. Jayshree Bajoria and Eben Kaplan, "The ISI and Terrorism: Behind the Accusations," Council on Foreign Relations, New York, July 16, 2010, http://www.cfr.org/pakistan/isi-terrorism-behind-accusations/p11644.

25. Brahma Chellaney, *Asian Juggernaut: The Rise of China, India, and Japan* (New York: Harper Business, 2010), 166.

CHAPTER 9: CONCLUSION

1. Ambrose Evans-Pritchard, "Will 'Chindia' Rule the World in 2050, or America after All?," *Telegraph* (London), February 28, 2011, http://www.telegraph.co.uk/finance/comment/ambroseevans_pritchard/8350548/Will-Chindia-rule-the-world-in-2050-or-America-after-all.html.

2. Niall Ferguson, "The Next Meltdown," *Time*, January 15, 2007, 60.

3. Robyn Meredith, *The Elephant and the Dragon: The Rise of India and China and What It Means for All of Us* (New York: Norton, 2007), 260.

BIBLIOGRAPHY

PRIMARY SOURCES

Ahmed, Sadiq, and Ejaz Ghani, eds. *South Asia: Growth and Regional Integration* (Washington, D.C.: World Bank, 2007).

Asia 2050: Realizing the Asian Century (Manila: Asian Development Bank, 2011).

Asian Development Outlook 2011: South-South Links (Manila: Asian Development Bank, 2011).

Bajoria, Jayshree. *Pakistan's New Generation of Terrorists*. Report, Council on Foreign Relations, October 7, 2010. http://www.cfr.org/pakistan/pakistans-new-generation-terrorists/p15422.

Fogel, Robert W. "Capitalism and Democracy in 2040: Forecasts and Speculations." National Bureau of Economic Research, Working Paper 13184, June 2007. http://www.nber.org/papers/w13184.

G-20 Mutual Assessment Process—IMF Staff Assessment of G-20 Policies for G-20 Summit of Leaders. Seoul, November 11–12, 2010.

India 2006 Article IV Consultation (Washington, D.C.: International Monetary Fund, 2007).

Indonesia: Environmental and Natural Resource Management in a Time of Transition (Washington, D.C.: World Bank, 2004).

Japan Economic Survey (Paris: Organization for Economic Cooperation and Development, 2006).

Joshi, Vijay, and I.M.D. Little. *India: Macroeconomics and Political Economy 1964–1991* (Washington, D.C.: World Bank, 1994).

Keidal, Albert. "China's Looming Crisis—Inflation Returns." Policy brief, Carnegie Endowment, Washington, D.C., September 2007.

Keidal, Albert. "China's Social Unrest: The Story behind the Stories." Policy brief, Carnegie Endowment, Washington, D.C., September 2006.

Kuczynski, Pedro-Pablo, and John Williamson, eds. *After the Washington Consensus: Restarting Growth and Reform in Latin America* (Washington, D.C.: Institute for International Economics, 2003).

Lall, Marie. "The Challenges of India's Education System." Brief, Chatham House, London, April 2005.

Loungani, Prakash. "Globalization by the Book." Policy Communications, External Relations Department, International Monetary Fund, Washington, D.C., February 5, 2007.

Pei, Minxin. "Corruption Threatens China's Future." Policy brief, Carnegie Endowment, Washington, D.C., October 2007.

People's Republic of China 2005 Article IV Consultation, November 2005 (Washington, D.C.: International Monetary Fund, 2005).

Podpiera, Richard. "Progress in China's Banking Sector Reform: Has Bank Behavior Changed?" International Monetary Fund, IMF Working Paper, Washington, D.C., March 2006.

Reddy, Y.V. Address by Dr. Y.V. Reddy, governor of the Reserve Bank of India at the Institute of Bankers, Karachi, Pakistan, Bank for International Settlements, 35/2005, Basel, May 18, 2005.

"Reforming China's Banking System." Federal Reserve Bank of San Francisco, FRBSF Economic Letter, no. 2002–17, May 31, 2002.

Rieffel, Lex. *Indonesia: Ten Years after the Crisis*. Report, Brooking Institution, Washington, D.C., June 28, 2007. http://www.brookings.edu/opinions/2007/0628globaleconomics_rieffel.aspx.

Rumo, Joshua Cooper. *The Beijing Consensus* (Beijing: Foreign Policy Center, 2004).

Singh, Sushank K. "India and West Africa: A Burgeoning Relationship." Africa Programme/Asia Programme Briefing Paper, Chatham House, London, April 2007.

Strategy 2020: The Long-Term Strategic Framework for the Asian Development Bank 2008–2020 (Manila: Asian Development Bank, 2008).

Tanner, Murray Scott. *Can China Contain Unrest?: Six Questions Seeking One Answer*. Report, Brookings Northeast Asia Commentary, Brookings Institution, Washington, D.C., March 2007.

Tellis, Ashley, and Michael Wills, eds. *Strategic Asia 2006–07: Trade, Interdependence, and Security* (Seattle: National Bureau of Asian Research, 2006).

Thayer, Carlyle A. *Southeast Asia: Patterns of Security Cooperation* (Barton ACT, Australia: Australian Strategic Policy Institute Limited, 2010).

Wang, Jian-Ye. "What Drives China's Growing Role in Africa?" International Monetary Fund, IMF Working Paper, WP/07/211, Washington, D.C., August 2007.

World Economic Outlook: Spillovers and Cycles in the Global Economy (Washington, D.C.: International Monetary Fund, 2007).

World Economic Outlook: Tensions from Two-Speed Recovery (Washington, D.C.: International Monetary Fund, 2011).

Yudhoyono, Susilo Bambang. Remarks by H.E. Dr. H. Susilo Bambang Yudhoyono, president of the Republic of Indonesia at Islamic University of Iman Muhammad Bin Sa'ud. Riyadh, Saudi Arabia, April 26, 2006 (Jakarta: Government of the Republic of Indonesia, 2006).

SECONDARY SOURCES

Articles

Anderlini, Jamil. "China Lifts Profile in Cambodia." *Financial Times*, November 5, 2010.

Anderlini, Jamil, and Mure Dickie. "Taking the Waters: China's Gung-Ho Economy Exerts a Heavy Price." *Financial Times*, July 24, 2007.

Anderson, Jonathan. "Bling! Bing! Boom! China's Stocks Zoom." *Far Eastern Economic Review*, December 2007: 9–13.

Ash, Timothy Garton. "Only Burma's Neighbors Can Stop Its Dictators: Beating Up the Buddha." *Guardian*, September 27, 2007. http://www.guardian .co.uk/commentisfree/2007/sep/27/comment.burma.

Bagchi, Indrani. "A Tale of Two Manmohan Singhs." *Current History*, April 2011: 131–35.

Barr, Michael D. "The Charade of Meritocracy." *Far Eastern Economic Review* 169, no. 8 (October 2006): 18–22.

Batson, Andrew. "China Says Its Moves Won't Rattle Markets." *Wall Street Journal*, March 17–18, 2007.

Bellman, Eric. "As Economy Grows, India Goes for Designer Goods." *Wall Street Journal*, March 27, 2007.

Benes, Nicholas. "Japanese Capitalism Hits a Tipping Point." *Far Eastern Economic Review* 169, no. 8 (October 2006): 48–52.

Bhagwait, Jagdish. "Coping with Antiglobalization." *Foreign Affairs* 8, no. 1, January/February 2002: 2–7.

Bosworth, Barry, and Susan M. Collins. "Accounting for Growth: Comparing China and India." Economics of Developing Countries Papers, Brookings Institution, Washington, D.C., December 6–7, 2006.

Breen, Michael. "Korea, Inc., Looks for a New CEO." *Far Eastern Economic Review*, December 2007: 31–34.

"Briefing Business in India: A Bumpier But Freer Road." *Economist*, October 2, 2010.

Brown, Kevin. "Malaysia on Hard Road to High-Skills Wealth." *Financial Times*, November 5, 2010.

Brzezinski, Zbigniew. "America and China's First Big Test." *Financial Times*, November 24, 2010.

Burton, John. "Arrests in Singapore for Burma Protest." *Financial Times*, October 9, 2007.

Burton, John. "Secrecy a Way of Life in City-State." *Financial Times*, September 5, 2007.

Burton, John. "Singapore's Wealth Fund Flattered by Imitation." *Financial Times*, September 5, 2007.

Cha, Ariana Eunjung. "Asians Say Trade Complaints Bring Out the Bully in China." *Washington Post*, September 5, 2007.

Cha, Victor D. "Korea's Place in the Axis." *Foreign Affairs,* 81, no. 3, May/June 2002: 79–92.

Cha, Victor D. "Winning Asia." *Foreign Affairs*, November/December 2007: 98–113.

"China's Luxury Boom: The Middle Blingdom." *Economist*, February 19, 2011.

Chipman, Stephen. "China's Reform Needs Foundation." *Financial Times*, July 19, 2007.

Cohen, Jerome. "The Slow March to Legal Reform." *Far Eastern Economic Reform*, October 2007: 20–24.

Cohen, Stephen O. "Shooting for a Century: The India-Pakistan Conundrum." *Current History*, April 2011: 162–64.

Cohen, Stephen P. "India vs. Pakistan: Asia's New Hundred Years' War?" *Current History*, April 2011: 162–64.

Dasgupta, Sunil, and Stephen P. Cohen. "Arms Sales for India." *Foreign Affairs,* 90, no. 2, March/April 2011: 22–27.

Davis, Sara. "China's Contested Ethnic Borders." *Far Eastern Economic Review* 168, no. 10 (November 2005): 48–52.

Deng, Yong, and Thomas G. Moore. "China Views Globalization Toward a New Great-Power Politics?" *Washington Quarterly*, Summer 2004: 117–36.

Dhame, Sadanand. "Playboy in Indonesia." *Wall Street Journal*, March 29, 2007.

Donnan, Shawn. "Suharto's Five-Pronged Principles Enjoy a Revival in Combat with Radical Islam." *Financial Times*, August 7, 2006.

Dyer, Geoff. "China Gives Corrupt Drugs Regulator Suspended Death Sentence." *Financial Times*, July 9, 2007.

Economy, Elizabeth. "The Great Leap Backward?" *Foreign Affairs*, September/October 2007: 38–59.

Elegant, Simon. "World Spotlight: China's Democracy." *Time*, October 29, 2007, 15.

"Emerging Markets: Climbing Back." *Economist*, January 21, 2006.

Engammare, Valerie, and Jean-Pierre Lehmann. "Can Asia Avert a Globalization Crisis?" *Far Eastern Economic Review*, March 2007: 7–10.

Fazl-e-Haider, Syed. "Pakistan's Economy Takes a Hit." *Asia Times*, January 3, 2008. http://www.atimes.com/atimes/South_Asia/JAO3Df06.html.

Feldstein, Martin. "There's More to Growth than China . . . India Has Awakened from Its Socialist Slumber." *Wall Street Journal*, February 16, 2006.

Fifield, Anna, and Sung Jong-a. "Seoul in Rethink over Foreign Investment Law." *Financial Times*, October 23, 2007.

Frisbie, John, and Michael Overmyer. "U.S.-China Economic Relations: The Next Stage." *Current History*, September 2006: 243–49.

Ganguly, Sumit, and Manjeet S. Pardesi. "India Rising: What Is New Delhi to Do?" *World Policy Journal*, Spring 2007: 9–18.

Gaz, Azar. "The Return of the Authoritarian Great Powers." *Foreign Affairs,* July/August 2007: 33–45.

Giles, Chris. "Wrong Lessons from Asia's Crisis." *Financial Times*, July 2, 2007.

Gimbel, Florian. "Beijing Sets Deadline for Banks to Implement Basel Accord." *Financial Times*, March 15, 2007.

Glader, Paul, and Peter Wonacott. "Why Private Colleges Are Surging in India." *Wall Street Journal*, March 29, 2007.

Glaser, Charles. "Will China's Rise Lead to War?" *Foreign Affairs* 90, no. 2 (March/April 2011): 80–91.

Green, Michael. "Fukuda, the Other Side of Koizumi's Magic." *Financial Times*, September 28, 2007.

Green, Michael, and Derek Mitchell. "Asia's Forgotten Crisis." *Foreign Affairs*, November/December 2007: 147–59.

Hale, David, and Lyric Hughes Hale. "China Takes Off." *Foreign Affairs* 82, no. 6 (November/December 2003): 36–53.

Hamlin, Kevin. "Remade in Singapore." *Institutional Investor*, September 2006, 70–82.

Hamm, Steve. "The Trouble with India." *Business Week*, March 19, 2007, 49–58.

Harris, Tobais. "Can Fukuda Rebuild Trust in the LDP?" *Far Eastern Economic Review*, October 2007: 38–40.

Heginbotham, Eric, and Richard Samuels. "Japan's Double Game." *Foreign Affairs* 81, no. 5 (September/October 2002): 110–21.

Holland, Tom. "Mining: Feeding China's Giant Appetite." *Far Eastern Economic Review*, June 3, 2004: 44–48.

Holtz, Carsten. "Will China Go to War Over Oil?" *Far Eastern Economic Review*, April 2006: 38–40.

Hook, Leslie. "Rising Fuel Prices Leave China's Drivers Stuck in First Gear." *Financial Times*, April 25, 2011.

"India: Hindu v. Hindu." *Economist*, June 12, 1993.

"India's Surprising Economic Miracle." *Economist*, October 2, 2010.

"Investment Banking: Stir-Fry Finance." *Economist*, October 27, 2007.

Ish-Shalom, Piki. "The Civilization of Clashes: Misapplying the Democratic Peace in the Middle East." *Political Science Quarterly* 12, no. 4 (Winter 2007): 533–54.

Jaffrelot, Christophe. "The Indian-Pakistani Divide." *Foreign Affairs* 90, no. 2 (March/April 2011): 140–45.

"Jasmine Stirrings in China: No Awakening, But Crush It Anyway." *Economist*, March 5, 2011.

Jisi, Wang. "China's Search for a Grand Strategy." *Foreign Affairs,* 90, no. 2 March/April 2011: 68–79.

Jopson, Barney. "Somalia to Win Bonuses on China Oil Finds." *Financial Times*, July 19, 2007.

Joshi, Shashank. "Why India Is Becoming Warier of China." *Current History*, April, 2011: 156–61.

Jung-a, Song. "South Korea's State Pension Fund Dips Toe in World of Risk." *Financial Times*, July 13, 2007.

Kane, Yukari Iwatani. "Sanyo Ends Era of Family Rule." *Wall Street Journal*, March 29, 2007.

Kaplan, Robert. "Attacks That May Signal a Pyongyang Implosion." *Financial Times*, November 24, 2010.

Kaplan, Robert. "Lost at Sea." *New York Times*, September 21, 2007.

"Kayani's Gambit: America, Afghanistan and Pakistan." *Economist*, July 31, 2010.

Kazmin, Amy. "Labour to Unlock." *Financial Times*, October 5, 2010: 11.

King, Stephen. "Sustaining Authoritarianism in the Middle East and North Africa." *Political Science Quarterly* 122, no. 3 (Fall 2007): 433–59.

Kingston, Jeffrey. "Abe Should Focus on Domestic Issues That Worry Voters." *Financial Times*, January 31, 2007.

Kiviat, Barbara. "They Really Do Own the Road." *Time*, October 29, 2007, 36–38.

Kux, Dennis. "India's Fine Balance." *Foreign Affairs* 81, no. 3, May/June 2002: 93–106.

Lague, David. "Bank of China IPO Raises $9.7 Billion." *New York Times*, May 24, 2006.

Lam, Willy. "Hu Jintao's Hollow Pledges." *Far Eastern Economic Review* 170, no. 9 (November 2007): 27–29.

Lamont, James. "France Nears $9 Bn Deal to Build Two Reactors in India." *Financial Times*, December 7, 2010.

Lampton, David M. "What If China Fails?: We'd Better Hope It Doesn't!" *Wilson Quarterly*, Autumn 2010: 61–66.

Leahy, Joe. "Banks Reap Rewards of Indian Frenzy." *Financial Times*, July 2, 2007.

Li, Lianjiang. "Driven to Protest: China's Rural Unrest." *Current History*, September 2006: 250–54.

Lieven, Anatol. "The Pressures on Pakistan." *Foreign Affairs* 81, no. 1 (January/February 2002): 106–19.

MacDonald, Scott B. "China and India: Same Road, Different Destinies." World Defence Network, November 2, 2007. http://www.defence.pk/forums/economy-development/8065-china-india-same-road-different-destinies.html.

MacDonald, Scott B. "Radical Islam Threatens Indonesia's Moderate, Democratic Unity." *Wall Street Journal*, April 2, 2007.

MacDonald, Scott B. "A Tale of Two Indias." *Society*, July/August 2006, 72–77.

MacDonald, Scott B., and Jonathan Lemco. "Japan's Slow-Moving Avalanche." *Current History*, April 2002: 172–75.

Maddox, Bronwen. "Forget Sanctions: China and India Hold the Key." *Times Online* (London), September 27, 2007. http://www.timesonline.co.uk/tol/news/world/asia/article2537021.ece.

Mahbubani, Kishore. "India: Emerging as Eastern or Western Power?" YaleGlobal Online, December 19, 2006. http://www.mahbubani.net/articles%20by%20dean/India%20emerging%20as%20eastern%20or%20western.pdf.

Mahbubani, Kishore. "Welcome to the Asian Century." *Current History*, May 2008: 195–200.

Masheshwari, Ritesh. "2006 Fire Dog Year Shines Brightly for Asian Banks." *Standard & Poor's CreditWeek*, February 8, 2006, 12–18.

Matthews, Eugene A. "Japan's New Nationalism." *Foreign Affairs* 82, no. 6 (November/December 2003): 74–90.

McGregor, Richard. "China Posed to Give More Cash to Banks." *Financial Times*, August 7, 2007.

Medeiros, Evan S., and M. Taylor Fravel. "China's New Diplomacy." *Foreign Affairs* 82, no. 6 (November/December 2003): 22–35.

Mehta, Pratap Bhanu. "Globalization and India's Sense of Itself." *Current History*, April 2007:

Melloan, George. "Asia's Tigers Are Back, with More Muscle." *Wall Street Journal*, June 1, 2004.

Montlake, Simon. "Singapore's Bid for Brainpower." *Far Eastern Economic Review*, October 2007: 46–48.

Murphy, Colum. "Pakistan's Last Bid for Democracy." *Far Eastern Economic Review* 170, no. 9 (November 2007): 17–22.

"Myanmar's Border With China: Good Fences." *Economist*, November 10, 2010.

Neary, Ian. "State and Civil Society in Japan." *Asian Affairs* 34, no. 1 (2002): 234–40.

Newman, Barry. "Pledging Allegiances: Indian Passport Law Reflects Global Trend." *Wall Street Journal*, December 15, 2006.

Overholt, William H. "Japan's Economy at War with Itself." *Foreign Affairs* 81, no. 1 (January/February 2002): 134–47.

Pei, Minxin. "China's Governance Crisis." *Foreign Affairs* 81, no. 5 (September/October 2002): 96–109.

Rachman, Gideon. "Do Not Panic over Foreign Wealth." *Financial Times*, April 29, 2008.

Ramo, Joshua Cooper. "China Has Discovered Its Own Economic Consensus." *Financial Times*, May 7, 2004.

Ramstad, Evan. "Korea Trade Focus: Cars." *Wall Street Journal*, March 29, 2007.

Restall, Hugo. "Financial Center Pipedreams." *Far Eastern Economic Review* 169, no. 8 (October 2006): 23–26.

Rid, Thomas. "Cracks in the Jihad." *Wilson Quarterly*, Winter 2010: 40–47.

Rodan, Garry. "Singapore's Founding Myths vs. Freedom." *Far Eastern Economic Review* 169, no. 8 (October 2006) 13–17.

Scheve, Kenneth F., and Matthew J. Slaughter. "A New Deal for Globalization." *Foreign Affairs*, July/August 2007: 34–48.

Scissors, Derek. "Deng Undone." *Foreign Affairs* 88, no. 3 (May/June 2009): 24–39.

Shih, Victor. "China's Uphill Battle for Stronger Banks." *Far Eastern Economic Review* 168, no. 10 (November 2005): 37–40.

"Singapore's Economy." *Economist*, October 27, 2007.

Slater, Dan. "China—Protectionist or Just Picky?" *The Deal*, April 2007, 52–58.

Tanaka, Naoki. "No Turning Back from Koizumi Legacy Despite Election Loss." *Nikkei Weekly*, August 13, 2007.

Terrill, Ross. "What if China's Fails?: The Case for Selective Failure." *Wilson Quarterly*, Autumn 2010: 52–60.

Timmons, Heather. "Japan and India to Announce Partnerships and New Business Initiatives." *New York Times*, August 20, 2007. http://www.nytimes.com/2007/08/20/business/worldbusiness/20iht-rupee.4.7186610.html.

Tucker, Sundeep, Joe Leahy, and Geoff Dyer. "Defying Gravity?: Asia's Continued Rise Spurs Debate on 'Decoupling.'" *Financial Times*, November 2, 2007.

Ulrich, Jing. "Transformed China Is Ready for Overseas Investment." *Financial Times*, August 8, 2007.

Unger, Jonathan. "China's Conservative Middle Class." *Far Eastern Economic Review*, April 2006: 27–31.

Walker, Martin. "Globalization 3.0." *Wilson Quarterly*, Autumn 2007: 12–19.

Ward, Andrew. "Chinese Building Boom Lifts Kone." *Financial Times*, April 25, 2011.

Warner, Jeremy. "America Not Yet Down and Out, or How the West Is Still Winning." *Telegraph* (London), February 28, 2011. http://www.telegraph.co.uk/finance/comment/jeremy-warner/8353283/America-not-yet-down-and-out-or-how-the-West-is-still-winning.html.

"Water Pricing in China: Bottling It." *Economist*, January 9, 2010.

Wessel, David. "As Globalization's Benefits Grow, So Do Its Skeptics." *Wall Street Journal*, March 29, 2007.

Willman, John, and Joanna Chung. "Big Spenders: How Sovereign Funds Are Stirring Up Protectionism." *Financial Times*, July 30, 2007.

Wright, Robert. "Western Retailers Shift Their Supply Chain Tasks to China." *Financial Times*, March 27, 2007.

Wright, Tom. "Aceh Leader Seeks to Drum Up Investment." *Wall Street Journal*, March 29, 2007.

Xie, Andy. "China's Bubble May Burst But the Impact Will Be Limited." *Financial Times*, October 17, 2007.

Zakaria, Fareed. "The Rise of Illiberal Democracy." *Foreign Affairs*, November/December 1997. http://www.foreignaffairs.org/19971101faessay3809/fareed-zakaria/the-rise-of-illiberal-democracy.htlm.

Books

Arrighi, Giovanni. *Adam Smith in Beijing: Lineages of the Twenty-First Century* (New York: Verso, 2007).

Barfield, Thomas J. *Afghanistan: A Cultural and Political History* (Princeton: Princeton University Press, 2010).

Baum, Richard. *Burying Mao: Chinese Politics in the Age of Deng Xiao-ping* (Princeton: Princeton University Press, 1996).

Bayly, Christopher, and Tim Harper. *Forgotten Wars: Freedom and Revolution in Southern Asia* (New York: Harvard University Press, 2007).

Bergsten, C. Fred, Bates Gill, Nicholas R. Lardy, and Derek J. Mitchell. *China: The Balance Sheet* (New York: Public Affairs, 2006).

Bhaqwati, Jagdish. *In Defense of Globalization* (New York: Oxford University Press, 2004).

Blomqist, Hans C. *Swimming with the Sharks: Global and Regional Dimension of the Singaporean Economy* (Singapore: Marshall Cavendish Academic, 2005).

Blustein, Paul. *The Chastening: Inside the Crisis That Rocked the Global Financial System and Humbled the IMF* (New York: Public Affairs, 2001).

Bootle, Roger. *Money for Nothing: Real Wealth, Financial Fantasies and the Economy of the Future* (London: Nicholas Brealey, 2004).

Braham, Laurence J. *Zhu Rongji and the Transformation of Modern China* (Singapore: Wiley, 2002).

Bush, Richard C., and Michael E. O'Hanlon. *A War Like No Other: The Truth about China's Challenge to America* (Hoboken: Wiley, 2007).

Calder, Kent. *Crisis and Compensation: Public Policy and Political Stability in Japan, 1946–1986* (Princeton: Princeton University Press, 1988).

Chanda, Nayan. *Bound Together: How Traders, Preachers, Adventurers, and Warriors Shaped Globalization* (New Haven: Yale University Press, 2007).

Chang, Gordon. *The Coming Collapse of China* (New York: Random House, 2001).

Chaudhuri, K. N. *Asia before Europe: Economy and Civilization of the Indian Ocean from the Rise of Islam to 1750* (Cambridge: Cambridge University Press, 1990).

Chen, Guidi, and Wu Chuntao. *Will the Boat Sink the Water? The Life of China's Peasants* (New York: Public Affairs, 2006).

Chua, Amy. *World on Fire: How Exporting Free Market Democracy Breeds Ethnic Hatred and Global Instability* (New York: Anchor Books, 2004).

Clark, Tim, and Carl Kay. *Saying Yes to Japan: How Outsider's Are Reviving A Trillion Dollar Services Market* (New York: Vertical, 2005).

Clifford, Mark L. *Troubled Tiger: Businessmen, Bureaucrats and Generals in South Korea* (Armonk, NY: Sharpe, 1994).

Cochrane, Janet, ed. *Asian Tourism: Growth and Change* (Oxford: Elsvier, 2008).

Cohen, Stephen P. *The Idea of Pakistan* (Washington D.C.: Brookings Institution Press, 2006).

Cohen, Stephen P. *India: Emerging Power* (Washington, D.C.: Brookings Institution Press, 2001).

Cooper, Robert. *The Breaking of Nations: Order and Chaos in the Twenty-First Century* (New York: Atlantic Books, 2003).

Corn, Charles. *The Scents of Eden: A Narrative of the Spice Trade* (New York: Kodansha International, 1998).

Crouch, Harold. *Government and Society in Malaysia* (Ithaca, NY: Cornell University Press, 1996).

Das, Gurcharan. *India Unbound: The Social and Economic Revolution from Independence to the Global Information Age* (New York: Anchor Books, 2000, 2002).

Day, Kristen A. *China's Environment and the Challenge of Sustainable Development* (Armonk, NY: Sharpe, 2005).

De Bary, Theodore, ed. *Sources of Indian Tradition*. Vol. 2 (New York: Columbia University Press, 1985).

Disney, Anthony. *Twilight of the Pepper Trade: Portuguese Trade in Southwest India in the Seventeenth Century* (Cambridge: Cambridge University Press, 1978).

Dreze, J., and A. Sen. *Indian Development: Selected Regional Perspectives* (Delhi: Oxford University Press, 1997).

Economy, Elizabeth C. *The River Runs Black: The Environmental Challenge to China's Future* (Ithaca, NY: Cornell University Press, 2005).

Edwards, Sebastian. *Crisis and Reform in Latin America* (New York: Oxford University Press, 1995).

Elvin, Mark. *The Retreat of the Elephants: An Environmental History of China* (New Haven: Yale University Press, 2006).

Fergusson, Naill. *The War of the World* (New York: Penguin, 2006).

Fewsmith, Joseph. *China since Tiananmen: The Politics of Transition* (New York: Cambridge University Press, 2001).

Fishman, Ted. *China, Inc.* (New York: Scribner, 2005).

Friedman, Thomas. *The World Is Flat: A Brief History of the Twenty-First Century* (New York: Farrar, Straus, and Giroux, 2006).

Garver, John. *China and India: Ancient Partners in a Post-Imperial World* (Seattle: University of Washington Press, 2007).

Gascoigne, Bamber. *A Brief History of the Great Moghuls* (London: Constable & Robinson, 2002).

Gifford, Rob. *China Road: A Journey into the Future of a Rising Power* (New York: Random House, 2007).

Gittings, John. *The Changing Face of China: From Mao to Market* (New York: Oxford University Press, 2005).

Guthrie, Doug. *China and Globalization: The Social, Economic and Political Transformation of Chinese Society* (New York: Routledge, 2006).

Haqqani, Husain. *Pakistan between Mosque and Military* (Washington, D.C., Carnegie Endowment for International Peace, 2005).

Heinberg, Richard. *The Party's Over: Oil, War and the Fate of Industrial Societies* (Gabriola Island, British Columbia: New Society Publishers, 2003).

Henderson, Callum. *Asia Falling: Making Sense of the Asian Crisis and Its Aftermath* (New York: McGraw Hill, 1998).

Hsu, Immanuel C.Y. *The Rise of Modern China* (New York: Oxford University Press, 1975).

Hughes, Elizabeth, and Scott B. MacDonald. *Carnival on Wall Street: Global Financial Markets in the 1990s* (New York: Wiley, 2003).

Hughes, Neil. *China's Economic Challenges: Smashing the Iron Rice Bowl* (Armonk. NY: Sharpe, 2002).

Huntington, Samuel P. *Political Order in Changing Societies* (New Haven: Yale University Press, 1968).

Hussain, Zahid. *The Scorpion's Tail: The Relentless Rise of Islamic Militants in Pakistan—and How It Threatens America* (New York: Free Press, 2010).

Hutton, Will. *The Writing on the Wall: Why We Must Embrace China as a Partner or Face It as an Enemy* (New York: Free Press, 2006).

Ikuta, Tadahide. *Kanryo: Japan's Hidden Government* (New York: ICG Muse, 1995).

Issenberg, Sasha. *The Sushi Economy: Globalization and the Making of a Modern Delicacy* (New York: Gotham Books, 2007).

Jacobs, Jane. *Dark Age Ahead* (Toronto: Vintage Canada, 2004).

Jacobsohn, Gary Jeffrey. *The Wheel of Law: India's Secularism in Comparative Constitutional Context* (Princeton: Princeton University Press, 2005).

Johnson, Rob. *A Region in Turmoil: South Asian Conflicts since 1947* (London: Reaktion Books, 2005).

Jones, Seth G. *In the Graveyard of Empires: America's Wars in Afghanistan* (New York: Norton, 2010).

Kaplan, Robert D. *Monsoon: The Indian Ocean and the Future of American Power* (New York: Random House, 2010).

Katz, Richard. *Japanese Phoenix: The Long Road to Japanese Revival* (Armonk, NY: Sharpe, 2003).

Kingsbury, Damien. *The Politics of Indonesia* (New York: Oxford University Press, 1998).

Kingston, Jeff. *Japan's Quiet Transformation: Social Change and Civil Society in the Twenty-First Century* (New York: Routledge Curzon, 2004).

Kohli, Atul. *Democracy and Discontent: India's Growing Crisis of Governability* (New York: Cambridge University Press, 1990).

Kurlantzick, Joshua, *Charm Offensive: How China's Soft Power Is Transforming the World* (New Haven, CT: Yale University Press, 2007).

Lardy, Nicholas R. *China's Unfinished Economic Revolution* (Washington, D.C.: Brookings Institution Press, 1998).

Lardy, Nicholas R. *Integrating China into the Global Economy* (Washington, D.C.: Brookings Institution Press, 2002).

Lincoln, Edward. *Arthritic Japan: The Slow Pace of Economic Reform* (Washington, D.C.: Brookings Institution Press, 2001).

Ma, Jun. *China's Water Crisis* (New York: Eastbridge, 2004).

MacFarquhar, Roderick, ed. *The Politics of China: The Era of Mao and Deng* (New York: Cambridge University Press, 1997).

Macpherson, W.J. *The Economic Development of Japan, 1868–1941* (New York: Cambridge University Press, 1995).

Maddison, Angus. *The World Economy: A Millennial Perspective* (London: Plagrave Macmillan, 2001).

Mann, James. *The China Fantasy: How Our Leaders Explain Away Chinese Repression* (New York: Viking Press, 2007).

Marti, Michael E. *China and the Legacy of Deng Xiaoping: From Communist Revolution to Capitalist Evolution* (Dulles, Virginia: Potomac Books, 2003).

McGregor, Richard. *The Party: The Secret World of China's Communist Leaders* (New York: Harper, 2010).

Meredith, Robyn. *The Elephant and the Dragon: The Rise of India and China and What It Means for All of Us* (New York: Norton, 2007).

Minchin, James. *No Man Is an Island: A Portrait of Singapore's Lee Kuan Yew* (North Sydney: Allen & Unwin Australia, 1986, 1990).

Mishra, Pankaj. *Temptations of the West: How to Be Modern in India, Pakistan, Tibet, and Beyond* (New York: Farrar, Straus, and Giroux, 2006).

Mulgan, Aurelia George. *Japan's Failed Revolution: Koizumi and the Politics of Economic Reform* (Canberra: Australian National University, 2002).

Nathan, Andrew J., and Bruce Gilley. *China's New Rulers: The Secret Files* (New York: NYREV, 2002).

Naughton, Barry. *Chinese Economy—Transitions and Growth* (Cambridge, MA: MIT Press, 2007).

Navarro, Peter. *The Coming China Wars: Where They Will Be Fought; How They Can Be Won* (New York: Financial Times Books, 2006).

Nussbaum, Martha C. *The Clash within: Democracy, Religious Violence and India's Future* (New York: Harvard University Press, 2007).

Ooms, Herman. *Tokugawa Village Practice: Class, Status, Power, Law* (Berkeley: University of California Press, 1996).

Osterhammel, Jurgen, and Niels P. Petersson. *Globalization: A Short History* (Princeton: Princeton University Press, 2005).

Pei, Minxin. *China's Trapped Transition: The Limits of Developmental Autocracy* (New York: Harvard University Press, 2008).

Pembel, T.J. *Regime Shift: Comparative Dynamics of the Japanese Political Economy* (Ithaca. NY: Cornell University Press, 1999).

Pomeranz, Kenneth. *The Great Divergence: China, Europe, and the Making of the Modern World Economy* (Princeton: Princeton University Press, 2000).

Prestowitz, Clyde. *Three Billions New Capitalists: The Great Shift of Wealth and Power to the East* (New York: Basic Books, 2005).

Pye, Lucian. *Asian Power and Politics* (Boston: Harvard University Press, 1985).

Pyle, Kenneth. *Japan Rising: The Resurgence of Japanese Power and Purpose* (New York: Public Affairs Books, 2007).

Rajadhyaksha, Niranjan. *The Rise of India: Its Transformation from Poverty to Prosperity* (Singapore: Wiley [Asia], 2007).

Ramage, Douglas E. *Politics in Indonesia: Democracy, Islam and the Ideology of Tolerance* (New York: Routledge, 1995).

Rasgotra, M.K., ed. *The New Asian Power Dynamic* (New Delhi: Sage Publications, 2007).

Rashid, Ahmed. *Descent into Chaos: The U.S. and the Disaster in Pakistan, Afghanistan, and Central Asia* (New York: Penguin, 2009).

Richards, John F. *The Mughal Empire* (New York: Cambridge University Press, 1993).

Ricklefs, M.C. *A History of Modern Indonesia C1300* (Stanford: Stanford University Press, 1993).

Riedel, James, Jing Jin, and Jian Gao. *How China Grows: Investment, Finance and Reform* (Princeton: Princeton University Press, 2005).

Roberts, Andrew. *A History of English-Speaking Peoples since 1900* (New York: HarperCollins, 2006).

Rotberg, Robert I., ed. *China into Africa: Trade, Aid, and Influence* (Washington, D.C.: Brookings Institution Press, 2008).

Salisbury, Harrison. *The New Emperors: China in the Era of Mao and Deng* (New York: Harper Perennial, 1993).

Sharma, R.N. *Indian Education at the Cross Road* (Delhi, India: Shubhi, 2002).

Shirk, Susan J. *China: Fragile Superpower* (New York: Oxford University Press, 2007).

Sims, R.L. *Japanese Political History since the Meiji Renovation* (London: Hurst, 2002).

Spear, Percival. *A History of India*. Volume 2, *From Sixteenth Century to the Twentieth Century* (New York: Penguin, 1990).

Spector, Ronald. *In the Ruins of Empire: The Japanese Surrender and the Battle for Postwar Asia* (New York: Random House, 2007).

Steyn, Mark. *America Alone: The End of the World as We Know It* (Washington, D.C.: Regency Publishing, 2006).

Stiglitz, Joseph E. *Globalization and Its Discontents* (New York: Norton, 2002).

Terrill, Ross. *The New Chinese Empire: And What It Means for the United States* (New York: Basic Books, 2003).

Tharoor, Shashi. *The Elephant, the Tiger, and the Cell Phone: Reflections on India, the Emerging 21st-Century Power* (New York: Arcade Publishing, 2007).

Trocki, Carl A. *Singapore: Wealth, Power and the Culture of Control* (New York: Routledge, 2006).

Vatikiotis, Michael R.J. *Political Change in Southeast Asia: Trimming the Banyan Tree* (New York: Rutledge, 1996).

Vohra, Ranbir. *The Making of India: A Historical Survey* (Armonk, NY: Sharpe, 2001).

Weaver, Mary Anne. *Pakistan: Deep inside the World's Most Frightening State* (New York: Farrar, Straus, and Giroux, 2010).

Werner, Richard A. *Princes of the Yen: Japan's Central Bankers and the Transformation of the Economy* (Armonk, NY: Sharpe, 2003).

Woodall, Brian. *Japan under Construction: Corruption, Politics, and Public Works* (Berkeley: University of California Press, 1996).

Yang, Benjamin. *Deng: A Political Biography* (Armonk, NY: East Gate Books, 1997).

Yoda, Yoshiie. *The Foundations of Japan's Modernization: A Comparison with China's Path Towards Modernization* (Amsterdam: Brill, 1995).

Zakaria, Fareed. *The Post-American World* (New York: Norton, 2008).

Zeilenziger, Michael. *Shutting Out the Sun: How Japan Created Its Own Lost Generation* (New York: Doubleday, 2006).

INDEX

About the Authors

SCOTT B. MacDONALD is the head of Credit and Economics Research, senior managing director and principal at Aladdin Capital Holdings, LLC, based in Stamford, Connecticut. He covers sovereign credit issues for both advanced and emerging economies and follows global credit conditions, with a focus on financial institutions. Prior to that position, he worked at KWR International; Donaldson, Lufkin & Jenrette; Credit Suisse; and the Office of the Comptroller of the Currency (Washington, D.C.). For several years during his time on Wall Street, he was rated as one of the top sovereign analysts by *Institutional Investor* magazine. Dr. MacDonald received his PhD in political science from the University of Connecticut, MA in Area Studies (Far East) from the University of London's Oriental and African Studies, and BA in History and Political Science from Trinity College in Hartford, Connecticut. He has traveled extensively in Asia, with a particular emphasis on Japan and Korea. Dr. MacDonald is also published extensively, with his more recent efforts being co-authored: *Separating Fools from Their Money* (2006, 2009) and *When Small Countries Crash* (2011).

JONATHAN LEMCO is a principal and senior analyst at the Vanguard Group, where his role includes the evaluation of sovereign risk in developed and emerging markets. Dr. Lemco joined Vanguard in July 2000. Prior to taking this position, he headed the sovereign research effort at Credit Suisse First Boston Corporation. Before that, he served as director of the National Policy Association, providing public policy forums and publications related to the NAFTA, and as professor at Johns Hopkins University School for Advanced International Studies, teaching courses on sovereign risk, public policy, and North American economic and political issues. Dr. Lemco has authored nine books and many articles on sovereign risk, comparative public policy, international trade, and related topics. A native of Montreal, Dr. Lemco has a BA from Clark University and an MA and PhD in political science from the University of Rochester.